SOLO
ON HER OWN ADVENTURE

EDITED BY **SUSAN FOX ROGERS**

SEAL PRESS

SOLO
ON HER OWN ADVENTURE

Copyright © 2005, 1996 by Susan Fox Rogers

Published by
Seal Press
An Imprint of Avalon Publishing Group, Incorporated
1400 65th Street, Suite 250
Emeryville, CA 94608

ISBN 1-58005-137-5

9 8 7 6 5 4 3 2 1

Library of Congress Cataloging-in-Publication Data

Solo : on her own adventure / edited by Susan Fox Rogers.— 2nd ed.

p. cm.

ISBN 1-58005-137-5

1. Outdoor recreation for women—Literary collections. 2. Wilderness survival—Literary collections. 3. American prose literature—Women authors. 4. Short stories, American—Women authors. 5. Women travelers—Literary collections. 6. Outdoor life—Literary collections. 7. Solitude—Literary collections. 8. Adventure stories, American. I. Rogers, Susan Fox.

PS648.O88S65 2005

818'.60808357—dc22

2005006574

Cover design by Gia Giasullo
Interior design by Domini Dragoone
Printed in Canada by Transcontinental
Distributed by Publishers Group West

For Teri

CONTENTS

Introduction

FIRST, A STORY. In the fall of 2001, I took a new teaching position at Bard College, a small school crunched against the Hudson River about one hundred miles north of Manhattan. When the attacks on the world trade towers rode the waves up the river leaving all in its wake sad and mourning, I did what I often do: I took to the woods. But not alone. Alone felt too much at that time. So with a friend, I tromped around a series of lakes in the Adirondacks. We listened to loons' haunting calls in the mornings and made mad dips into icy waters. In four days we didn't cover a lot of miles, but the woods had their effect: I was feeling stronger physically, and I knew that would sustain me back in my other life.

As we crested the final small mountain on our last day, a woman came chugging up the other side, her hair pulled back in a determined ponytail, sweat dripping from her cheeks, and a napkin clutched in one hand. On it, someone had drawn a crude map of the area, outlining the trail we had just hiked, but in reverse. This woman was out for a day hike. I've been that woman, taken advice from someone in the local diner and headed out with faith and energy, only to be stopped by someone who knows better, who warns me that I've bitten off too much, that I can't do what I've decided on, or who offers other words of caution. Whether I need these words or not is not a question: As a woman traveling alone, I am a target for all sorts of advice. Nothing irritates me more. And yet I started to do just that: offer advice. "You might want to cut off here, eliminating about five or six miles," I suggested. The woman nodded. I recognized that nod: She was not going to follow my directions. She would come stumbling out of the woods, in the dark, exhausted and elated. I kicked myself, wished her well, and headed down the trail.

A white rental car nudged our car in the dirt parking lot. "Hey look," my friend said, pointing to the back seat. And there lay a copy of *Solo*. I laughed and slipped an apologetic note under her windshield wiper.

This is perhaps my favorite story, but there are many others. Chance encounters, letters from women adventuring around the world, students who tell me the book changed their lives, have all made me realize that this book has an adventuring life of its own. For an editor nothing could be more satisfying.

Nine years have passed since *Solo* first appeared on bookshelves. I'd like to say something grand now, something about the state of women and the outdoors, or about women writing about the outdoors. But if there's something important to say—such as, women now, as never before, are heading solo into the outdoors full of confidence and with impeccable skills; or, women writers have taken on subjects and themes men only dream of—I'm not the one to say it. I read, I kayak. I hike and pretend to still rock climb. I've even edited another collection of solo stories, *Going Alone: Women's Adventures in the Wild*, but I don't feel qualified to make any big pronouncements.

But if not me, then who? I have as good a perspective as anyone, and why not say it? We are adventuring out in greater numbers (I don't need statistics from a central source to know this—all I have to do is go out and hike or ski or paddle and I will, almost inevitably, run into another woman alone), on more daring adventures (I think of the middle-aged woman from Wisconsin I met this summer in McCarthy, Alaska, who had spent twenty-eight days alone in the wild Wrangell Mountains), and in a greater range of sports. To back up my bold assertions are two of the three new essays I've included in this edition. Barbara J. Euser writes about being the first woman solo sailor in a 2,120-mile race from San Francisco Bay to Hanalei Bay in Hawaii and Val Van Brocklin writes of flying solo into the wilds of Alaska and hunting for several days. Nine years ago, women were sailing and flying and hunting, but the scale of these two adventures is bigger, and both women, implicitly or explicitly, have taken strength from knowing of other women's feats. They knew what they were doing was possible, perhaps from seeing men do it, but the translation to *I can do it, too*, came more easily—maybe even naturally—because they had images of women who had also gone solo to call upon for strength.

And yet, as I began to pull together my thoughts for this introduction, I opened *The New York Times* on a lazy post-Thanksgiving weekend and read: "For Women, Easy Does It. Adventure trips are yielding to tours that focus on shopping, spas, and spirituality." I groaned and opened to the article. Full of doubt, I began to read. "In recent years, companies specializing in women's tours emphasized adventure: the chance to surf, climb mountains, or sail in all-female groups. Adventure is still popular, but sybaritic pursuits are gaining ground." *Gaining ground.* They will never catch up. *In groups.* None of the women in this collection is a part of a group. The point is solo. And so no data bank, no statistic-loving company will find us.

But more troubling than the idea that women are giving up adventure trips to shopping is the idea expressed in the article that shopping, spas, and spiritual trips allow women to "get in touch with their feminine side." What still needs a bit of revision is what is feminine—or rather, where can we feel or be feminine? Why not on a mountainside? I, too, can shop with the best of them, it just so happens that the stores I choose are called Rock & Snow or Appalachian Outdoor House.

Identifying women as "shoppers" or even as "outdoor women" limits us all. The essays in this collection testify to the range of identities (as daughter, as teacher, as mother, as explorer), and in contacting the contributors for this new edition, I was struck by the range of life experiences, how steady some lives were and how transformed others had become. First, all of the women in this collection are nine years older. Most are still out there hiking and paddling, and some—like myself—are coming to grips with what it means to be "middle aged" and still out there. Going out alone is never simple, and that's why these stories remain vital; they all grapple with the complexity of these experiences as women. This collection is about being feminine and not. Strong and not. Afraid and not.

Here's what I can say (without exaggeration or invented facts): Nine years ago, now, and nine years from now, the issues that women wrestle with, and the reasons to adventure solo, have not and will not change. We head out to find solace, happiness, peace, self-knowledge, and the land we belong to. This is why anyone goes solo. But for women, there are other elements, and these will fluctuate, but never vanish. One of these is fear. Fear of the adventure, of animals, of men. This fear is only a sign of sanity—there *are* real things to fear. In the essays I've added to this collection, that fear takes on greater proportions as Val Van Brocklin describes her plane's engine cutting out. What could be more frightening?

Susan Marsh puts forth several of these timeless ideas in beautiful ways as she travels to the desert Southwest and, because alone, can see that land in new ways. That ability to "look out," to really see, was an element of solo travel I found harder to find when I searched for essays nine years ago. Women spent—still spend and will always spend—much solo time engaged in an inner search, one that is both frightening and rewarding. That inner journey often takes over, leaving the land a bit neglected. With Marsh, the land as well as the self is clearly seen.

When *Solo* appeared in 1996, the country had one major event that focused us on outdoor adventure, and that was a disaster on Everest, the scale of which has never, thankfully, been repeated. Nine people died, and the rescue of those who lived took on epic proportions. This tragic event had a heroic chronicler in Jon Krakauer, who saw friends die and was able to write about it with stunning clarity. But a strange thing happened after that event: It didn't warn people away from outdoor adventure; more people wanted to go. And more people wanted to dream about going. Reading is a part of that dreaming.

That same year, another tragic event colored my personal world more darkly: the death of two young women on the Appalachian Trail in Virginia. Reporters called me and asked, "Well, Miss Solo, what do you say to women now?" I pulled myself together and repeated, "Go now, and go solo." But their deaths followed the trail to where I then lived in the Berkshire Mountains of New York State. For months, seized with a fear I had never known, I couldn't walk alone. I read about their deaths, I researched other deaths, I read accounts of women being attacked. Statistics told me my fear was out of proportion to reality: Since 1974, fifteen people—men and women—have been killed in national parks, which cover eighty-three million acres. But my fear was not only for my own safety; no one in the woods should be killed. What seemed sacred had been violated, and I remained paralyzed. And then, with time, I worked my way out of this fear when I found some perfect hiking partners. My new duo-status led to a different anthology, *Two in the Wild: Tales of Adventure from Friends, Mothers, and Daughters.*

That fear has now dulled, and I am back to traveling mostly solo. My freedom has expanded. This revised edition is a part of that expansion. To readers, I offer the freedom these stories offer.

SUSAN FOX ROGERS
MARCH 2005

SUSAN MARSH

Gifts of Vacant Land

FOR ELLEN MELOY

I WAS TWENTY-ONE AND ON THE ROAD IN THE BOISTEROUS COMPANY OF FIFTEEN FELLOW STUDENTS OF GEOLOGY, ALL PALE-SKINNED NATIVES OF THE PACIFIC NORTHWEST. The landscapes that passed from the windows of the university van were utterly different from the rainforest of coastal Washington, a province so cloaked in green we could have walked right over a mossy outcrop of bedrock and not known it. Even the place names of these new territories were those of a savage and alien world: Skeleton Cave and Newberry Crater; Furnace Creek and Devils Postpile. We stayed no more than one night at each spot until we reached the desert east of Las Vegas, where the Mojave Desert's volcanic ranges lapped against the red-rock fantasia of the Colorado Plateau. The desert had bedrock in spades, brazenly bare and splayed across the land like a steak on a spit. The folds and faults and sedimentary layers couldn't have been more readily observed, and thus our professor had chosen Nevada's Muddy Mountains for instructing us in the fundamentals of geologic mapping.

For nearly three weeks, we camped in a sand gully called, unglamorously, West End Wash. Twenty days in the desert—halfway to the biblical forty. From our chapped and bleeding lips, molars grinding sand with every meal, and sunburn mitigated only by the fine dust that coated our unbathed bodies, it might as well have been forty years. The following morning we would break camp and head for showers, laundry, groceries, and most important—cold beer. Next stop: the Grand Canyon.

One evening, on the way back to camp from Callville Bay, where we re-filled water jugs, I was staring out the van's window. Shadows settled into the rumpled hems of the Muddy Mountains and crept across the desert floor like smoke. Barren ranges stood on the far horizons in shades of soft blue and hammered gold. A crimson haze danced above them, its sultry eyes on me.

I called to Bob at the wheel. "Hey, let me off. I'm going to walk the rest of the way."

He shot a puzzled glance over his shoulder, and I verified my intention with a smile. He slowed the van and pulled over.

"Thanks," I said. "See you later."

I dropped to the roadway and the van sped away.

The engine's hum faded, and I confronted the trackless desert I planned to cross alone. Utter silence awaited. This was not the quiet of mid-day, when insects scurry and the windblown sand grains gently pepper my open map. It was nothing like the quiet of the Pacific Northwest mountains, where, from the highest ridges, I could hear the distant roar of rushing creeks and waterfalls. Here was no source of sound: no water, no wind. I started walking away, and the highway slipped behind a mound and with it went the only hint that humans had ever inhabited this austere land. Who would blame them for such wise avoidance? The loneliest, emptiest sweep of terrain I could imagine lay before me dotted with thorny shrubs and bronzed by the long light of sundown. Tiny round pebbles at my feet snapped into sharp relief, each casting a shadow as long as a pencil. Unless I counted the imperceptible lengthening of pencils, nothing moved.

The territory held no sense of scale. I spotted a dark crease in the plain a mile or two ahead—the broad, shallow wash that sheltered camp. No sooner had I started for it than doubt began to boggle my steps. The subtle fold might be ten miles distant, in which case I'd never reach it before nightfall. It blurred as I squinted toward it, then vanished altogether. I looked away, and when my gaze returned, the crease reappeared. It occurred to me that it might be an illusion, that the crease was only a mirage or a shadow trailing eastward from the Muddy Mountains. Any possibility was as likely as the next, for I'd been here long enough to understand that what I once considered a hallucination, the product of a feral imagination, was simply part of the natural landscape.

I'd begun to expect a certain sequence in the way my perception shifted as I encountered the desert. At first, my eyes reported some new wonder and my mind began to balk. I moved closer and looked again. Forgot my assumptions and the meanings I once assigned to certain forms or colors, and looked again. Only then did reality sink in: That dab of azure on the cliff face was in fact a natural arch, round as an owl's eye; that smudge of showy wildflowers on the ridge—coral, scarlet, teal—was in fact the color of the rock.

I angled for the dent in the desert, navigating by faith as much as what scant information I could glean from the view. The Muddy Mountains fed the wash where we'd made camp so I knew my destination was somewhere in their direction. But between myself and the treeless escarpment lay only vacant land.

Why had I been struck by the urge to hop out of the van and walk to camp alone? At the time, I understood implicitly with no need for contemplation or words to fix the reasons in my mind. I can answer this question better now, after thirty years have passed, but I knew back then, as I walked in the desert plain, that several facts hovered on the edges of my mind like a distant range of mountains. That evening was my last in the V formed by the southern tip of Nevada as it wedged between California and the Colorado River, and for all I knew, I'd never see the country again. I needed its silence and emptiness and solitude. I wanted to say goodbye to a harsh district that, to my surprise after twenty days of wind in my hair and sand in my food and the various deprivations of field camp, I had come to love. Further, I was following a lifelong pattern of abandoning the company of others and striking off alone. Last, I had something to celebrate: the calm that had taken up residence within me since I'd been footloose and on the road. The previous winter had been relentlessly dreary with weeks of chilling rain and clouds that hung over Puget Sound like a wad of soggy dishrags. I had endured my first failed love affair while struggling through a heavy load of science courses and dealing with the emotional volcano of an alcoholic mother. When had I last enjoyed an unfettered thought? When had I last lived fully in the moment without any thoughts at all?

Alone in the desert I wandered slowly, my mind as clear as the land. Without my conscious understanding of what was happening, I found serenity.

The urge to hike back to camp alone was triggered by the quality of light as the sun began to set. I'd been leaning against the large window in the back of the van from which I could watch the scenery perfectly well. But seeing the desert from a speeding vehicle was like taking in the autumn colors by going for a drive instead of walking through an aspen stand, inhaling its smoky musk, listening to the gently talking leaves, and holding my face toward the sun to feel its warmth. Scenery wasn't what I needed, but complete immersion, a full-body baptism.

It wouldn't have worked had someone else decided to join me, even if we agreed to walk apart without a word. I sought a degree of communion with the land only possible if I went alone.

Walking toward that vague crease in the plain—yes, I saw by now that it was definitely the wash that held our camp—my consciousness of self dropped away. I became hyper-alert, my senses on fire, but not for fear of losing my way in the approaching darkness or being bitten by a snake. My condition was a spontaneous mix of inner peace and sensory alacrity, a state that I had never known. I tasted my first true measure of the largeness and complexity of nature and my own unplumbed depths. The wild world held much for me to apperceive, and without effort, I was absorbing it.

Before that evening, I had traveled in the wilds with what I considered an appropriate degree of reverence and heed, but also with the self-absorption of a kid, that childish premise that one could somehow be the center of it all. It was more about developing my skills at route-finding, wild-flower identification, and summit-bagging than the mountains themselves. Now, aware that I was not the center of anything, I walked with profound appreciation and undiluted joy. This new way of walking in the world has since become the only way for me. I don't seek to go higher, farther or faster, nor to name and thus diminish each miracle of native flora, but to sojourn, informed by humble observation, gratitude, and grace.

Grace: This is what the desert held. Grace is what it offered me.

Without knowing it, for twenty days I'd been preparing for that evening. The geologic mapping exercise required a daily ramble across the low hills and canyons within a few miles of base camp. The assignment: to observe with a single aim, to measure and map the surface exposures of geologic strata, and draw conclusions about how they got there. I struggled to unravel the processes that had assembled vermilion sandstone, green and purple shale, ash-gray limestone, and charcoal fingers of basalt into an apparently chaotic jumble. With a hand-held transit and protractor, surveying tools not so different from those once used by geologist and Colorado River pioneer John Wesley Powell, I climbed bald ridges and hogback buttes to locate my position on a topographic map. From each vista, I carefully triangulated and drew thin lines with indelible India ink (my first mistake), trying to depict on a two-dimensional sheet the folded, tortuous layers of rock as they intersected cliff bands, arroyos, and crenulated slopes. I scratched my head over a tilted bed of rainbow shale, each bright stratum rippling across a set of gullies like a sidewinder.

Discouragement came quickly as I watched my fellow students' geologic maps progress, neatly rendered and somehow making scientific sense. We'd each been given a topographic contour map on which to draw and there were no extra copies. Though I erased gingerly, I did it often, and my map began to look like a moth-eaten coat.

Dutifully, I marched with compass, map, and clipboard to the outcrops every morning. But the land held its distractions and they offered me welcome company and solace: fence lizards, chuckwallas, rattlesnakes, horned lizards, desert tortoises, ring-tailed cats, and jackrabbits. Creosote bush studded the wide plain with sprays of pale-yellow blooms, whose fragrance drifted on eddies of warm air. I swayed to the music of the botanical name: *Larrea tridentata*. Its cousin bloomed nearby: *Larrea divaricata*. These plants were the desert's poetry.

Cholla cacti raised blond medusa-heads as the morning sun backlit their slender spines. Desert indigo waved its bright purple flowers among tiny silver leaves. As I stopped for a closer look at the pealike blossoms, a pale green twig began to twitch. I stood back on my heels as it took a step forward, and all at once I was eye-to-eye with a six-inch insect, a walking stick.

The rockscape was no less fantastic than its plants and creatures. Sharp-edged and raw, this was a land still under construction. Silence and emptiness attenuated its distances, and these qualities drew me most of all. Each morning I left camp in the company of two or three others but soon split off, following the direction that appealed to my senses and my heart. I was led not to ground I needed to cover in order to complete my geologic map, but to places that promised far vistas or the remote reaches of a tributary wash. Places where I could spend the day alone.

From the time I was a child, I'd been a loner, but only here had I been able to indulge my penchant for exploration and long lingering, day after day. I could stop to sketch a flower or climb a hill with no one waiting for me.

By the second week, my geologic map was growing hopelessly sloppy. Though it mattered to my professor, the precise degree of strike and dip was not what mattered to me; what did was the unclothed beauty of the land. Exposed rocks flaunted their ripples and striations and dramatically steep dip slopes. Some beds were overturned, recumbent. I delighted in these geologic terms, as well as the structures they described; both were decidedly immodest. Variegated shales of blue and green and tan bled like sweat-softened rouge and eye shadow down the faces of low bluffs. Sandstone the color of a bad sunburn reclined in shapely curves, as if to beg for more.

In counterpoint to the reclining female forms, a gypsum dome burst through the earth's surface like a blunt-nosed whale. Rising thirty feet above the desert floor, it shed plates of hydrous calcium sulfate in single crystals three feet long. They were feather-light and clear as glass; I held one over my clipboard and could read the scribbling on my goofy geologic map.

On my way back to camp from the gypsum dome, I found what I hoped would be a shortcut, a slot canyon penetrating the end of a long sandstone ridge. I entered its cool darkness, and soon I was looking straight up without a glimpse of blue beyond the overhangs. I walked the quarter mile in a state of rapt amazement, touching both walls with my fingertips.

The clipboard remained in my daypack more frequently as I wandered deeper into that strange land. Trying to improve my map left me helpless with frustration, but while I despaired of my future as a field geologist, something else began to happen. I came to know the rocks on a sensory level after I quit trying to confine them to a flat representation in India ink and colored pencil. Weathered limestone was rough as sandpaper and had a faint salty odor when scratched. Fine-grained volcanics held large phenocrysts of twinned feldspar that mirrored one another like facing pages of an open book. I learned something of the physical characteristics of the rocks, their singularities, and their wild and ancient souls. Slowly, in my daily ritual of solitude and attention, I found the land opening to include me. My morning shadow splashed the base of a cliff as if it had been doing so for years. I stopped to watch the antics of a barrel-rolling raven until the horizon drew my gaze. When I wasn't watching anymore, I began to see.

I began to see something about myself as well. I wasn't suited to descriptive science; whether struggling through chemistry lab or baking a cake, I had little patience for anything that required precise measurements and complete concentration. In order to carry out a complex task with some degree of proficiency, I had to discipline my mind and shut out whatever competed for its attention. In that fantastic place, I couldn't. Didn't want to. In its thirst to absorb the desert's wonders, my mind was as disciplined as a rank colt.

I'm glad I let my imagination have its head. It was the key to a contentment I have known ever since when wandering alone in wild land. Most of my classmates found living in the desert inconvenient on good days and increasingly miserable as the month of May wore on, with its wind and heat and unrelenting sun. Most of them never returned. But the weeks I spent there, energized by solitude in a land so vast and empty I could look around and see there was no one else within ten miles, induced me to return as often as I could.

The more I learned of the arid Southwest, the more places I came to love: Arches, Canyonlands, and Zion National Parks; the unprotected BLM lands in between; cliff dwellings and slickrock; the delicate early buds of single-leaf ash. The more I knew, the more I wanted, and when I could not be in the desert, I turned to the writings of those who knew and loved it best: John Wesley Powell, whose journals I read before paddling a canoe down the Green and Colorado Rivers; the heart-rending poetry of Richard Shelton; the curmudgeonly rants of Edward Abbey; love letters to the desert from Terry Tempest Williams; wild worlds opening from the pen of Ellen Meloy. The rust-red of a flash flood ran through the veins of these writers—their unyielding devotion to this hardscrabble land helped the rest of us learn to love it, too. Shelton let tarantulas wander up his walls (indoors) and made snakes the subject of his verse. I once asked Ellen Meloy if she ever considered moving from Bluff, Utah, back to Montana, where we both had lived for many years. Vigorously she shook her head. "The rocks are the wrong color," she said.

The arid lands of the Southwest have been called America's empty quarter. Empty of roads and settlements and agriculture, save the occasional cheatgrass pasture for cactus-munching beef cattle. Empty of what we are told should matter to civilization—commerce; towns (even a lonely, alkali-bitten cabin); sources of wealth other than what can be heedlessly exploited and, most often, hauled away. For most of the purposes of society this is worthless, vacant land.

My dictionary defines vacant mostly in terms of what it isn't. Unclaimed, uninhabited, unoccupied. Empty, but also free. Farther down the string of meanings is reference to a vacant mind: free from occupation or preoccupation. Walking in the desert on a still evening, I find my state of mind matching the state of the land.

The empty quarter of America is anything but empty. It is filled with size and silence, sunlight and sky. If invited, it will fill the wanderer with grace.

The evening I walked to camp alone across the desert, I ended up staying out until well past dark. The dusky wash had loomed close as the sunset paled, and I picked up my pace. But then I found a stone. A rust-colored lump projecting from the pavement of black gravel, it looked like a crumpled steel can. In the still heat of sundown, I bent to pick it up.

It wasn't a rusting metal scrap at all. It lay cool and heavy in my hand, some kind of solid ceramic figure. Its faces were carved into complex ridges and ruffles—the petrified swirling skirt of a flamenco dancer. I examined it in disbelief, first tapping it to produce the hollow ring that would certify it had passed through a firing kiln, then peering into my magnifying lens for any sign of tool work. No evidence of hand sculpting greeted my inquiry. It was only dense, dumb stone. I realized that if this rock had been carved, it was by the elements, not by human hands. I flushed at my surprise: Hadn't I spent the past three weeks among the most stunning ornaments imaginable, all of them crafted by nothing more than wind and water and sand? Still, I couldn't quite believe this rock.

The size of my fist, it resembled a lopsided pyramid with four sides and four points blunted by their exposure to the wind. Etched furrows ran along the surface, a mirror of the ridges and slot canyons of the land. The furrows abutted one another and twisted into pleats and curls like Vitruvian scrollwork. They converged upon a wrinkled eye—the center of the pyramid.

I kept examining the rock in the failing twilight, still searching for evidence of handicraft. Finding none, I groped toward science from which to spin a story.

A nodule of chert, I guessed by its considerable weight, but the outer ribs were surely sandstone. Two rocks in one—how could that happen? What had carved the fanciful designs? I recalled an odd specimen from my childhood rock collection, one of those pre-made cardboard trays whose labels favored rock hound vernacular over scientific names. Among the Fool's Gold and Apache Tears was a singular specimen called Desert Rose. Like a tea rose, the specimen was small, not much larger than my thumbnail. It was pale-pink and appeared to have been formed from sand. Its petals were imbricate, offset, and stacked—a bit like the rock I held in the desert of Nevada.

I supposed that what I found was a bulky and misshapen Desert Rose. I still have bewildering questions about it, such as, "How did it arrive here, miles from the nearest outcrop or sand dune, where around it lay only a uniform pavement of black basalt?" If I were a real geologist, I would have smacked it with a rock hammer, destroying it to know it. Instead, I took it back to camp and buried it in my duffel.

Because of that evening in the desert, I came to love the study of the earth, and managed to earn my degree in spite of a geologic map of the Muddy Mountains that brought snickers from my classmates and a C- from the professor. It was the reason I chose Utah for graduate school and the reason I leapt at the invitation to travel to Escalante, Utah, for a weeklong hike through a place called Death Hollow during the first week of August and peak color in the wildflower parks near my home in the Tetons.

Not only did I return to the desert through the years, but I was increasingly impelled to defend that which I had come to love, for such an unpopulated place was considered ideal for secreting away what no one wanted—nuclear waste, spent military ordnance, and toxic mine tailings. I wrote to congress in favor of wilderness proposals for the public lands in southern Utah, protested plans to transform the West Desert into a grid of bulldozed racetracks for the MX missile system, and gave up hiking in some of my favorite places after they became too popular, places where my footsteps would make a lasting, unwanted impression.

Perched on my writing desk, my Desert Rose remains a souvenir of the great parade of earth history in all its beauty and violence. It is a souvenir of the time I struck out alone across the desert and changed the way I experienced the world. In a land where the wondrous was ordinary, I discovered that nothing was common. I hold the rock sometimes, to feel its weight and roughness and cool, unyielding pressure, to renew my resolve to speak on behalf of wild and empty places—places only able to endow us with great spiritual cheer because of their untrammeled immensity. What they offer to those who go alone in search of them are these: size and silence, sunlight and sky. Gifts of vacant land.

BARBARA J. EUSER

Singlehanded TransPac

"TURN RIGHT AT THE 'A' IN 'GALE.'" Up and down the Corinthian Yacht Club docks, sailors repeated this dark joke. Most of us—the twenty-four participants in the 2004 Singlehanded TransPacific Yacht Race—had dutifully printed out the National Weather Service's morning weather forecast before heading to our boats. We would start our 2,120-mile race from San Francisco Bay to Hanalei Bay in Kaua'i, Hawaii, in gale force (twenty-five to forty mile-per-hour) winds. The first few days offshore compose the roughest part of the passage between San Francisco and Hawaii. During that time, beating into the wind, the boat pounds into the waves. In ideal weather—ten to fifteen knots (11–15.5 mph) of wind—it is an unpleasant beat. In a gale, it would be much worse.

But there was nothing to be done about the weather. The race was scheduled to start at 10:00 AM on June 26, and the Race Committee had no intention of delaying it. Dressed in full foul-weather gear, we readied to confront the elements.

Each of the twenty-four skippers at the start had been preparing for this race for months. To meet the stringent race requirements, every one of us had upgraded electronics, sails, and communications and safety equipment to pass inspection by the Race Committee. The race sponsor, the Singlehanded Sailing Society, had conducted monthly seminars since December 2003 to prepare potential participants. Local experts lectured on medical emergencies, sleep deprivation, food provisioning, sail choice and repair, emergency rudders, radios and telephones, route strategy, and arrival in Hanalei.

Even though I had sailed my family's boat, a Bristol 34 named *Islander*, twice across the Atlantic Ocean, I had made numerous purchases and improvements to qualify her for the race. So whatever I had done was done and whatever I had left undone would be up to me to improvise. After the start, all I would have available was what I had put on board.

The Singlehanded TransPac Race has been run every even-numbered year since 1978. More than two hundred sailors have competed in fourteen races. Of those, I was the tenth woman to make it to the start line—and getting to the start line is no easy feat—and the only woman entrant in 2004. When asked, "Why do you want to do it?" my short answer was, "It's something I've wanted to do for years, and now I'm ready." But why did I want to sail alone for days on end? Ever since reading Joshua Slocum's *Sailing Alone Around the World* as a teenager, I had dreamed of what it would be like to take off on a solo passage alone at the helm. My idol, Sir Francis Chichester, at age 65, sailed his *Gipsy Moth IV* around the world. To me, sailing alone seemed like the ultimate adventure. I would be the only one responsible for my movement across the ocean from start to finish. I needed to see if I could actually do it on my own, without the assistance of crew. An added benefit, no one would be able to criticize whatever mistakes I made. I did not see myself confronting the elements. Instead, with grace, the elements might permit me to pass through their undisputed domain. At age fifty-five, I wanted to make the attempt while still feeling young and strong. Having accumulated several thousand miles of offshore experience and hundreds of miles sailing alone, I was eager to try.

The Race Committee had wired and sealed each boat's propeller shaft. Thus, we could not use our engines to propel us toward the finish, though we could still run our engines to refill batteries to provide power for instruments and lights. To get to the start line, beginning at 8:30 AM, the Race Committee towed each boat out into Raccoon Straits, where we raised our sails and milled about, waiting for the gun.

Pow! A stream of boats flowed past the start. We headed for the

Golden Gate Bridge, the first marker on our way. In my mind, the second marker was Mile Rock; the third was getting through the shipping lines. Then there was nothing but open ocean to the Hawaiian Islands.

By afternoon, I had sailed out of sight of the coast. I sighed with relief. My worst fear is running into something. Once well away from land, I breathed easier, as I prefer sailing surrounded by deep water on all sides. I trust *Islander*. She was built in 1975 by Bristol and designed by Halsey Herreshoff to sail offshore. Her hull is thick and strong. She weighs a lot, one reason I was rated second-slowest boat in our fleet.

It took all day to sail beyond the shipping lanes. The Monitor, a wind vane self-steering system, was at the helm, keeping *Islander* on course in relation to the relentless wind. Condensation inside my foulies made me cold and damp. The boat pounding in the choppy seas made me violently seasick for the first time in my life. Then, as the gray skies darkened at the end of the afternoon, I saw that my jib was coming unstitched along its base. About three feet of binding flapped. I pulled the jib in on its roller furler to keep the damage from getting worse. The rough seas prevented me from hauling it down and replacing it with my working jib. I continued sailing under mainsail alone; progress slowed, and *Islander* wallowed in the waves.

By law, ships must maintain a constant watch. Sailing alone, that is physically impossible. To me, "standing watch" meant that every twenty minutes I checked to make sure the wind was still blowing in the same direction, the mainsail was trimmed, and that no ships loomed on the horizon. Night closed in. Too sick and exhausted to take off my foul-weather gear, I spent the night fully dressed, leaning back next to the chart table, my feet propped on the companionway stairs. I pulled a Dacron comforter over my legs, set the egg timer for twenty minutes, and tried to sleep. Each time it shrilled, I opened the hatch, climbed up to the cockpit, checked the compass and mainsail, and looked around 360 degrees for ships. Then I dropped down below. And set the egg timer again.

At one in the morning, the wind shifted. I clipped in to my tether and carefully climbed aft of the cockpit. The Monitor likes to be adjusted in small increments. Turning the wheel that rotated the Monitor's vane, I gradually worked us back on course.

The twenty-minute increments became a blur of dozing and waking just enough to make a quick check, then falling back into a shallow sleep. At 3:20 AM, I pulled myself up for a quick look around, looked, then looked again. Yes, there was a ship off to port. I could see the bright lights of the bridge, but couldn't make out a colored light—red for port or green for starboard—to tell me which way it was headed. I ducked below to grab binoculars. The compass in the binoculars allowed me to check the bearing of the ship. I huddled next to the dodger for the limited protection it offered from the wind. In five minutes, I checked the ship's bearing again. It seemed to have changed. That meant we were not on a collision course. But I checked again and again to make sure.

I had survived the first night but, exhausted, all I wanted was to sleep. Sleep would have to wait as roll call started at 9:00 AM. I checked the GPS and wrote my coordinates in *Islander*'s logbook. According to our communications plan, everyone would tune in to a specific channel on their single sideband radios. Rob MacFarlane on *Tiger Beetle* emceed.

On Sunday, June 27, Rob opened roll call and asked if *Dogbark* copied. Al on *Dogbark* responded, "This is *Dogbark*. This is *Dogbark*." He recited his latitude, longitude, boat speed, direction, and distance to finish. Rob repeated it, then said, "I spoke with Ryan on his satellite phone," and gave *Surfinn*'s position. "*Rusalka, Rusalka*, are you there?" Erik responded with his coordinates in the prescribed order. Rob worked his way through the list of twenty-four boats. The boats were listed by division and by handicap within their divisions. *Islander* was next to last. Rob called *Islander* and I tried to respond. But when I spoke into the microphone, the radio dial read, "Hi SWR," short for "high standing wave radio"—not a hello at all. I said,

"This is *Islander*. This is *Islander*. Rob, do you copy?" I repeated this three times, but it went nowhere. Then Rob called *Islander's* name again. "Well," he said, "We have no word from *Islander*. Let's move on. *Haulback, Haulback,* are you there?" My radio, which had transmitted clearly at the dock twenty-four hours before, was not working.

At the end of roll call, Rob asked if anyone needed clarifications on any positions. Several boats asked him to repeat latitude or longitude of various boats. As he did so, each one of us, alone at our chart tables, was noting our competitors' coordinates. I had created a separate sheet for every roll call with blanks I could fill in as the positions were given. But that first morning, I was so sick to my stomach and bleary with fatigue I didn't even look at my roll sheets. Then Rob opened the radio meeting to conversation. I hung on to every word I could understand. Not everyone's radio transmitted with the same clarity. Only mine did not transmit at all.

I had a problem. I needed to let the Race Committee—and my family—know where I was. Greg Nelsen, commodore of the Singlehanded Sailing Society, had already dropped out of the race because of ripped sails. Wen Lin, a diabetic, was so seasick he couldn't keep down any food: a life-threatening situation. Alan Hebert, on *Wisdom*, reported "oil-canning" problems with his hull. By contrast, I was not in any difficulty—and I definitely didn't want anyone to worry about me.

When I purchased it in 1999, my back-up communications system was cutting-edge technology. Now the GSC (Global Satellite Communications) was outdated. Happily, I reactivated it. I sent a short email to my husband, Dean, and Rich Ray, chairman of the Race Committee, giving my position and confirming that I was safe, though seasick. Dean had promised to forward my messages to our two daughters and other family and friends. The GSC carries messages using a limited number of satellites. I pushed SEND. My unit showed the message in queue. When a satellite from the system passed overhead, my machine would transmit the message.

That didn't happen until three that afternoon. Finally, the message flew from my machine to a satellite. When the satellite passed over a ground station, it downloaded my message. From there, the ground station sent the message to Dean's and Ray's computers.

At 6:00 PM, I tuned in to the weather broadcast. Don Anderson, an accomplished amateur forecaster, had volunteered to give our fleet a daily update on the location of the Pacific high. His broadcast came through loud and clear. The location of the high would help us determine our routes to Hawaii. In choosing a route, the type of boat mattered. Lighter boats could afford to sail extra miles in pursuit of the best wind. Heavier boats, like mine, traditionally stuck close to the rhumb line, the shortest distance between the start and finish. After giving the weather, Don asked for comments or questions. Mark Deppe of *Alchera* announced that when he emailed everyone's position to Rich Ray, Rich replied that he had received an email from *Islander*. Relief washed over me. Messages had flown back and forth across the water and folks knew where I was. Invisible waves connected me to family and friends.

The wind remained strong. The relatively relaxed day darkened into night. Well beyond the shipping lanes, I extended my sleeping time to thirty minutes between checks. Even at that, it was misery. At three in the morning, the wind had shifted about thirty degrees. As I scrunched down in the cockpit, it gusted to thirty-two knots. Fighting the wind, I adjusted the Monitor onto course and *Islander*'s motion gradually smoothed. There were no stars in the cloud-filled sky. No time to sit outside and dream. I eased myself below and reset the egg timer.

The next morning, as Rob worked his way through the 9:00 AM roll call, I filled in the blanks giving each boat's location. When Rob got to *Islander*, he said, "Good morning, *Islander*. We know you are out there and wish you a very good day." Surrounded by infinite gray sky and dark waves, my eyes filled with tears.

Days assumed shape: twenty-four hours divided into three-hour increments. Nine AM roll call, 6:00 PM weather, and 9:00 PM roll-call highlights; log entries at noon, three, six, nine, midnight, three, six, and nine. Nights were infinitely harder than days. I woke up each half hour to check all around. During the day, figuring *Islander* was visible, I allowed myself up to three-hour naps.

On Tuesday, June 29, I ventured onto the foredeck with my storm jib. As soon as I set it, *Islander*'s balance improved. The sun came out. With thirteen knots of wind, *Islander* rocked along making more than six knots under a partly cloudy blue sky. I opened up the hatch to dry below decks; solar panels recharged the batteries. Relaxing, I began to enjoy the passage.

The next day, I dropped the storm jib. I pulled the damaged jib off the roller furler and replaced it with an 85 percent jib—the working jib I had brought to use when running downwind. To keep from creating a mess of lines, or making a potentially dangerous mistake, I moved slowly and deliberately. Before I tackled any project, I thought it through step by step, movement by movement. Terribly fatigued, operating at less than 100 percent, I spent hours changing each sail. Once I raised the working jib, I shook the reef out of the mainsail. Then the wind dropped to seven knots. Two days after a gale, I wished with all my heart for more wind.

That night, after listening to Don's evening weather report, I heated a quart of fresh water and took a sponge bath. I pulled on clean clothes. How civilized! I stretched out on the settee and for hours read one of Patrick O'Brian's seafaring adventures—punctuated every thirty minutes by a check outside.

Measuring the days in miles from the Corinthian Yacht Club, as well as miles remaining to Hanalei Bay, I passed the one-quarter mark on July 1. Chronically preoccupied with my speed, I feared arriving in Hanalei after the official end of the race and being classified DNF: Did Not Finish. Rich Ray had emailed, reminding me that providing my whereabouts by email did not constitute "checking in" as required by the sailing instructions. I was being penalized one hour for each day I did not check in. In order to arrive within the twenty-one day duration of the race, I had to average five knots (five nautical miles per hour) for every hour of every day. Considering my accumulating penalty, I needed to average even better than that. Each day, the rest of the fleet stretched farther ahead of me. As Dean pointed out before the race, I had never averaged five knots on any previous passage. This time, I prayed, would be different.

On July 4, eight days after the start, I reached the trade winds. At last, I could set twin jibs to sail downwind. Attaching my spinnaker pole to the working jib and poling it out to starboard, I lifted the pole on its topping lift. A foreguy attached to the lower bridle kept it from going too high. Next, I set the storm jib and pulled it out to port. The mainsail was also flying to port, covering the storm jib. However, the storm jib created a flow of air in front of the mainsail, pulling the boat forward. This was not the twin sail arrangement I had envisioned. In fact, these twins were so small they looked silly. But until I figured out how to repair my larger jib, I was flying all the sail I had.

Hooking up the electric self-steering device allowed me to sail nearly directly downwind. My Wheelpilot 5000 wouldn't start, but my older, smaller Autohelm 3000 connected right away. That evening, the wind picked up considerably. Double-reefing the mainsail, I left the twin headsails flying. With twenty knots of wind, the Autohelm could not keep *Islander* on course. I set up the Monitor and headed up into the wind just enough so the Monitor would work.

Day by day, the weather grew warmer. I traded foul-weather gear for shorts and a tank top. The nonskid deck covering, a beige material that absorbs heat, burned my bare feet. Wary of sunburn, I slathered myself with sunscreen and wore a safari hat with a neck curtain. I looked ridiculous—and didn't care one bit.

I spent hours in the cockpit, *Islander's* living room. The view extends to the horizon in all directions. This huge living space changes constantly. Dramatic colors and cloud patterns herald sunrises and sunsets like theatrically staged events. On the horizontal plane, the swell throbs like the ocean's heartbeat. During dark, stormy days, I hid below to avoid the endless whitecaps. On calm, sunny days, I sat outside and marveled at the immensity.

On previous passages, I spent watches in the cockpit. Sailing solo, I kept watch differently. Desperately trying to reduce my sleep deficit, I spent much more time below decks napping than I would have preferred. At times, I thought I heard the whoosh of a whale or the sigh of a dolphin, but I missed seeing those that must have passed.

Eleven days out, on July 7, a white spinnaker billowed up over the horizon. The West Marine Pacific Cup race from San Francisco Bay to Oʻahu had started the week after the Singlehanded TransPac. These larger, fully crewed boats would pass through our fleet. This was the first sailboat I had seen since leaving San Francisco. At last, I had an opportunity to speak with someone. My VHF radio operates only for short line-of-sight distances. For fifteen minutes, I tried to raise the white-sailed boat. Why wouldn't it respond? At last, the captain answered. *Icon* was indeed competing in the Pac Cup. Excitedly, I explained I had spoken to no one since leaving San Francisco and asked him to contact the Singlehanded TransPacific Yacht Race Committee to confirm *Islander's* location. The captain was not inclined to chat. He could not have realized what that short conversation meant to me.

Two days later, on July 9, I painstakingly repaired the jib. Using an awl, I pulled whipping cord through the holes in the stiff, reinforced foot of the sail, and tied the ends together. I tacked it together at four locations—enough, I hoped, to keep it together for the final 700 miles.

I moved the sails around, first bringing in the storm jib. After adjusting the working jib and the large jib, my boat speed increased by a knot. For the first time during the passage, I had the sails in the positions I had planned. I headed for the finish line.

The fastest boats in the fleet were crossing the finish line, one or more a day, while I was a week behind. *Tiger Beetle* finished and Bill Merrick on *Ergo* took over roll call. *Ergo*'s signal had never come through as well as *Tiger Beetle*'s. I couldn't hear roll call any more at all. Those friendly words had given me a sense of belonging. I deeply missed my daily greetings from the fleet.

On top of that, emails were not leaving my GSC. Faithfully, every twelve hours I wrote an email giving my position and a couple of sentences about the day's events. The emails stacked up in my Out box. It seemed like a personal failing. My mother, in particular, was worried about my sailing alone. I didn't want her to suffer. I felt miserable and, for the first time, terribly alone. Rationally, I knew it was all a matter of satellite coverage of the area—obviously incomplete. I had been physically alone since I crossed the start line, but I had had a sense of being connected. Even though I hadn't spoken, except for the brief exchange with *Icon*, I had been able to communicate. Now I was isolated. I felt more vulnerable than I had since sailing out into the opening gale. If anything happened to me, how would I let someone know?

At noon on July 12, 450 miles from the finish line, with twin headsails flying, I was down below when a terrific gust of wind shook the boat. I heard a loud crash and raced outside. The large jib had back winded and bent the pole at a right angle. In a flash, I realized there was no way to repair it; my downwind sail was over.

In mourning, I unhooked the ruined pole and clipped it to the lifeline stanchions. I dropped the working jib and carried it back to the cockpit. The finish line had seemed so close. Now, forced to sail on a broad reach with much less sail area, it had receded dramatically. During the downwind days, I had felt fairly confident I could arrive before the official end of the race at midnight on July 17. With this latest setback, I was no longer so sure.

On July 14, a satellite picked up one of the emails that had been sitting for days in my Out box. I hoped it would relieve my family's fears. I wished I could hear from them but I hadn't received an email since July 8. Although I had to believe people were trying to contact me, my mailbox consistently read EMPTY. In frustration with the single sideband radio, I had given up trying to pick up roll call. I was getting very tired of being completely alone.

The wind blew directly toward Hanalei Bay, but I was forced to sail in long zigzags to approach the finish. I sailed west until I crossed the rhumb line, then headed south. By heading south, I could pass close to O'ahu before turning west to Kaua'i. As the sun rose on July 15, I searched the horizon for a dim shadow of land. There it was! The mountains of O'ahu rose darkly from the waves. Mentally, I cheered.

At 2:30 in the early morning dark, I had double-reefed the mainsail. Now I was glad I had. With twenty-two knots of wind, I gybed and skimmed west along the coast of O'ahu toward my final goal. Using my VHF radio, I called the Coast Guard on O'ahu to request communications assistance. The friendly voice agreed to contact Dean and the Race Committee with my coordinates. Talking with someone infused me with a burst of strength and enthusiasm. I had less than one hundred miles to go.

As soon as I reached seventy-five miles out, I commenced calling the Race Committee by VHF radio. I expected to arrive at the finish line in the middle of the night and wanted to make sure the Race Committee would guide me into reef-protected Hanalei Bay. In the distance, I could see the blue silhouette of Kaua'i; as it got dark, the island disappeared into a bank of clouds. I headed to a point north of the island, searching for the Kilalei Point light to guide me in.

At midnight, I still had not reached the Race Committee by VHF. After all these days at sea, would I end up crashing into the reef? Feeling very nervous, I contemplated turning back out to sea until daylight.

The only other piece of communications equipment I had on board was my cell phone. The Race Committee had monitored its satellite phone as long as other boats were out there. But the last boat had arrived at least two days ago—and the Race Committee knew I did not have a satellite phone. Desperately, I dialed. A phone rang and rang. "Hello, Race Committee? This is Barbara Euser on *Islander*." "Barbara, this is Dean." I nearly dropped the phone.

Dean had arrived on Kaua'i that afternoon. He woke the Race Committee, and I communicated with them by VHF. Folks drove to the bay, jumped into a motorized skiff, and headed out to meet me. Once the committee member at headquarters confirmed that I had crossed the finish line—forty-five hours before the end of the race—the skiff pulled alongside. Five men scrambled aboard: Rich and Bill of the Race Committee; Greg, commodore of the Singlehanded Sailing Society, who had dropped out of the race on day two; Napoleon, helmsman of the skiff; and Dean.

Rich took the helm and instructed me to take a seat and relax; the Race Committee would take it from there. This was the same reception each of the other boats had received upon crossing the finish line: relief at the helm, escort into the bay. Once the wires immobilizing the prop shaft had been cut, the motor started, the jib furled in, and the anchor attached to its rod, all six of us assembled in the cockpit. Bill lifted his backpack to his lap and pulled out a bottle of champagne. He poured it into plastic glasses and proposed a toast: "Congratulations to the first woman to finish the Singlehanded TransPac 2004!"

E. A. MILLER

Equipment and Pretense

I DIDN'T WANT TO HIKE ANYPLACE WHERE THERE WAS HISTORY. My father, an inveterate hiker himself, thought I should go to the White Mountains—well-traveled ground for both him and our family. My brothers, in their self-appointed roles as consultants, thought I should go to the Berkshires. Everyone thought I was crazy when I chose the Adirondacks, a five-hour drive from my home in eastern Massachusetts.

But I didn't want to go where my family had already been. This was not a trip about family history; it wasn't even a trip about larger history—I rejected western Massachusetts because I had read captivity narratives set there. I wanted something unknown to me, unknown to history. I wanted to be self-centered, to have the trip revolve around my experiences, to not come home and hear, "Did you take the loop up Pinkham's Notch?" Or even to hear my own mind talking back, *Hmm, this must be around where Eunice Williams was taken in 1704.*

I wanted my own story. And so I began my first solo overnight hiking trip in the Adirondacks.

I had been hiking before, and done any number of solo day trips, but I had never camped overnight by myself. The camping trips I had done had generally been with men—in the man's tent, sleeping bags gathered together, the thrill of making love half-in and half-out of the tent. I had been on nine such trips with four different men, and they bore remarkable similarities. The pre-trip planning was for me to prove that I knew about hiking, that my stories about my father and brothers (avid hikers) were not for naught, that my family's trips in the White Mountains were not done out of the car, that I was the logical, pragmatic being I presented myself as.

Or at least this is what I thought the pre-planning was about. The actual trip of course was about two things—the daytime "I can carry as much as you can and walk as quickly as you do" and the nighttime "See, I'm just as sexy here in the wilderness as I am in my negligee in the city." The best of these trips was two weeks in Canada, canoeing and camping on our own exclusive island and eating the "real-people" food (steaks and Czechoslovakian pastries) that his mother insisted we bring. The worst of these trips combined the arrival of an early period with the California Coast. Try making tampons from seaweed and you'll see what I mean.

I've only camped once with a woman friend. That time, I actually was the most experienced person as she had never been camping before. It was dreadful. Not only was her basic temperament more suited to hotels and waiters than to tents and campfires, but we also had the worst weather I've ever experienced—four solid days of rain. We cut the trip short, but not before everything we owned had been soaked, and not before discovering that four days earlier we had locked the keys inside our rental car. It was another long, wet hike to the town to get a locksmith.

All of these trips had two things in common—borrowed equipment and pretense. It's a little easier to talk about borrowed equipment, so that first. Despite my family's love for the outdoors, I didn't own my own pack or tent. I did own my own sleeping bag, purchased before the first expedition with a man—in fact, we bought matching down bags, one a left-zip and one a right-zip so they could be put together (that man is long gone, but the left-zip lives on). My brothers used to purchase new equipment and lend me their old packs, and either the man would have a tent or I'd borrow one from my family. My family is opposed to purchasing anything new when it can be borrowed, so it happened a couple of times that one of my brothers would express-mail his pup tent, and I'd express-mail it back after the trip. It wasn't a big thing, but it meant I always had a pack that didn't fit well, a tent I had set up only once before, if that, and equipment I wasn't sure about. This came to a head on that Canadian camping trip, when the tent I had borrowed from a brother, which was checked out by my teenage nephew, turned out to have a broken zipper. I spent the first evening of the camping trip apologizing to my then-boyfriend, trying without success to fix the zipper and finally resorting to sewing us into the tent at night so that the mosquito netting could have some effect.

When I announced my plans to purchase my own equipment for this trip, wanting everything I had to be mine alone, my father told me that I should save my money for when I got married, because "your husband might have a tent."

Your husband might have a tent. Somehow, in spite of my family's frugality, the men in my life (brothers, father, future husband) were expected to own equipment. And somehow, although my mother and I were expected to be "good troopers" while hiking, making camp, and identifying wildlife, we were expected to do these things only in the company of men. My brothers and father went on trips together and alone, but my mother and I were always unequipped, and when I would express my desire to take a solo trip, the physical lack of equipment grew into a gender lack: "The world is too dangerous for you to go by yourself." In America, ownership is power. And in my life, men were the owners.

If the men in my family owned the equipment, I owned the pretense. By all rights, I was an experienced hiker and camper, and I wanted to be seen by men as competent and knowledgeable, but I didn't think of myself in that way. So I pretended. I pretended about real events and real experience and real competence. And how was anyone to know differently? After all, if anyone questioned my pretense, I had none of the physical evidence to back me up—where was my backpack, the tent, the walking stick? If anything, my pretense of the real was suspicious.

I acted in this way longer than I want to admit, pretending to boyfriend after boyfriend that I could light a fire with one match, snow-shoe into the Poconos and winter-camp, read a compass and a topo-graphical map, steer a canoe. Of course I could do these things, so the only person I was truly pretending to was myself. And by the time that last, best camping trip came along—on the Canadian island with a zipless tent—I had almost stopped pretending.

Almost because, after all, I was still in the company of men. All of my performances, pretense and reality, had an audience. And so it was that I decided, in my thirtieth year, to go solo, to abandon the audiences of family, of history, of romance. If I were going to perform, it would be by myself to an audience of one.

I decided to hike in the Pharaoh Lake Wilderness Area of the Adiron-dacks, a collection of small ponds and smaller mountains (my trip, my mountain size), a short, three-night jaunt that would make a loop around eight of those ponds and one bump of a mountain. I planned my trip and supplies with care, and then went to a local outdoor store to buy myself a tent and pack. Oh what joy! I bought an adjustable internal-frame pack that was designed for a short-waisted woman and had it fit to my short-waisted measurements right in the store. Then I bought a two-man (or one-woman and a dog, as the case was) lightweight, three-season tent. I was ready.

Well, not quite. There was the matter of armament. Even though I was going in October, a month chosen for a high probability of good weather and few people, and even though I was taking my dog Honig, an overly protective golden retriever with a bark that makes mailmen cower and fellow dog-walkers scoop up their Scotties, this was not enough for my family. From my father came a piercing whistle, strung on rugged cord, which I was to wear around my neck. It had, he carefully explained, a dual purpose: to ward off would-be attackers and to at-tract rescuers if I were to fall and break my leg. He also provided a worn, wooden walking stick with a sharpened steel tip at the bottom and a concealed space for a small dram of whiskey (he didn't say whether I should poke or toast those I encountered). My brother Doug sent me a bone letter opener *cum* dagger which he had carved from an elk horn. The thick handle curved downward into a mean-looking blade; "the better," my brother explained, "to put your weight behind the thrust." By the time I signed in at the trailhead, I felt less like a pretend hiker than I did like a pretend Rambette.

In fact, I would meet no one during my hike, but the walking stick was wonderful to let slide up and down in my right hand as I stepped forward; the whistle could almost sound like a loon, my finger muting and releasing the air; and the bone blade proved the exact curvature of an apple, the peel falling off in looping red circles.

I saw no one, and I was not afraid. At least not of getting lost, nor of bears or other animals, nor of fellow hikers, nor of bad weather. But I was afraid of myself.

The first day proved miserable. And there was nothing wrong. The pack was not too heavy, my legs felt fine, the dog was good company. But my practice of pretense had deprived me of knowing real sensations, and so I worried about the smallest of things: *Should I take a break now? Should I go to the third lake today? Should I eat something?* Behind these questions lurked comparatives: *Would my brothers stop now? Would a "real" hiker camp here?* It was as if fatigue and hunger were just pieces of ill-fitting equipment, not to be trusted, just patched over and forgotten.

As a consequence, I saw nothing. And chased by invisible demons of competitiveness, I hiked, without resting (throwing dog bones to Honig along the way), from 8:00 AM until 4:00 PM, when I finally stopped to make camp. I wish I could say that this was the moment I came to my senses. But it wasn't. I did everything properly, hung my food up away from the tent, made my fire and ate my dinner, got into my sleeping bag.

There in the tent, the dog curled up at my feet, my pack at my right side, a flashlight pointed over my journal, I wrote that I had failed.

The next morning, things seemed better. I woke early, chased the dog out of the tent and stood in my long johns on the broad rock cropping out from the lake. The rock was cool and moist under my feet, two shades darker than the grey sky; the rock flecked with mica and the sky with early pieces of light. I stood in the V-stance and began the first pattern. Tai chi on Rock Lake.

The mist was rising and the sky had whitened into birch bark. There were fallen birches in the lake, their branches reflected in the water, a dark tangle against blue. I moved into White Crane Spreads Its Wings, and turning, saw my tent, its light-green tarp stretched out, a leafhopper caught on a bare branch.

But after breakfast, hiking up Treadway Mountain, watching for the red diamonds of the trail, trudging again in vague restlessness, the sense of unease caught up to me. Here I was, doing the very thing I had set out to do, and yet, I felt like a failure. Without an audience, without someone to direct my response, I was at a loss, unable to frame my own experiences. I might have rejected history in choosing my hiking place, but history had not rejected me. It was my family history of competitiveness that had kept me hiking all day, the fear of my brothers labeling me a "wimp" or worse yet, their "wussy" little sister. But I hadn't failed that test. I had hiked all day. I was alone. I was carrying a fifty-pound pack (dog food is heavy). I was meeting the expectations of family history. It was literary history that I had failed.

I had failed to meet the rules of narrative. That to prove my competence, I had to endure a physical trial—rescue a small child from an avalanche; hike ten miles on a broken leg; subsist for five days on ground nuts and wild mushrooms. That to prove my solitude, I had to experience a miracle—hear the voice of my mother (dead for five years now) laud me for my independence; wake to write an inspired masterpiece by sunrise; remember, in the light of the campfire, a long-forgotten commitment to dedicate my life to the poor.

In short, captivity and conversion.

As a girl growing up in New England, I had read as many captivity-and-conversion narratives as I could find, imagining myself as Mary Rowlandson on her eleven-week forced march, walking with no shoes in the frozen snow, eating only acorns and rancid bear meat, being mindful to pray daily and resist the vice of pipe smoking. I also had a recurring fantasy that on our next family camping trip we'd be caught by a blizzard, and I would lead my family to safety by sheer dint of will, despite my hunger and frostbitten feet, having given up my shoes and meager rations to my parents.

Or I'd pretend to be William Bradford, looking at the dark woods, "no lights to greet us," with the darker sea behind. He knelt at the sight of that vast and unyielding wilderness, and in my version, I'd bushwhack to the river that ran behind our house, crouch down in the frozen mud and commit my soul and the souls of whatever pets had accompanied me to God.

I learned how to be a "good American" from these accounts: to be independent, to have fortitude and faith preserve me through hardship, and, most importantly, to spin a good yarn. I'm still a sucker for these tales: modern conversion narratives like Annie Dillard meeting the spirit of Rimbaud in the woods or modern captivity narratives like the story of the man who, having been pinned by a felled tree, cut off his own leg with his penknife and crawled six miles to help.

But after two days in the woods, I struggled with neither my body nor my soul. There was no blizzard, no broken leg, no capture by Indians, no desire, upon seeing that first sunrise, to commit either my soul or Honig's, no spirit of Rimbaud. I was still wrestling with pretense. I was so uncomfortable with my own perceptions that they were only real if they could be translated into narratives of faith and fortitude—even if those narrative models made me feel like a failure! So much for a solo hiking trip—I had brought along a vast audience, crowded with family, old lovers (even the thought of which can make me suck in my stomach), and literary critics. Talk about ill-fitting equipment: an invisible audience and borrowed stories.

I came to hike to find a story, but stories are products of past history and future audiences. I didn't know how to attend to the present. While I was doing all of this pondering, I hiked up and down Treadway (I said it was a small mountain) and was heading to Grizzle Ocean. My feet, apparently, had a life of their own and good navigational skills because I cannot recall one detail of Treadway's terrain despite the fact that the guidebook says the mountaintop is a bare dome of milk and rose quartz.

It was at Grizzle Ocean that I came to my senses. The dog plunged into the lake; I threw sticks to her, and with each wide sweep of my arm, I dismissed my audience and vowed to spend the rest of my trip in hedonistic attention.

There are no stories to tell from the rest of the trip. I felt quiet and calm, and the dog, probably exhausted from her two-day forced march, was game to stop and rest whenever I sat and watched. We saw some wild turkeys rustling in the path, and a small black bear crouched in a hole. Everybody was just content to look.

I left the wilderness area on the morning of the fourth day and was signing out at the trailhead when the ranger came by. He looked at Honig, tiredly puddled against my legs, and said, "1 don't think your dog is going to make it on your hike." I didn't tell him that we had already been there and back. I was glad the shape of stories didn't shine through me, that I could have secret faith and silent fortitude.

As it turned out, both of my brothers had gone hiking that same weekend. One had fallen and broken his collarbone; the other, drinking whiskey by the campfire, felt renewed. They told their captivity-and-conversion narratives over the telephone. When they asked for my story, I just said everything went fine. There are no narratives for competence and observation. I'm planning another solo trip for March—after all, I own the equipment now.

BRIDGET QUINN

The Cliffhanger

ONE OF THE HARDEST THINGS TO TEACH BEGINNERS IS TO POINT THEIR TIPS
DOWNHILL. It goes against nature to take two slippery sticks and the unsteady body on top and turn them willfully toward possible destruction, to
ignore the threat of gravity, hurl yourself headlong toward the abyss,
and not cling to the familiar safety of the uphill. I can understand that fear,
though I never experienced the moment for myself. I learned to ski too
young, when walking and skiing required equal leaps of faith. I don't remember learning to ski and I don't remember learning to walk. They
were just there, whenever it was that consciousness broke in on me. I
was a girl. I walked. I skied.

I don't get to ski much anymore, have only done it a couple of
times in the last ten years. I've turned to other sports: rock climbing,
mountain biking, in-line skating. But it doesn't matter. Skiing is still with
me. I learned from it: how to be alone and be happy, how to point myself downhill (or up a rock face) and go, how to trust the outcome and
enjoy the ride.

At eleven I've skied by myself for years. In a family of nine children, at my
age, I'm a leftover. My older brothers and sisters ski together or with
friends. They don't want me around, I'm too young. I don't care. I love to
ski alone. It's the only time I'm ever by myself.

I avoid being thrown in with other people on the lifts. In line,
when someone raises their pole and yells, "Single!" I don't scoot up to
join them. But the operators don't like to see me get on the chair alone,

as if someone so small might not be able to hold her seat, might get swept away by the hard winds that pick up through the gorge and make the chairs sway, sometimes bringing the whole lift to a stop. The people caught above can't be rescued and have to stay there, freezing, sometimes for hours.

Maybe the operators are afraid such a little body will panic up there or need comforting. I love the gorge, the wide-open white on white, the way the mountain suddenly shoots away under my feet, the craggy rock faces hanging with icicles, the shallow trails of snowballs that start rolling down the slope, then plunge over the edge, the tiny skiers, little dots of color, racing over the snow bridge that crosses the frozen creek. I would love to swing high above there, all eyes on me, but not seeing me. Alone, but on stage.

I had never been to New York before. My family and friends in the West thought I was crazy. "Why New York?" they wailed. "It's dirty. It's so violent. Aren't you scared?"

I had never lived in a city before. I welcomed the solitude.

One of my first nights out, I was robbed in the subway. Standing in line, waiting to buy tokens, I clutched a twenty-dollar bill. When I got to the window, as I handed my money to the teller, I was pushed hard from the side by a kid of about eleven or twelve. Another kid, behind him, grabbed the twenty and they both took off up the stairs. I chased them. I didn't have a bank account yet, had no other money with me. I didn't know anyone.

Slamming up the two flights to the street, all I saw were the white sweat socks above white high tops of the kid in front of me. The whole way up I yelled at those shoes, "You'd better stop! You'd better stop!" When we broke onto the street I shrieked "STOP!" in a voice so maniacal the boy with the money froze. He turned around slowly, his arms out by his sides. By the time he faced me, two men had also come to the top of the stairs. He held out the money. I reached out, snatched it, and he ran.

When I resubmerged back underground, money in hand, people in the station started clapping. I bought my tokens and pushed nonchalantly through the turnstile. On the subway, going back downtown, I was still breathing hard. I felt exhilarated, excited, strong.

"That was so foolish," my mother said. "You could have been killed."

At the last minute, I'm pulled up to join a man skiing with another man and woman, a couple wearing matching ski outfits. He's annoyed to be forced together for fifteen minutes with some kid. People feel that way a lot. They don't like it on airplanes and they don't like it on ski lifts. He doesn't say anything for the first several minutes as he knocks his boots together to get the snow off his skis. Then he looks all around, examining the trees as we go past, checking out the sky, craning his neck to watch the pulleys as we bump under them, like it's the first time he's seen any of this, and maybe it is.

Silence makes people nervous, even around kids. "Look at that Indian," he says. He points with his pole. I look. I see B., long, glossy hair flowing behind him, doing freestyle tricks off moguls, showing off as he passes under the chair lift. "That's my brother," I say, proud. B. can do things on skis most people can't do walking. I'm not clear about racism yet, or about his being adopted. The man looks at me, blue-white as the snow, purple lips and blond hair scraggling out around my face. He looks away and snorts, doesn't say anything to me for the rest of the ride, calls rowdy things to the couple in front of us.

Before I could live in graduate housing, my own sterile, utilitarian cubby-hole plopped down amid the hedonistic outlandishness of St. Mark's Place, I had to be immunized. I waited over an hour at the university's medical center. I was finally taken into a curtained room where a young, blond doctor, not much more than a student himself, was reading through the Xeroxed questions I had filled out. "Your name's Irish," he said. "So's mine." I smiled, nodded.

"I tell you," he said, ripping the cellophane off a new syringe and filling it, squinting at the contents, "it's so nice not to have another Jew in here. They're just everywhere around this place, aren't they?"

I sat there. He jabbed the needle into my arm. When he was done I grabbed my jacket and stood up. "What you said," I sputtered. "I don't agree with you." He looked at me. I left.

I filled out a complaint, but felt dirty, complicitous.

I see people freak out on the mountain all the time. Sometimes they won't even get off the lift and it's funny to watch them pass you going down. I think that would be awful: pitched downward like that in an open chair. For me, the only scary thing about skiing is getting ready in the morning.

My father wakes us early, hours before it's light out, pounding on our doors, bellowing, "Reveille, reveille, it's daylight in the swamp!" There's a certain way to do things and not much time. Things not done right are punished with temper tantrums. "Son of a bitch!" he bellows, slamming doors. Or: "Damn this snake farm!" Or: "I oughta have you skinned alive!" Or scariest, most mysterious of all: "How would you like me to ostracize you?"

I have to get everything together quick. There are two bathrooms for the eleven of us and I have to get in and out of there fast. We each have a plastic bag with our name on it. Mine has mittens, hat, goggles, socks, and my pass that fastens to my jacket with a big horse-blanket pin. Today nothing's missing; I've checked my bag three times, know it's all there. I go to the smokehouse, where we eat his huge, dry pancakes in shifts, then cram into the van. For the next hour and a half I'm pushed around by crabby teenagers and everything I say is stupid.

I had to learn to walk differently when I came to the city. At first, I'd stop in the wrong places, suddenly, and people would come crashing into me from behind, like a pile-up on the freeway. I waited too long at lights, until they actually said "Walk," then would get cut off by turning cabs and never make it across before the lights changed again. Or I'd get caught behind slow goers and couldn't figure out how to get around. I'd drop into the street and scurry around parked cars before hopping back onto the sidewalk, running into people coming the other way.

But I quickly adapted. I learned to storm the sidewalk. I had a pair of low-cut granny boots whose square, elongated heels I particularly enjoyed mashing against the concrete, as I propelled myself from their height forward onto my toes, taking long, burly strides. I came to a new understanding of my body in space, careening off thousands of other bodies, weaving myself and whatever parcels or attachments (backpacks, book bags) I might be carrying, through and around everyone else's. I roared through crowds, around obstacles, with the power and precision of a race car driver. I slalomed down Broadway.

When we make the last turn of the winding, sickening road to the top, the mountain suddenly opens up in front of us, towering, wide, white runs hemmed in by green. As soon as the van stops, we push out, falling over each other to get out. My father steps down from the driver's side and stretches, happy to be away from the pressure and craziness of job and home. He's a big man in a big landscape, and he finally looks comfortable.

I understand how it is with him. I feel easier on the hill, too. In my big jacket and mittens, hat and goggles, people I know don't know me. I don't usually tell them. A lot of people think I'm a boy, and I like that. Growing up in a big family in a small town, everyone thinks they know you already. Here, I'm not my family. I'm not even a girl. I don't have to be myself, whoever that is.

My graduate advisor was a famous art historian—as famous as you can get as an art historian. He's mentioned more than once in Andy Warhol's diaries. My last presentation was in his seminar on neoclassicism. I spoke for nearly two hours on the work of Adelaide Labille-Guiard, almost-forgotten female portraitist of the French Revolution. She was a woman who painted, not a painter of women. Or, not necessarily.

I ended the talk buzzing with excitement and a sense of triumph, for myself and for my subject. In the darkened room no one could see my sweaty hairline, my flushed face, lipstick gone, mascara smearing. I was barely illuminated by the last slide, still up, Labille-Guiard's monumental *Self-Portrait with Students*—an eighteenth-century woman, heroic-sized, bound up in a voluminous blue silk gown. Sitting before her canvas, palette in hand, two female students watch from behind her chair. Her gaze is locked outward, challenging the viewer to question if this task is appropriate to women. She is an artist. She is a woman. She is very powerful. She is a model for her students and for me.

From somewhere out in the dark, the voice of my professor: "But how is her work significant?"

I have red-, white-, and blue-striped skis. One has a smiley-face sticker at the tip, so I know which is the right and which, left. I've had them for a couple of years, but I still like them. My brother J. has a poster of hippie motorcycle riders and one of them has a helmet with the flag on it. My skis remind me of that. They're the only new piece of ski stuff I've ever gotten. Everything else is hand-me-downs, and most things don't fit exactly right. But my skis fit me perfectly.

When I slide off the lift, I take a minute to get my mittens through the leather loops of my poles. The man I was riding with and his friends have poles with molded rubber grips and they're off right away, laughing and talking loud, daring each other to go fast, to ski hard. I wait another minute, then push off after them.

I cut close to the woman who was in the chair in front of me, plant my pole, and push off a mogul, landing with a thump on the other side. I plant my other pole, turn, and do it again. I finally catch the men near the bottom of the face, where the meadow opens up. I crouch into a tuck, go straight the rest of the way, and whiz past them as the run crosses under the lift. I hear people cheering above me. I look back. The men pull up, wait for their woman friend, as if they weren't trying to go fast.

I make it on the chair alone next time.

I found the city strangely comforting. The mob, the noise, the squeezed space felt familiar, reminded me of my family. Except that here, I was anonymous. New York had no expectations, no preconceived notions, required nothing of me. I felt safe in the crowd, sheltered and brave.

But graduate school, the reason I'd come to New York, was boring, frustrating, seemed dead next to the excitement of the city. One night, home late from the library, lights off, votive candles I'd bought at the corner bodega flickering around the corners of my bedroom, the Velvet

Underground crackling from my boom box, I ate chocolate chip cookies washed down with beer, stared out my window at the people and cars and lights, and wondered why I ever wanted to study art history. Half a six pack—tall boys—and a second VU album later, I realized: *I want to be an artist, not study them. I came to New York to become a writer.*

It was a terrifying thought. I felt sick. I blew out the candles and went to bed.

After only a few runs my eyes are burning. I'm wearing goggles but they're not tinted. They keep out wind, not sun, and the sky, huge, bigger than the mountain, is blazing bright blue. The snow shines back even stronger so it doesn't make things clearer, but harder to see, like car headlights shining right at you at night. But I keep skiing. After a while, the burning goes away.

During finals one semester, I noticed a hard bump in my left eye. I went to an ophthalmologist on Park Avenue. He did several creepy, in-my-eye tests with skeletal, high-tech equipment. Left me alone and blinded by substances he'd dropped in my eyes, for what seemed like a long time, then came back into the darkened room and asked, before he'd even closed the door, "How long did you live near the equator?"

I can never be outside without sunglasses again, sun or clouds, or I might lose my sight. But sunglasses in New York are chic, rain or shine.

I've skied every run on the mountain a hundred times, except one. I've never been told not to ski the Cliffhanger, but I know I'm not supposed to. I think they just think I never would. It's steep, the steepest on the mountain. Last year three people were killed in an avalanche on it.

It's awful to think of dying that way, like underwater, only it takes a lot longer. I'm a good swimmer; I don't think I could drown. But when you're buried in an avalanche, you don't know which way is up. Even if you can dig, if your legs aren't broken or something, you probably won't go in the right direction.

The Cliffhanger is closed a lot because of avalanche warnings. I've heard that sometimes the ski patrol goes out and starts avalanches on purpose, so they can open the run, even though it's not skied much. I don't know how they do that or how they don't get caught in one themselves.

I ski all morning without going into the lodge, up and down, fast as I can. There are almost no lines. I like to try different things. One time down, I leave my poles at the top. Or I make rules: only two turns, or: as many turns as I can make, or: straight the whole way, or: make jumps out of everything, or: close my eyes for as long as I can.

But after a while I want something new. There isn't anything new. I've done the same runs, the same way since I was a little kid. Next year I'll be in junior high. I want to feel the challenge of skiing. I can't remember pushing my limits.

I find myself at the opening to the Cliffhanger. There's a rope tied between two trees and a sign hanging from it that reads: *Closed, Dangerous Conditions*. I look behind me, and there's no one around. It's nearly one. Most people are eating lunch. Most of my family's probably in the lodge now, pulling sandwiches and cookies out of big brown paper bags. No one will see me.

I'm not sure why I want to do this. I never do things I'm not supposed to, not really. I crouch down, lay back onto my skis, and slide under the rope.

My skis make a hissing sound as I glide through the deep snow. No tracks. I'm the first one here. That's already something new. I stop right at the edge and before looking down—still not sure I'm really going to do it—I look out.

The Cliffhanger faces a different direction from all the other runs. I see the Little Belt Mountains from a new angle. I can see sides and unusual faces I've never seen before.

I don't look down. I push off and immediately I'm going too fast. My tips feel more behind me than underneath, like I'm skiing the inside of a spoon. But I get control before I fall, make wide arcing turns to keep my speed down and to make it seem less steep. No one's been on the slope before me. I have to choose my own way.

I've never skied in powder before, though everyone knows it's supposed to be the best. "The ultimate," my sister P. says. It's deep, I can barely see my skis beneath the snow. It's soft, velvety, and it's not hard to turn in like you'd think it would be. I start to sing to myself, a song from the radio I've had in my head all day. It's fun to sing loud where no one can hear me. I ski slowly, carefully. I want to make it last.

The boom nearly knocks me over. The ground is trembling and at first I think it's an earthquake because I've heard about those in Montana before. Then I know what it is and before I can think about anything else I'm in a tuck and I'm going straight down. It's way faster than I've ever gone before. Snow is blowing up everywhere around me and I can't see. I keep going.

MONIQUE COLE

I Did Iditasport

THE NORTHERN SKY SWALLOWS THE LIGHT OF MY HEADLAMP AS THE STARS SHINE BACK FROM LIGHT-YEARS AWAY, MOCKING THE INSIGNIFI-CANCE OF MY TEN-FOOT BEAM. I'm on Alaska's Iditarod dog sled trail in February—on a bicycle. Alone in this silent expanse of wilderness, I feel completely confident and surprisingly at peace.

When I told friends and family about my plans to enter a 160-mile ultra-marathon called Iditasport, the unanimous response was, "Why?"

I tried "It sounds like fun" a few times, but that sounded insane even to me. I guess I wanted to test my theory that most of my athletic limitations were self-imposed; that I was capable of much more than I believed. As a child in Hawaii, I was hit by a car. Both legs were broken, and later, complications left me with a torn knee ligament, one leg three-fourths of an inch longer than the other, and scoliosis between my shoulder blades.

In my teens and early twenties I avoided land sports, escaping to the ocean where my asymmetry went unnoticed. After moving to Colorado, I tentatively delved into rock climbing, snowboarding, and mountain biking, slowly chipping away at my fears and self-doubts. But the final blow would require an extremely difficult physical challenge. Iditasport was the answer.

On Saturday, February 18, at 10:30 AM, I set off into the unknown of Alaska's outback. This moment, months in the making, inspired an ecstatic "Yahoo!" Elation turned to concentration as I learned to maneuver my bike over the punchy snow across Big Lake, where the race started. Pedal, pedal, sink; pedal, pedal, sink. I was developing quite a rhythm doing the Iditasport two-step whenever my back tire became mired in soft spots. Progress was slow, but I didn't mind. I was innocently optimistic about what lay ahead.

New challenges greeted me as I left the lake to follow a roller-coaster trail along a survey line cut straight through the taiga—a spider's web of stunted spruce, frozen swamps, and braided streams. When the forest opened into a swamp, the snow got softer, forcing me out of the saddle to push. And unfortunately the numerous stream banks came in pairs. The careening downhills were exhilarating, but were always followed by a steep climb on the other side. Pushing an overfilled shopping cart up a ski jump would be a similar feat. Iditarod champion Martin Buser shouted encouragement as he mushed past with his dog team. Now that's the way to travel, I thought to myself.

Michael Bane, a friend and fellow writer from Colorado, pulled out a pair of crampons to ascend one particularly steep and icy stream bank. I was almost to the top when an Italian racer offered to help, pulling the handlebars while I pushed from behind. His chivalric gesture seemed a bit ludicrous considering the fact that I had entered a 160-mile wilderness race. I suppressed my feminist prejudices ("I ain't no damsel in distress, Buster") and gave him the benefit of the doubt ("Maybe he's demonstrating camaraderie, not male chauvinism"). Using one of the few words I know in his native tongue, I said, "*Grazie.*"

"*Ciao,*" I would later say as I rode past him walking his bike. You see, I had the advantage of superior equipment. I had begged, borrowed, and sewn to collect my Iditagear. Floatation is the key to success in bicycling on a trail of snow packed by snowmobiles and dog sleds. Two things increase your floatation: a larger wheel "footprint" and a lighter load. One friend had an extra pair of Snow Cat EB-3 wheels. The extra-wide rims were developed by Fairbanks locals for riding on snow and can be used on any bike without frame modifications. The larger wheel-print means the weight of bike and rider is distributed over a greater surface area than covered by normal wheels. The Italian didn't have the wide wheels and scratched from the race before the first checkpoint.

In order to succeed in Iditasport, I also had to acquire a lightweight bike and the camping gear required by race regulations. To my Barracuda aluminum frame I strapped two quarts of water in insulated containers, a sleeping bag and pad, bivy sack, stove and pot for melting snow into drinking water, and food. Everything but the water and food were lent by various outdoorsy friends.

Some of the more serious racers skimped on the quality of their survival gear in order to trim ounces from their load. They were betting on the fact that they would be moving fast and would not need to camp out. I had less confidence in the kindness of the weather and my own ability to stay on-course, warm, and hydrated. So I strapped extra layers of fleece (pieced together on my trusty Singer) and a down coat onto my rear rack. My bike began to resemble a gypsy wagon. Mountaineer Vernon Tejas once told me that people carry their insecurities on expeditions: the greater the number of insecurities, the greater the amount of equipment. Comparing my gear to that carried by my comrades, I judged that I had an average, perhaps healthy, amount of wariness.

At least I didn't pack any firearms. A fear of moose inspired Don Cuerdon (a.k.a. Captain Dondo), an editor for *Mountain Bike Magazine*, to carry a Colt .45 automatic during the 1988 race. His fear was somewhat well-founded: Moose prefer to walk on the trail rather than wallow through deep snow and they belligerently refuse to yield the trail to humans. Several cross-country skiers and sled dogs have been trampled to death by moose in Alaska. However, locals pointed out to Captain Dondo that his little pistol could never bring down one of those two-ton members of the deer family. But if he encountered a wild beast, they teased, he could use it to shoot himself in the head for a quick, painless death. He carried the gun despite the jeers and dropped out partway through the race. To his credit, the Captain returned and finished the following year, his load lightened by leaving behind some of his insecurities and all of his weaponry.

That twenty-seven-mile stretch to the first checkpoint redefined my concept of distance. A twenty-seven-mile training ride on snow-covered dirt roads takes four hours at the most. But in four and a half hours, I had traveled only fifteen miles. I was spending as much time pushing my bike as I was riding it.

Iditasport is a multisport affair, with a one-hundred-sixty-mile course for bikers, skiers, and triathletes (who bike, ski, and run) and a *short*, seventy-mile trail for runners and snowshoers. Voices carry very well over snow, I discovered as I heard two snowshoe runners gaining on me. One of the voices belonged to Roman Dial, a biology professor at the University of Fairbanks who was pontificating to athlete/journalist/archaeologist Chris Kostman on the nuances of animal urine in the wild.

"Bad day for bikes," Dial said as he passed me pushing my bike uphill, once again. Then I remembered the sage advice of former Iditasport champion Gail Koepf at the start line: "Take the time to adjust your tire pressure; it's worth it." I flattened my tires to almost zero and started *floating* over the soft stuff. Reluctantly, I said goodbye to my heavier companion, Michael.

Now my solo adventure had begun. My personal pace was apparently unique: Most of the sixty other entrants were in front of me and a few stragglers were behind. The voluptuous Mount Susitna kept me company, though. The mountain's resemblance to a recumbent woman inspires the nickname "Sleeping Lady" and a local legend. A young woman falls asleep while awaiting her lover's return from battle, the tale goes. But her soldier dies and her family lets her sleep on . . . indefinitely. No longer naive about the difficulty of Iditasport, I envied her state of ignorant bliss.

When I rolled into Big Su, the first checkpoint, my spirits lifted. Cheers and hugs from my friends, Marge Stoneking and Lynelle Kukowski, greeted me there. Thanks to working as a volunteer the previous year, I knew most of the race staff. I lingered too long basking in the warmth and fellowship of the sweat-scented racers' tent. I must have said, "Okay, I'm going now," at least ten times. When I finally did leave at sundown, Marge and Lynelle sent me off with more cheers, votes of confidence, and promises of beer when I returned to Big Su, which was also the last checkpoint on the lollipop-loop course.

"Boy, this trail is great," I said to myself, "I feel so light, I'm just hydroplaning over the trail." No wonder I felt so light: I had left my fanny pack at Big Su. Gloves, food, water, and stove are not the kinds of things you want to go without, so I doubled back. "You all gave me such a great send-off, I decided to come back for an encore," I joked to my confused friends. Marge marveled that I had retained my sense of humor, but hey, what's a couple miles of backtracking on a one-hundred-sixty-mile course?

My spirits remained high for the next fifteen miles of hard-packed trail. If Disneyland had an Iditabike ride, this would be it—banked turns, rolling moguls, phantasmagoric arches formed of fallen spruce frosted with snow. The full moon still rested below the horizon, and there were no city lights to drown out the perfect sky. There were so many stars, it was almost easier to count the black spaces between them than the heavenly bodies themselves. The only sound was the constant whirring of my wide wheels on the snow.

I stopped often to soak in the sheer joy of being alone in the Alaskan bush at night. If something happened—an encounter with a belligerent moose, a breakdown of my bicycle or my body—I had to depend upon myself to survive. It could be hours before I was missed and race organizers sent someone on a snowmobile to look for me. And if I strayed off the course into the maze of trails, it could be even longer before I was found.

Instead of being frightened, though, I felt prepared, independent, ready for anything. With me I had a knowledge of moose etiquette and outdoor survival, a bike repair kit complete with extra spokes, inner tubes, nuts, bolts, screwdrivers, and hex wrenches, and enough clothing and gear to survive for several days. Besides, I had trained hard, both mentally and physically. All fall and winter long, I rode my mountain bike for twenty to one hundred miles at a time. Neither snow storms, nor forty-mph headwinds, nor total darkness could keep me out of the saddle. I had learned to read my body, controlling my body temperature through calorie intake, clothing layers, and increased exertion. And I had learned how to fight the urge to give up.

After a few hours of lonely night riding, the purr of a generator broke my reverie and signaled my proximity to Eagle Song, the second checkpoint. Inside the warm cabin, two tall, handsome, young blonds (checkers, not hallucinations) signed me in as I wondered how many women dropped out at this checkpoint. Next door, at the lodge, I gorged myself on chili, reindeer sausage on a roll, chips, and juice. Tearing myself away from a conversation with Kostman and Dial, who had since moved on to topics more scintillating than animal excretions, I finally crawled into a warm bunk. Exhausted as I was, I had no trouble succumbing to sleep amidst the happy snores of my comrades. Most would only allow themselves two or three hours' rest before pushing on. Not me. My strategy was to sleep and eat as much as possible and to treat the race like a very rugged inn-to-inn tour.

Seven hours later I arose, eager to continue my journey. In the early morning hours my sleep had been fitful, plagued by the persistent fear, "You've only gone forty-two miles, you might not make it." I had seventy-five hours to complete the course before race officials would disqualify or evacuate me. I didn't care if I came in last; I just wanted to finish. In my haste, I neglected to check the temperature before leaving. The mercury had plunged to twenty-below while I slept, and the rising sun provided only psychological warmth. "It'll warm up soon," I lied repeatedly to myself as I pedaled, shivering feverishly. It was the classic Catch-22: To put on extra clothes, I needed to stop riding, but I had to keep moving to stay warm. So I dismounted and danced the circulation jig, stomping my feet while adding a layer of fleece to my head, hands, and torso, and windproof gaiters to my feet.

The nine miles to the next checkpoint sped by—I guess the fear of death by freezing was a good motivating factor. At the Rabbit Lake aid station, the temperature was frigid, even inside the tent, and did not inspire lingering. I spent only a few moments there and pushed on toward the race's halfway point, Skwentna, another twenty-two miles away.

This was the stretch I feared the most. Historically it had proved to be a death march for cyclists who were forced off their bikes by soft snow, deep moose prints, and the unyielding moose themselves. But the previous night's low temperatures allowed the trail's crust to "set up" into a rideable surface, and I saw no signs of a rumored belligerent moose. Three bikes abandoned along the trail bore eerie witness to racers who had braved the cold night only to give up the race and their hundred-dollar evacuation fee for a snowmobile ride to safety. Despite the sympathy I felt as I passed the road kill, I couldn't hold back the satisfied shout, "Hah, I've made it farther than you!"

However, it still was a long, lonely twenty-two miles. After the first day of playing leapfrog with other racers, this day I felt completely alone, passing only two other people in nine hours. The monotony of swamp,

trees, swamp, trees was broken by Heartbreak Hill, a small geological pro-
tuberance that afforded a spectacular view and a screaming descent. I had
passed by the foot of Sleeping Lady, careful not to wake her, and now had
a more vertical mountain to admire—the 23,320-foot-high Mount
McKinley. Basking in the pink morning light and dwarfing her neighbor-
ing peaks, she truly lived up to her native name of Denali, The Great
One. I stopped often to amuse myself by photographing Denali and
snow formations that resembled cartoon characters—at least they did at
the time. I surprised myself by thinking, *I'm having fun!* The sky was a
perfect azure and the temperature was a moderate 25°F by midday. I
felt lucky considering that in this region clear skies usually mean below-
zero weather.

I knew there were two cyclists just ahead of me—they had left Rabbit Lake as I arrived—and I could see their tire tracks. When the trees
opened into swamps and the snow softened, I was reduced to walking. But
I could tell by the tire tracks that my predecessors were riding. "If they can
do it, I can," I said to myself. So I softened my tires and stiffened my resolve. It took every ounce of strength in my legs to maintain enough
momentum to float, but I did it. At least ninety-five percent of this section
was rideable; I had expected to walk at least seventy-five percent.

In a cheery mood, I arrived at the familiar cabins of Skwentna, where
I had volunteered as a checker in 1994, along with Jay and Bill Laxson.
After so many lonely hours, my own voice startled me as I greeted the Lax-
sons, who had also returned. They pampered me with a shoulder massage
and the best bunk in the house. I ate everything in sight: fat-filled chocolate muffins, dinner rolls slathered with butter, hot beef stew, and a pizza
pocket from my re-supply bag.

Each racer had prepared two "drop bags" with extra clothing, batteries, food, hand warmers, and other necessities that were delivered by
single-engine plane to Big Su and Skwentna. Rookies often pack only

energy bars and liquid-replacement powders. I knew better and filled my bags with *real* food: pizza, peanut butter and jelly sandwiches, bagels with cream cheese. The frozen delectables could be defrosted and toasted on the wood stove found at each checkpoint.

After a two-hour "power nap," I left in the twilight with another cyclist, Jim Bowron. It's amazing what eight thousand calories and some rest can do for your attitude. We hooted and hollered with glee as we flew down the frozen Skwentna River at a whopping nine miles per hour. One of the checkers at Skwentna had sent us off with this blessing: "May the trail be hard-packed and the wind at your back." I never had the chance to thank him.

Fifteen miles later we reached River Song Lodge. Pulling aside a bear hide that insulated the door, I entered the warm amber glow of this elegantly rustic log cabin retreat. "What can I get you?" asked Mark Flanum.

"That looks good," I said, pointing to a wineglass in his hand.

"Laurel Drews has been asking about you," Mark said as he served me moose stew and homemade bread with my glass of Merlot. Radio reports had kept her informed that I was closing the gap between us. Out of four women who started, two had dropped out at the first checkpoint. Even at my tortoise's pace I was in contention for the women's title. But I resisted the urge to turn my tour into a race. Mine would be a victory over self-doubt, not over Laurel, who I had come to see as a comrade, rather than a rival.

With those thoughts in mind I prepared for another full night's sleep. A sink with running water provided the luxury of clean hands and face; a lumpy mattress on the floor, and I thought I was in heaven. It's the little things you learn to appreciate on a trip such as this.

Monday morning I awoke, dressed, and sat at the breakfast table sipping coffee and reading the paper. Just like home. Only it was the

Sunday paper (what do you expect? I was in the middle of nowhere) and I had the surreal experience of reading about a race I was still a day from finishing. Overcast skies foreshadowing a snowstorm added urgency to the morning's departure down the frozen Yentna River. A few inches of fresh snow could mean sixty miles of walking. Brian, a triathlete from San Diego, whose last name I will withhold for reasons that will become obvious later in the story, joined Jim and me for the river-running.

Being slightly slower, I urged Jim and Brian to go on without me. I preferred traveling at my own pace, stopping when it pleased me. Besides, the time differential in rest stops made me experience penis envy for the first time ever. They didn't even have to get off their bikes, whereas I had to dismount, sort through my various layers and squat with my hind end exposed to the elements. Inevitably, all those objects I was keeping thawed under my shirt—camera, Snickers bar, batteries—would tumble out as I pulled my pants down. Jim and Brian politely pulled ahead but remained within sight. Their silhouettes against the overcast sky reminded me of sepia-tinted photos I had seen of stampeding gold rushers who actually bicycled down the Yukon River in the winter of 1901.

My mind hummed with the drone of perpetual motion. I had often wondered what hallucinations or imaginings would be inspired by spending hours alone in the wilderness. But my mind's eye only saw the present—the vastness of the landscape, the needs of my body, the distance to the next checkpoint—or nothing at all. For entertainment, I pondered what my parents back in Hawaii were doing while I traveled through the Alaskan bush. *Dad's probably trying to decide if he should go for a swim or a walk on the beach.*

It was day three of my trip, and I had not yet covered two-thirds of the course. So I kept pedaling and rationed my rest stops. When my odometer read one hundred miles, I celebrated by stopping to eat an oatmeal cookie and sip some water.

Yet another friend, Walt Landgrebe, was waiting for me at Yentna Station, the site of a surprise gear check. After verifying that I still carried the equipment necessary for survival, Walt ushered me into the family-run lodge where a cat and a three-year-old vied for my attention. The hours spent hunched over my handlebars were taking their toll on my scoliosis-plagued spine. I begged Walt for a neck rub, and he obliged. Indiscreet moans of pleasure escaped my mouth as he untangled the muscles that were beginning to resemble a macrame plant hanger. It pays to have friends in remote places.

Another fifteen miles on the Yentna River separated me from the last checkpoint, Big Su. A few miles out, I caught up to Dan Bull, who was skiing the course. It was partially Dan's fault that I was there. He was the founder of Iditabike, which grew into Iditasport. Besides competing in several Iditabikes, in 1990 Dan had also biked all the way to Nome, eleven hundred miles, on the heels of the Iditarod sled dogs. He flew me up to Alaska to help write a book about winter cycling and somehow talked me into doing the race.

At Big Su, Lynelle, a woman of her word, offered me and the rest of the stragglers a cold brew. Raising our tin cans high in the racers' tent, we toasted the final leg. Dan squeezed my quadriceps and said, "I didn't think you were this tough."

"I didn't either," I countered. I had suspected the fortitude was in me, but had to prove it. Dan looked a lot worse than I felt. Not much of a skier, he had basically shuffled the entire way, sleeping about seven hours in two nights.

It was twilight when we left the last vestiges of civilization that we would see until the finish line. We had heard of other racers losing the trail in this section and were all in various stages of delirium, so we left together. This was the stick of the lollipop loop—a repeat of the first twenty-seven miles. Fatigue had negated any bike-handling skills I may have once had, making my descents on the numerous stream banks almost as slow as my ascents.

The smile and good mood that had been my steady companions throughout the race were replaced by a determined stare and semi-comatose drive to finish. Almost immediately after leaving Big Su, Jim pulled ahead with another racer, leaving Brian and me behind.

"I can't believe Jim left us," Brian whined. "I thought since we rode together for so long, we'd have a gentlemen's finish and cross the line side-by-side."

"We'll be okay, there's two of us," I reassured him. "Jim probably just got tired of going so slow."

The hours dragged by as we pushed our bikes over a rideable trail because Brian's knees hurt too much to pedal. I tried to pass the time with conversation but my questions were met with monosyllabic utterances. Why couldn't I be stuck on the trail with a philosopher or poet? I wondered to myself. I had the feeling of being stranded at a party late at night waiting for a ride home—the buzz had worn off and the hangover was setting in. I yearned for the previous days of traveling solo, but Brian was disoriented and did not want to be left alone. I had heard too many stories of Iditasport camaraderie, of people helping each other when egocentricity could spell death. So I dedicated myself to keeping Brian in motion, gently urging him to ride in granny gear when he wanted to walk and sharing my trail mix because he had no food.

Alaskans believe in insta-karma. A man once told me that if you see someone stuck on the side of the road in winter, you stop to help—even if the guy has been screwing your wife. You could be the one stranded tomorrow, he explained, and he could be your savior. This willingness to help others in need is an odd complement to the independent, often reclusive, tendencies of Alaskans. This dichotomy, I suppose, is the perfect representation of life on America's last frontier.

"I quit! Take me to Big Lake," I teased Richard Larson, who was patrolling on a snowmobile in search of lost Iditasport victims, and whose boots I had borrowed for the race. We were about fifteen miles from the finish and Richard informed me that Laurel was not too far ahead and walking because of a sore knee. I had a chance to catch her; my legs could still pedal. Temptation reared its ugly head but I resisted the urge to abandon Brian and push ahead to take the women's title.

We reached the shore of Big Lake, five long miles from the finish, where we saw Richard again. He warned us of a flashing light at the Klondike Inn, which was luring in racers like moths to a light bulb. The finish was at Big Lake Lodge, about a mile farther. "One of you is going to be the last cyclist," Richard said as he handed Brian some water. "Now's your chance, Monique. You could take off and let Brian be the Red Lantern."

"I couldn't do that," I said, thinking how much I'd like to. "After coming this far, we might as well finish together." I waited for Brian to finish drinking, and we continued on. With the end in sight, I began to allow myself to feel the effects of overexertion. It was all I could do to remain upright as I pedaled over the soft trail at about four miles per hour. Brian, on the other hand, got a second (or was it a hundredth?) wind and took off across the lake. I shouted ahead to inform him that he was thundering off in the wrong direction. Once back on course, he dusted me again.

"What a hypocrite," I muttered to myself. "So much for a gentlemen's finish." Actually, I was happy to be alone again. It seemed appropriate after going solo for most of the race that I finish it alone. This had been a personal race for me.

Just before I rolled under the race banner at 3:30 AM, I saw an object in the snow glimmering in the light from my headlamp. I stooped over to pick up a party tiara that read, "Happy New Year!" Taking this as a sign of new beginnings, I placed it on my head for the finish. My time was sixty-five hours, fourteen minutes—almost forty hours later than winner John Stamstad, and only two hours after Laurel. But time meant nothing compared to the fact that I reached my goal. I finished.

At Big Lake Lodge, I downed another beer before heading to one of the sleeping cabins. First, I took the best shower of my life, then started making a nest among some of my slumbering fellow finishers. "Is that Monique?" a woman's voice asked. My affirmative response inspired a screaming, "I'm so glad you made it!" The next thing I knew I was locked in Laurel's embrace. Despite our exhaustion, we stayed awake another hour talking excitedly about our various experiences. Her tales topped mine. She had pushed through the first night without sleeping and had run out of headlamp batteries the next night, having to stop and wait for another racer to avoid getting lost. I was sincerely glad she won first place. She wanted it more than I did and sacrificed much to get it.

"You look pretty good for someone who rode and pushed a bike for one hundred sixty miles on snow," I said to my reflection in the mirror Tuesday night before the awards banquet. I was showered, combed, and decked out in a short party dress and stockings. There were quite a few other racers at the banquet, limping on their frost-nipped feet and struggling to keep their sleep-deprived lids open. Each of us finishers received an engraved *ulu*, which aside from being a great Scrabble word, is also a half-moon-shaped Eskimo knife. When I was called to the podium to receive my award for placing second in the women's bike division, I thought of something my mom once said. "Back when you were lying in that hospital bed with two full casts on your legs, we never would have dreamed you'd end up being the athlete of the family."

Iditasport redefined what I believed I was capable of accomplishing, and not just in the physical realm. It inspired me to apply this new self-confidence borne of solo survival to all aspects of my life. Days after the race, I realized that completing an ultramarathon is much like birthing a baby. During the process you swear you'll never do it again, but later the joy of your achievement obscures your memory of the pain and you find yourself saying, "Next time . . . "

Icebergs in My Dreams

I WATCH MATT'S BACK RETREAT, ACROSS THE FERRY TERMINAL PARKING LOT AND UP THE RAMP; he reboards the ferry M/V *Columbia* under the black Southeast Alaska sky, dotted with dim stars whose light shines dully through the spaces among scattered clouds. Darkness provides cover for my tears. *The great adventurer has opened her big mouth once too often*, I think. *Now I have to follow through.*

My plan had seemed natural, even logical, at the time. Sitting on a drift-wood log with Matt and Stan at our campsite on Kolosh Island, holding in my hands a cracked wooden bowl filled with rice, I listened to them plot their plans now that our four-week expedition together was almost over.

"I'd like to do some backpacking in the mountains around Juneau," Stan said. "I've heard a lot about that country."

Matt frowned. "My job starts soon," he said. "To make it back to Seattle in time, I have to catch the September 12 ferry from Sitka."

They both looked at me. Four weeks of their frequent unsolicited advice had taken a steep toll. I remembered Stan instructing me in how to hold my kayak paddle. I had been working as a whitewater river guide for three seasons; this was his first summer kayaking. I remembered both of them standing over my white sixteen-foot Chinook kayak, *Ozzy*, and telling me how to arrange my stuff-sacks. I remembered the morning I was cooking a huckleberry pancake, and Matt appeared and said I should turn it over now. I turned it, and Stan strolled over, peered into the pan, and pronounced that it had not been ready to turn over yet. That was the day I stopped cooking. After that, when either of the men began a meal, I wandered away from camp to read, pick berries, or talk with the ducks and seals who live at the margins between beach and sea.

And I remembered Audrey Sutherland's talk at the Mountaineers Club in Seattle. She had autographed my copy of her new book, *Paddling Hawai'i*, with these words: "For Sheryl: Paddle south of Sitka—down to Goddard. Aloha, Audrey Sutherland." Her advice had been followed: Here we were, camped offshore of Goddard. It had been excellent advice. At both the beginning and the conclusion of her talk, Audrey told her listeners, "Go now, and go solo."

I flexed an arm grown hard and muscular through these many weeks of paddling and thought of my guide friends back home. "Arms like tree trunks" expressed the common standard we held to. I looked at Stan and Matt. "I don't have to go back yet," I said. "I think I'll get off at Petersburg and paddle solo down to Wrangell." Stranded without comment, they contemplated the steam swirling over their tea mugs.

Matt and I parted company with Stan in Sitka a few days later. I had not been sorry at the parting. I had known Stan only casually before joining this trip. A strong and experienced outdoorsman, he had nonetheless shown a penchant for cruising off alone, out of sight of the other two kayaks. During a storm in Windy Channel, Matt and I had stayed overnight at Goddard and did not see Stan for over twenty-four hours. The worry had kept us awake all night. "What do we do if he's missing or dead?" we had asked each other. Tightwads ever, the experience even brought up a conversation about buying marine-band radios. Although Matt and I had argued over many other points during this trip, we agreed that Stan's nonteam attitude was dangerous and put all of us at greater risk than necessary.

After Stan left, Matt and I cruised the Siginaka Islands for several days, savoring the fuchsia sun setting over Mount Edgecumbe's collapsed crater like rhododendron petals settling into a brandy snifter. As his remaining time in Alaska dwindled, Matt grew less argumentative, more meditative. He treated me to dinner, at twelve dollars apiece, too expensive by kayak bum standards. We sat at the windows in the Sea Glory dining room the night I was to disembark at Petersburg. The fact that the ever-thrifty Matt paid for my dinner indicated the depth of his concern over my solo venture. Gazing across the rims of our wineglasses at the glow cast by the moon over low-hanging ice fields, we enjoyed each other's company almost as we had in the beginning, before our mutual insecurities surfaced and ground against each other like icebergs turning, abrading in their night channels.

Stuff-sacks, paddles, ammo can: All are piled around my rubber-booted feet. *I'm alone, in the dark, in the rain.* I feel less alone, though, than the day I hollered a route question to Matt under the howling wind while rounding Povorotni Point in whitecaps. Flinging the chart and compass bag out of his cockpit toward me, over eight-foot waves, he yelled, "It's your chart; learn to use it!" Now the ferry horn blasts twice, a sound that usually churns the blood through my veins. Tonight, though, in it I hear a double death knell, and fix on the word *solo* as a saltwater mantra. . . . *solo, solo, so low, here I go.* I plant my Therm-a-rest and sleeping bag under the ferry terminal overhang to wait for dawn's light. Despite the racket from the disco across the street, sleep falls like a river rapid descending its glassy tongue.

I wake to the sounds of bottle glass smacking pavement. "Muh' fucker," a man's voice yells. A woman mutters something incomprehensible, and the next sounds I hear are those of police sirens addressing the parking lot. A glance at the watch under my Capilene sleeve reveals that it's only 4:00 AM. I shrivel down into my sleeping bag and hope the police won't notice me. My wide eyes stare at the stitching inside the bag. I long for daylight.

Dawn and rain arrive together, the drops making pock marks in the bay's leaden surface. I depart Petersburg's harbor as a cruise ship anchors. Resting the wooden paddle across my spray-skirted lap, I munch an apple and look at the people on the upper decks. A man trains his video camera on me, and I feel like a member of an endangered Alaskan species, captured on film before it's too late. *Time to get outta town.*

Paddling south along the east coast of Mitkof Island, I welcome the familiar rhythms settling in: push, pull, inhale, exhale. Shoulders, arms, wrists, waist: They move themselves like actors playing their parts for the thousandth time. Rain lightens to drizzle, then stops altogether. Strengthening sunlight reveals the whorls of my paddle blades reflected on the water. Birds wheel and call, brown kelp bulbs bob, sea swells cradle the boat, and over all things hangs the crusty pungency of salt. All afternoon I crawl alongside steep cliff walls, which plunge unrelieved to the water line. After several hours, my muscles begin to tire; time to consider tonight's campsite. Another hour's paddling and my upper arms are jammed with lactic acid. The underpaid actors start to grumble. Around a head wall, a long, gently sloping beach offers itself. I land the yak and disembark to look for the high water mark. The woods behind this beach are too densely overgrown to yield a tent space. I settle for pitching my tent as high as possible, but the encrusted rings of algae and kelp in this zone make me nervous. Scanning the tide table, I see it will be close, with the highest water due just after midnight. A pile of driftwood logs higher than my head looks like a stable stash for *Ozzy*, and after hoisting her over my head into the log nest, I lash her bow to the trunk of an overhanging cedar tree. The whole assembly reminds me of the absurd osprey nests I saw in the Florida Keys, big batches of sticks with pieces of clothing and sometimes even towels cascading out, riding the random breeze.

As I cook rice over a tiny climbing stove, eight curious seals bob offshore, their smooth gray heads echoing the shape of beach rocks smoothed by tides. Ball bearing–size saltwater beads slide down their whiskers and drop into the sea. In the slanting rays of the day's last sun, I see random squirts from a clam colony. Far across Frederick Sound, a cluster of icebergs rides the tide out to sea. I don't need the chart to tell me that the ice exits from Le Conte Bay, melting pot for Le Conte Glacier, the southernmost tidewater glacier in the United States. The ever-lowering sun mutates colors on the berg surfaces: green, blue, pink. Through coffee steam, I gaze at the beautiful danger, feeling the pull of those crystal layers compressed by thousands of years of weight.

In that ponderous weight hangs the bergs' principal danger to kayakers. The portion of an iceberg visible above the water line may be less than one-fourth of its total mass, and its instability due to uneven melting creates the potential that it will roll suddenly. When a couple of tons of ice roll over, the motion generates a huge wave. Even larger waves follow the fall of a chunk of hanging ice, maybe as big as a house, into the water. The Tlingits, Southeast Alaska's aboriginal people, call the sound made by calving ice "white thunder." A sixteen-foot kayak riding into such thunder has about as much chance of survival as a toothpick tossed into a flushing toilet bowl. From such primitive physics flows the advice that a kayaker's minimum safe distance from a hanging glacier is one-half mile.

My musings about iceberg dangers and rapture over kaleidoscopic ice colors do not transcend my anxiety as to this camping spot. *What could go wrong? The tide could wash into my tent door while I'm asleep and soak all the gear, or wash it out to sea.* I cram everything except one foam pad and my sleeping bag into the boat. Sleep brings fitful dreams, in which I dance naked across purple icebergs that shift in time to the spouting of humpback whales.

Morning's heavy mist conceals the icebergs, so I content myself with watching the squirting clams, circling gulls, and seals playing offshore. Frederick Sound is calm, the color of split shot. After brewing a cup of coffee, I settle onto a boulder to weigh the risks of a solo crossing of Frederick Sound against my desire for closeness to those icebergs. The chart shows a three-mile stretch of open water between me and Camp Island. The island forms a partial border between the Sound and Le Conte Bay. If I go, sooner is better, as the stronger winds tend to whip up in the afternoon in Southeast Alaska. The beings who camp in my brain begin their debate:

You told Matt you were taking the east coast of Mitkof. They'll never find the body.

The water is calm; there's no wind.

You don't have a rudder.

It's only three miles.

You've never tried an Eskimo roll with a fully loaded boat.

I may never be in this place again.

And so it goes for about ten minutes, the conservative versus the wild woman. Ultimately I don't know why I let them engage in battle; I knew from the moment I saw those icebergs that I would alter my original route plan and cross the Sound.

Decision made, the packing proceeds swiftly. I settle into the cockpit and tug the skirt around the coaming. The paddle cuts through the water as easily as a ski tip lifts through new powder snow, and soon I spy through the lifting haze the tribe of ice beings trekking toward me on their journey from Le Conte Glacier, where they cleave from the mother ice, fall into the bay, and slide through the outlets at either end of Camp Island into Frederick Sound, diminished by melt water as they go. They range in size from baseball-size chips to freeform, sculpted chunks longer than my boat. Some carry seal mothers and pups, serving as nurseries secure from landlubber predators. The largest piece I can see is about the height of a one-story building. I keep my distance, even from the smaller ones. An abruptly flipping iceberg could swamp my boat.

Perhaps the most compelling feature distinguishing solo kayak travel from a group trip is this absolute zero margin for error. If my boat should roll or swamp, I cannot rely on an altruistic porpoise to appear at the right moment and carry me to a safe beach, although those stories appeal to me and even seem believable, from dry land. Other than this greater requirement for self-reliance, and the satisfaction that meeting it brings, I haven't figured out all the reasons why people travel alone.

Alone applied to travel seems a questionable idea when consideration is given to genetics, upbringing, friends, mentors, cartographers, boatmakers, and equipment suppliers who all have contributed something to the journey. And, many travelers upon return from their solo journeys publish photos and articles telling other people all about their experiences. Do our adventures exist outside the zones of memory and imagination? Are our solo travels real if they are not told to others? The solo theme, after all, formed the basis for Sutherland's talk to a well-attended meeting of Seattle's Mountaineers and an inspiration for my being where I am right now.

Where I am: in a floating seal nursery, though smaller and less populated than the one in Johns Hopkins Inlet of Glacier Bay, where I once floated blissfully with two other paddlers in the iceberg-choked inlet. There, every other ice bit supported a group of mothers and pups. We laid our paddles perpendicular to our yaks, across the spray skirts, and wordlessly watched the glistening seals. The Alaskan maritime sun blazed down onto our slightly bowed, hatless heads. To watch seals, one must look at them while aiming the eyes elsewhere, slightly off-angle. A mother seal alarms so easily that direct eye contact will cause her to plunge abruptly from her ice haven into the water.

The silent seal watching proceeded for about ten minutes. Then the fourth member of our group caught up. "Hey, you guys!" his voice boomed across the bay. Four seals plunged. "You hafta be really quiet in here—the seals are nursing." The other three of us exchanged glances, and picked up our paddles. The difficulty of even two human beings deliberately not speaking for any significant length of time often precludes wildlife sightings. The animals know we're coming long before we've turned the corner into their neighborhood. The solo traveler has much better chances to see animals, especially by the quiet kayak mode of travel.

I think about these aspects of solo travel while noting that I haven't seen another boat all morning, simultaneously an omen of a high-quality trip and a risky one. I can see Camp Island's shoreline clearly now, and the nearer I get, the faster and closer together the iceberg shards drift toward me. Also, the tide is ebbing fast, and I have to land soon or risk being marooned in the dreaded Stikine mud flats until the next tide change, a six-hour cycle, which would then require paddling after dark. When Matt and Stan got stuck in the Stikine mud, they just sat in their yaks and read books until the tide came up. But they had lots of daylight.

I increase my paddle speed and point the bow for a landing just below a weathered gray cabin I see about a hundred yards back in the grassy clearing above the beach. After lashing *Ozzy* to a huge driftwood log, I climb out of the cockpit. With the blue neoprene spray skirt and red life jacket still around my waist, I lurch toward the house in water-logged rubber boots. Maybe this is how walruses and seals feel when they have to navigate out of water.

Through the panes, a red-and-white checked tablecloth under several wine bottles welcomes. By custom, many Alaskan cabin owners leave their places unlocked for use by those in need of shelter; in turn, the travelers are expected to leave the place cleaner and/or better stocked than they found it. The vandalism that plagues modern times threatens this extended grace with extinction. The Camp Island cabin has not yet been so dishonored. A note written on the back of a dried-food label says the 1986 Vouvray was left by kayakers, so drinking it will not deplete the owners' supplies. Deciding the wine will taste better chilled, I unload my gear and then hike around the island in search of ice. On the east side, two dozen bergs lie on the mud flat under a bright rainbow, stranded by the outgoing tide. The icebergs talk, in a way. Like Rice Krispies popping, they spit and crackle as they melt. I bend my ear to a glistening surface to hear the story. The ice tells where it began, what icefields it calls family. How it was loosed from substrate to slide downhill. How it was dumped into the bay and landed here. Maybe this is a story only the solo traveler hears.

I stroll among the stilled ice chunks, choosing a whale-shaped one dripping fast. My pail placed into the sand under the icy head catches melt water for drinking. Glacier chips drop into my cup. I want to see these icebergs moving again, weaving and dancing to the tide's rhythm, but the smaller ones will not last for the next tide. I turn back to the cabin, where I light a candle on the front porch and lounge with my glacial wine, listen to the dusk music of owls, tiny frogs, soft wind, and lapping waves, and watch the sun go down over Frederick Sound.

The tock of a hand-wound clock on the kitchen table is the only human-made sound available here, other than noises I make myself. Maybe lack of human conversation is one of the misgivings people have about solo travel. "If I don't miss the sound of other people's voices," I ask the clock, "does that mean I'm antisocial?"

Tick-tick-tick. The clock won't commit.

Hunting magazines, bullet casings, and duck decoys decorate the shelves and windowsills. In the cross piece of the front window hangs a little banner which says GATEWAY OFFICE OF AGING. Wine or people? Hunting cartoons and a dart board add to the ambience.

On the living room wall over the sofa hangs a pair of men's jockey shorts. Tacks hold the shorts spread out like the pelt of a wild thing. In the center back, a large, brown liquid-fart spot is labeled with careful black felt-pen letters: TYPICAL L.A. BRIEF.

The Camp Island cabin: so companionable that I spend a second day, lounging naked outdoors in the eighty-degree sun and writing poetry. Because the Vouvray is long gone, I drink vin rose sprinkled with Le Conte ice chips. The night is cold, though, so chilly I wear a wool watch cap to bed. Huddled in the narrow bunk, I know the weather gods will slap me in the face if I don't keep moving toward Wrangell.

In the morning, I haul away a bag of trash for the duck hunters. I feel I know them now, the way I know my own siblings after years of being allowed to hang around in their rooms, snooping in their stuff: the marbles, comic books, zit medicine, and gum wrappers that mark adolescence. "Thank you," I say to the walls and the clock, picking up the last load of gear and heading for the beach where *Ozzy* waits.

Another beauty of paddling solo is that I don't need to time my departures around the readiness of companions. I have my loading routine down so precisely that today I eyeball the rate of the incoming tide, carry the empty boat down to where I think the tide will catch her, stuff all my gear in while the tide swirls over the toes of my rubber boots, position my body with my back to the sea, fasten the spray skirt, grab the paddle, and grin; after less than two minutes, the draw is sufficient to carry me away. I hear the chewing of icebergs as they crowd Le Conte Bay. Small chunks already appear at the north and south channels, making their way into Frederick Sound. I paddle away fast because I can't bear the thought of waking up tomorrow without icebergs visible.

The usual contingents of birds and seals accompany my southward travel. I used to try to count the seals, but the moment I would make eye contact with one, she'd duck under. Another two or three would pop up on the periphery of my vision; if I turned toward them to get a count, they'd go under and others would pop up in a direction I wasn't looking. I don't try to count them anymore; now I sing or whistle. They stay above water longer for Beethoven than for Peter, Paul, and Mary. Critics everywhere. The occasional drone of a distant motorboat syncopates the mix.

The sun's pulse throbs hard enough that, for the first couple of hours, I can paddle without a shirt under my life vest. As I cross the strait between Dry Island and Little Dry, wind whips the water like a hand mixer beating egg whites. I put my shirt on and maneuver hard to keep my bow pointed into the foamy crests of the waves. Off starboard, a long, brown barracuda shape barrels toward me—a log escaped from its boom. My eyes pick out another off port, about ten o'clock; then another. Huge logs have broken their cables and now race for the open sea. Maneuvering to avoid the mavericks, I look for the channel that will lead to the camp shown on Little Dry Island's chart. Wind shrieks around my head. Wind twists the paddle blades; I tighten my clutch. *Only about an hour 'til dusk, Koknuk Mud Flats stretch for miles, tide's going out too fast . . .*

The system of mud flats off the Stikine River mouth supports a marshy shoreline, swampy plains cut with deep channels. Reaching the forested parts where cabins and good campsites lie requires threading my way up twisting muddy channels until I find one that goes all the way in, like having to eat the edges of the cookie before the chocolate drop in the center can be gobbled. On this cookie, however, I can't always see where the edges are. I paddle up-channel against the wild wind, threading close to the six-foot-high silt bank to take advantage of the weaker current. I bottom out, step out, and drag the boat, step into a hole, filling my left boot with mud and water. *Fuck. Arms ache, dusk near, damn wind . . .* To lighten the boat, I take out three dry bags and the ammo can, and stash them on a high outcrop of beach grass for later retrieval. Drag the yak upstream some more. *Arms on fire.* There, in a tiny clump of trees, I can just make out a Forest Service cabin, still several hundred yards away. *Wasn't on the chart.* I can't pull the weight of the fully loaded boat through this muck anymore. I haul one armload up to the cabin, dump it, sigh, curse, and sling a flashlight around my neck. There's maybe fifteen minutes' more light and another hour of hauling, in my fatigue. Back to the boat for more gear, through waist-high grasses. Mud holes for roots.

Too dark now to see the boat or find the stashed bags, I have to search by following my own boot holes back through the marsh. Looks like these early fall tides give little slack time. Almost as fast as the sound sucks itself back, it comes flowing in again. My boot holes begin to fill with incoming tidewater. Whole damned marsh will be under within the hour. I find the boat, and at the thought of having to move it all that way I feel tears rising. Looking at the ground, tidewater seeping into the depressions around my boots, I command my left foot to take a step. It barely moves. Muscle ache anchors me in mud and dark. *How in hell am I going to find that gear I stashed, gotta get it, too dark . . .*

Light floods the swamp, a sweeping gleam as though cast by a thousand icebergs. I throw back my head and open my arms wide to embrace the light, as over the ridge tops rises the fullest, roundest, most brilliant of all moons: the moon that lit the balcony when Romeo wooed Juliet; the moon that shone under the feet of the astronauts who first walked there; the moon that glints over the flukes of feeding humpbacks. I laugh, and sing to the sky an old John Prine song: "That's the way that the world goes round, you're up one day, the next you're down, it's half-an-inch of water and you think you're gonna drown, that's the way that the world goes round."

An hour later, I lift the last cargo out of the yak: two cans of Foster's Lager, just the right amount to wash down three Advils. I sit on the porch of the Forest Service cabin, muddy stuff-bags piled all around, crusty paddle pants and jacket drying over the rails. In all this baggage rides the essence of seals and whales who have accompanied me on open crossings, the smell of salt-spray crust on my face and hands and its taste on my tongue, the tales of old companions, the advice of mentors, and the gleaming dream visions of violet ice. Waves lap at the rocks a few yards away, and I inhale the salt smell. Gulls weave their aerial night patterns. "Ki-ree, ki-ree," they call. I can't see them, but I know the smooth, gray heads of seals bob offshore and will be there at dawnlight, their huge, curious eyes translucent like the marbles we called puries when I was a kid. To the southeast twinkle the electric lights of Wrangell, where tomorrow I will attempt a solo traverse through the streets of a town filled with people.

Eight Reasons Not to Paddle up Le Conte Bay
(*from notes in a kayak journal*)

1. Cedar fringes at treetop
    blow back toward my face.

2. Like a dog chewing rawhide, wind chaws
    the rudderless kayak.

3. I want to see my grandchildren born,
    and when they are teenagers, give their mom advice.

4. I can see Le Conte Glacier
    in pictures taken on a sunny day—
    the color will be better.

5. Without a survival suit,
   a perfect Eskimo roll might not be good enough.

6. Icebergs gather thick in the bay.

7. Paddling solo is a fine route
   to meditative death.

8. Three reasons are too many.
   I pour another cup of coffee and give thanks
   for the steam that clouds my vision.

LUCY JANE BLEDSOE

Above Treeline

I LIFTED MY BACKPACK OUT OF THE TRUNK AND PROPPED IT AGAINST A
TREE, PLEASED THAT I'D MADE TRAILHEAD SO EARLY IN THE DAY. The
sky was an icy autumn blue and a breeze made the golden aspen leaves
talk. Late October, snow would soon fall, could even fall this week.
This would be the last trip of the year during which I'd feel soil
beneath my boots.

And the first of the year in which I'd finally be alone. Most years I
make at least two solo trips, one in the winter and one in the summer, but
this year all attempts at solitude had been thwarted, and now my need for
it was intense.

As I taped my feet, a Cherokee Jeep towing a horse trailer pulled into
the parking area. I sped up my foot-doctoring. Three men, sparking
with enthusiasm, jumped out of the Cherokee. I've seen these kinds of
guys in the wilderness a lot, making their yearly trip with the boys, away
from wives and children. Two of them looked like my brothers-in-law,
professional family men. The soft blond one had more than the usual
middle-age chubbiness. A lawyer, I guessed. The tall stern one, with
square plastic glasses, was surely an accountant. I noted the gold bands
on their ring fingers, the expensive wool shirts. The third man, a guy with
a long mustache and shag haircut, looked different. I decided he was a
musician, an old college chum of the lawyer and accountant. Behind his
back they'd discuss his unwillingness, or perhaps inability, to settle
down, how he still lived as if he were twenty. I imagined the lawyer and
accountant resenting his independence, their wives liking the handsome, loose musician a little too much. And yet out here in the wilderness,

Above Treeline 75

he became their center. The professional family men orbited around his louder, wilder energy. He was the instigator of a good time, the perfect excuse.

"Russell," the lawyer clapped his back, "you're not bringing that whole bottle of brandy, are you?"

Russell grinned. Then he noticed me across the parking lot.

"Howdy." His eyes raked across my car, backpack, body. "By yourself?"

I nodded.

Russell kept grinning and glancing at me as he unloaded the fishing poles, then the first gun. I was surprised. These guys didn't look like hunters. The Cherokee Jeep and other high-end gear made it clear they didn't need the meat. Hunting for sport appalled me.

But I eat meat, I reminded myself. *Doesn't that make me a hunter who makes others do the dirty work?*

I have hunted, once. About twenty years ago, on a trip in Alaska's Wrangell Mountains, my hiking partner and I ran out of food. People hunt in Alaska. They think you're out of your mind if you go into the backcountry without a gun. We didn't have a gun, but Wendy and I spent a lot of time on that trip talking about guns and killing. We heartily agreed that hunting was evil and that we could never kill.

Then we got hungry.

After three days of nothing but oatmeal, the concept of good and evil seemed ridiculously superfluous. Our best bet were ptarmigans, big birds reputed to taste like chicken. They were plentiful in the Wrangell Mountains and better yet, far too stupid to realize someone was trying to kill them. I'd read that they were easy prey: Simply hit them on the head with a rock. The drawback was that these big birds, who sat up on tree branches often no more than ten feet above ground, had tiny heads. Wendy and I, salivating for roast bird, found stones and fired them at the pinheads. I felt no remorse as I tried to kill. Even a little bit of hunger can alter a person in dramatic ways. As it turned out, I never hit my target, though we did get to taste ptarmigan. We soon ran into a trail crew who fed us a breakfast of hot coffee, powdered scrambled eggs, toast, and fire-roasted ptarmigan. It was delicious.

Who was I to judge these guys about to hunt in the Trinity Alps?

I hefted my pack and set out on the Upper Canyon Creek Trail, ignoring Russell's final salutation, figuring I would make tracks to put distance between the guys and me. In spite of my aching heel—a problem the podiatrist recently said was twenty years in the making, and then shrugged when I told him I'd jump the bridge if I couldn't hike and ski—I felt the familiar euphoria settle into my cells. Alone at last.

The air hinted at snow, a feeling of icy warning. With every few hundred feet I gained in elevation, the deciduous leaves changed color. The evergreen boughs sagged, heavy with the year's bumper crop of toasty-brown cones. The undergrowth on either side of the trail rustled with constant noise, the sounds of animals hurrying to pull together the last of their winter stores.

I walked fast and let my mind roar through the complications of the summer. No wonder those men's guns made me uneasy. I had felt hunted during the whole trip in Montana's Beartooth Mountains. Katie and I had set out expecting yet another joyful two weeks in the Rockies. I was apprehensive about going in August rather than our usual September, because of the crowds, but hoped to get off-trail quickly and leave all signs of civilization far behind.

We stopped in Salt Lake to pick up Katie's New Yorker sister, Peggy, at the airport. That night our gear—the tent, stove, boots, backpacks, clothes, hundreds of dollars of food, and much, much more—was ripped off from my car.

I live in the city. I've been mugged, my home has been broken into several times, and cars are picked off my street regularly. These are violations. But my *backpacking* gear. I felt as if the thief had ripped off my soul. I felt hunted.

At least—as I've been told by dozens of well-meaning folks—gear can be replaced. Well, sort of. I've collected my backcountry gear for over twenty years. True, some of my stuff should have been replaced, such as the threadbare wool pants or the stove that worked only when I said *abracadabra* and tapped on the wind screen three times, but some things, such as the twenty-year-old rag wool hat that's been in thirty of the fifty states or the perfect cook pot that no one sells anywhere, can't be replaced. And I'm nothing if not hopelessly sentimental about my gear. My first reaction, which lasted for several days, was that I'd give up backpacking. I wanted to go home. But the Deamer sisters were intent on continuing with the trip, which meant a several-thousand-dollar shopping spree at Salt Lake's REI.

Those hours in REI were a nightmare. I hated all that newfangled gear we bought, and spending that kind of money terrified me (though in the end Katie was right; our insurance did pay for it). Already, I knew this wouldn't be a wilderness trip no matter how deeply we penetrated the Beartooth. For me, wilderness has been a long, slow relationship, built over my thirty-eight years. The gear should be as transparent as possible, serving my backcountry travel but not dominating it. Too many outdoorspeople are gear junkies, enjoying the new technologies more than the wilderness itself. The brand-spanking-new tent, sleeping bag, wool pants, and polypro underwear made me feel ridiculous, like a made-for-TV explorer.

However, I knew I had to get over it. It was a bit like getting right back on the horse after it throws you. Someday (thirty years hence?) this new gear would have its own history. Backcountry travel with others requires teamwork, so I tried to let go of my bad feelings.

Once on the trail, I did relax. Though we were hiking during the busiest month of the year, in a popular area, we soon headed off-trail and found a gorgeous and secluded base camp at a high alpine lake. We planned to stay there several nights, exploring the surrounding peaks and high plateaus. I couldn't ask for much more—except for some time alone. We three had been together, without a break, for a week straight.

One afternoon, the Deamer sisters went off fishing and I at last had solitude. After hiking and climbing and reading all afternoon, I returned to camp at dusk. On the hillside, not far from the cook area, was a shaggy, white mountain goat. I sat on a small rock outcropping and watched it munch its way down the hillside—toward me.

I was amazed the goat didn't run away. They're the shyest mountain animals. You're lucky to see them at a distance. I credited myself for creating this special opportunity. I've always had an affinity with animals. I'm the one who everyone's cat chooses to sit on. Now the mountain goat was just ten yards away! This was the magical moment that would unlock all the distress of the trip. The goat had lovely curving horns and neat little hooves. Its coat was long and elegantly snowy.

Then the goat came yet closer, and I became a little uncomfortable. For one, I couldn't help but notice its obscenely large balls. Billy-goat balls. The look in its eyes was, well, not exactly hostile, but more like crazed or determined. This was a billy goat gone off in the head. No mountain goats came this close to people.

When the Deamer sisters returned to our private lake basin carrying a string of rainbow trout, the goat finally scurried back up the hillside. They didn't see the goat and I didn't tell them about him. I wanted something for myself this trip.

That night, I slept out alone. There was no moon, just a dark night and a canopy of stars. Just as I was falling asleep, I heard a grunting sound. I got up on one elbow and saw, not ten yards away, a big white phantom. The billy goat. He looked ghostly in the starlight. What was he doing here now? I couldn't help but think of those gargantuan balls. Somehow this whole scene—the boldly sexualized goat haunting me—was reminiscent of the Eastern European folktales I so loved as a child. Strange things happened between people and mythical animals. I wanted the goat to leave now, but nothing frightened him, not sudden movements nor loud noises. Once, after I'd drifted off to sleep for a few minutes, I awoke to see him standing immediately next to my sleeping bag, gazing down at me. Again, I felt hunted.

The next morning I told my hiking partners about the goat and they told me that while fishing they'd met someone who told them about this particular goat. Apparently he was well known. I've heard of camp bears, even camp elk. But camp mountain goats? Even this most elusive, proud species had stooped to become a garbage scavenger. So much for magical moments.

Later that morning, fishermen began swarming over the hill into our private lake basin. They were with an outfit that brings folks in on horses and gives them maps to the best fishing lakes in the Beartooth. Apparently, our lake was one.

I gave in and pretended I was traveling in the Middle East, and that meeting people from other cultures was fun. I chatted with more than a dozen of these old coots and had a decent time. But it wasn't a back-country experience.

Later, when the Montana State game warden set an elaborate trap to discover we had two fisherwomen and one license, and then busted us, we were too slaphappy from the string of trip disasters (besides the ones already reported, Peggy lost her glasses, I fell into a river, and Katie treated us to the longest bad mood I've ever witnessed) to even care. We photographed the warden ticketing us, died laughing at his suggestion that he impound my car until we paid up (like how many folks carried sixty bucks into the backcountry?), and eventually convinced him that we'd hike out immediately, drive straight to Red Lodge where the judge resided and pay our ticket in court. Which we did. We photographed that event as well.

Today, hightailing it up the Upper Canyon Creek Lakes Trail in the Trinity Alps, I realized for the first time that the Beartooth trip might actually make some great stories someday. Someday. For now, I wanted only to send those memories on their way into the precise autumn air, make them sail up into the mountaintops, above treeline, free.

I wanted to make my five days in the Trinity Alps last. So, although it was early in the day and I could have easily made it to Upper Canyon Creek Lake, I decided to camp when I found an enchanted meadow with a stream running through it, next to old-growth forest. I wasn't far off-trail, a hundred yards, but it wouldn't matter at this time of year. Who else was here?

My euphoria evaporated as quickly as my sweat. I tried to make my camp cozy by setting out the stove and ground cloth, but a column of fear rose inside me. Sheer terror, actually. I didn't get it. This easy trip was supposed to be a comfort, my release. After all, I had snow-camped alone, bushwhacked alone, traveled in African and Middle Eastern countries alone. This was a warm little trip with a well-marked trail. Fear didn't make sense. Yet I was overwhelmed by it.

I wandered, but the golden, late afternoon sun on the meadow didn't dislodge the tightness in my chest. I tried to meditate to the creek's music, then rubbed myself up against on old cedar's thick life, my cheek scraping along its feathery bark. Nothing helped. I could only think about how I had hours ahead of me, alone with my strange pain. I couldn't even place the pain. I took walks in every direction: across the creek into the brush until it was too thick to go on, then along the creek until I encountered a log jam which, another time, I might have delighted in scrambling over. I felt too tired now and hated myself for feeling such despair.

By dusk, I was sitting on a big boulder in the middle of the meadow, sobbing. Their voices alerted me. "It's on the other side of the meadow," one called out. I recognized Russell's voice. "Oh, hi!" he shouted, seeing me on the boulder.

I forced a bright smile, feeling like the lame caribou hiding from the wolf. I had to look healthy and capable, and whatever I did, not show fear. Inside, though, I seethed. The three hunters headed across my meadow to a campsite that, I gathered from their conversation, they used every year. The Trinity Alps covered thousands of acres and they had to choose a campsite a couple hundred yards from mine? As they hiked past my meadow boulder, I opened my mouth to suggest they move on, but didn't speak. I knew they wouldn't do it. They sagged under their heavy packs, and despite the icy air, sweat poured off the pudgy lawyer. Russell grinned at me. As the horse walked by, it left a large pile next to my boulder.

Listening to the fellows settle into their camp, I waited for darkness, then crawled into my sleeping bag and took an over-the-counter sleeping pill. Part of my problem, I knew, was exhaustion from the previous week's work. Day one on trips was often difficult. I had four more. Things change, especially my moods.

In the morning, I realized that with the horse, the men wouldn't be going to my destination, Upper Canyon Creek Lake, because it was just above treeline and horses weren't allowed above treeline. I packed up my gear and headed out rather late, due to the sleeping pill, but thankful for the twelve hours of sleep. The fellows were long gone.

As I climbed the final pitch to Upper Canyon Creek Lake, I began getting excited about where to make camp. The map showed a bar of land between Upper and Lower Canyon Creek Lakes. I hoped to find a spot on that bar where I'd have a long view down the valley. For three days, I'd sit and stare, explore, and read.

I crested the hill and got my first look at Upper Canyon Creek Lake. A huge granite wall bordered the far side of the lake. The water looked cold despite the sunshine. I hiked out across the bar of land separating the two lakes and, to my amazement, found the three hunters setting up camp. "Great view," Russell said.

Disappointment strangled my voice at first. Finally, I asked, "Where's your horse?"

Russell pointed down to Lower Canyon Creek Lake. "Tethered down there. We wanted a view." He shook his hair and ran his hands through it. I noticed his slim hips. Rock musician, I decided. My presence seemed to embarrass the other two who busied themselves with their rifles.

Russell saw me looking at the guns, so I asked, "Deer?"

"Yeah. So far, we've gotten one every year." He looked down the valley where the light muted the greens and blues. "I backpack, too, but there's nothing like tracking big game. It puts you in a relationship with the land like nothing else." He looked me in the eye, challenging. He was more like me than like other hunters, he wanted to tell me. He also wanted me to know that I didn't understand. He was right. I didn't. I've heard the argument before, how hunting provides a deeper, more rigorous wilderness experience, one that makes aimless wandering, the kind I do, look flabby.

"Have a good trip," I said, as if I didn't know I'd see them again, and then hiked back and forth across the bar of land until I was sure they had the only level campsite. It was getting late. Because of the enormous granite wall on the other side, my only choice was to camp on the small beach on the far end, below and in full view of my friends. I should have hiked back down to Lower Canyon Creek Lake, but I felt a combination of stubbornness—I wanted to camp at this lake—and defeat. What did it matter where I camped? Wilderness was dead. Solitude was possible only in the heart of winter or north of the Arctic Circle.

I had just finished setting up my tent on the spit of beach, as far from the lake as possible, and put on my soup, when they came tromping around the lake. They pretended to be taking an evening walk, but I knew they were coming to welcome me to the neighborhood. As they fingered my tent, asked questions about its construction, and commented on the size of my pack, I felt a prickling up my neck. They came in too close, touched too much. I'm a big woman with short hair—men don't usually bother me. But to these men, on this weekend, this was wilderness. They were playing at being primitive. Hunters. Maybe even animals themselves. Out here I was Woman. The only one.

I smelled the brandy, a lot of it, on Russell's breath when he said, "We're building a campfire when we get back to camp. Why don't you join us?" The lawyer and accountant looked out at the lake, maybe embarrassed at their lack of social grace, maybe grateful to Russell for being their spokesperson, maybe wishing he'd shut up.

"Maybe." I was afraid to say no outright.

After they left, my own thoughts embarrassed me. These guys were just friendly chumps out on a camping trip. *They* weren't resentful about sharing the lake with *me*. Their neighborliness made me feel like a cranky old mountain dweller, the kind who made her own liquor and chased people off the land with a shotgun. I told myself to get over my absurd antisocial fear and enjoy myself.

Still, all night long I felt like their phantom campfire guest. Their raucous conversation carried across the lake and though I concentrated on not listening, I heard "she" and "that girl" several times. Once I clearly heard one, I suspected the righteous, stern accountant, say, "She's out here for some peace and solitude, after all. We should keep it down." After that, they were quiet.

See, I told myself, *these guys are even considerate.*

And yet I didn't sleep in my tent. I set it up as a decoy, then climbed into the boulders above my camp and found a tiny shelf where I spent the night. Just in case.

Early the next morning, I packed a stuff-sack with day-trip supplies, and began climbing the ridge above my campsite. I hoped to get a view down into Stuart Fork, which I'd hiked up a few years before. I'd spent a magical couple of days at Sapphire and Emerald Lakes, which I hoped to glimpse today. I didn't, but it hardly mattered for all the other spectacular views. I climbed and sweated and breathed hard and allowed myself to be just body. I felt better, though the heaviness, that plug of unspecified fear, didn't loosen.

I tumbled back into camp in the afternoon. I hadn't yet decided whether to have a snack, take a nap, or read a book. I stood looking at the hard, flat surface of the lake and where it stopped at the hard, flat surface of the granite wall on its far side. The gunshot tore open the sky and slammed against the mountainsides. My body felt like a dropped glass that, at the last minute, didn't break.

I moved fast, stuffing my tent, stove, and food bag into the backpack. I knew by the angle at which the light sliced through the cold air that it was too late in the day to move camp, but I was way outside rational. I felt as if I had to outrun the next bullet.

I didn't see the hunters as I skidded down the trail into the valley. They could have been anywhere among the trees, stalking their big game. Or maybe they'd hit an animal with that bullet and while one man (Russell? the accountant?) butchered, another went to get the horse. The undergrowth was silent now, as if every creature in the area, except for me, was standing perfectly still, awaiting safety.

A couple of miles below Lower Canyon Creek Lake, I saw a faint trail heading up another canyon. I remembered seeing Boulder Lake on the map, settled in a stark basin far above treeline. I clawed my way up that trail as if Boulder Lake were the Holy Grail. I thought I could still hear the echo of that explosion ricocheting between the ridges. Phantom pain jabbed at my brain, as if I'd been struck by the bullet. If I could get above treeline, *well* above treeline, I would be able to escape the possibility of a hunter's bullet finding me instead of a deer.

I wondered what other animals, if any, had taken this exact escape route. Bear? Fox? I remembered the previous winter, skiing up Rock Creek Canyon in the eastern Sierras, how I'd followed coyote tracks for miles and wondered then why they were going above treeline in the winter. When I made camp at a frozen lake below the highest peaks, I could see the coyote tracks continuing right up to a pass on the Sierra crest. Visiting family in the valley on the other side? Just loved the view?

Now, as I hunkered up that rocky trail toward Boulder Lake, shouldering my unevenly packed load, exhaustion finally slowing me down, it began to dawn on me that I was acting irrationally. I'd felt that gunshot far too deeply. I knew that although deer hunters kill backpackers every year, the odds were on a par with being struck by lightning. I also knew that the danger of Russell and his friends was negligible. Yet, this awareness didn't take away my need to climb, to escape feeling hunted. I moved up, rejoicing in each inch of altitude gained. My legs, though tired, had a will of their own, springing from rock to rock. I felt bathed, cleansed, by the sweat running off my head and down my neck. I took comfort in knowing that I carried everything I could ever need on my back. The trail petered out at treeline and still I climbed, grabbing the last scrubby spruce for handholds, hungering for the clean, rocky basin I could see still far above me.

I arrived at dusk, my head bursting with exertion and relief. Boulder Lake sat in a barren bowl, circled by the steep walls of blackening mountains. One lone snag, as gray as the granite, leaned out over the water. I set up camp on a tiny ledge above the snag. A perfect patch of sand would cushion my night. There wasn't another person in sight.

My relief was total. Here was rock and water and one stark snag. The dusky sky twitched occasionally, and I had to look hard to make out the flap of wings before they disappeared, like the coyote tracks, to even higher elevations. As darkness wrapped around me, I let all my fear and anxiety drain away. The power of these huge rocks was absolute, as was the cold blackness of the impending night.

I didn't put up my tent. Nor did I sleep much or even think much. I lay in my toasty sleeping bag on the pad of sand, and looked up at the stars. Here above treeline, I was nothing more than sweat and iron, muscle and bone, blue and gray, silence and song. Nothing more and nothing less.

At dawn, I watched the sky gray over. The last few stars tickled my eyes, then vanished. I knew it would be a couple of hours before sunrise. I lay very still and watched it arrive, second by second.

SUSAN EWING

Antelope, Annie Oakley, and the Screaming Demons

I Sing along with the Sweethearts of the Rodeo, accelerating westbound out of Bozeman. Behind the seat in my little pickup are chains for all four tires, an emergency sleeping bag, my rifle, and my knife. And of course my purse, which looks as if it got on the wrong bus. Feeling like a wolf in sheep's clothing (in polar fleece, actually), I sip a double cappuccino and think about antelope meat.

Pat, the man in my life, loves to eat antelope. So do I. It's an honest protein that brings native grace to a western table. The fact that you have to get it yourself is part of that grace, something I am coming to more fully understand in this, my second, hunting season. And there is much to understand. Each revelation brings another question, each emotional high strikes a resonant low note.

Last year I started the season feeling like an adolescent: awkward and unsure. This year I feel like a woman who hunts. Fall brought an unexpected flush of hunter hormones and I find myself hungry to be out. Hunting.

The sun is shining and now Emmy Lou Harris is singing about happy endings as I turn off the interstate. One of the things I like about traveling alone is the music. I crank it up and sing along, or drift without interruption into melodic daydreams as the landscape speeds by—lulled by the movement, moved by the music. In this peaceful, suspended state I can drive almost forever. The sense of suspension is what I like about hunting, too; just walk, look, think. So life is good, rolling down the road with my Remington and two boxes of tunes.

The Montana season is long and generous and I hold enough permits and licenses to make a poker hand. On this trip, I will play the antelope card, down by Red Rock Lakes on the Montana–Idaho border. It's fitting to go there alone—I was by myself when I first found the place. I didn't live in Montana then, but that night, watching the night sky strobe with lightning, I knew I would someday. I didn't hunt then either, and would have been surprised to hear I would be back years later, intending to shoot a warm-blooded wildflower; a prancing prairie smoke.

Doing things by yourself—traveling, hunting, whatever—is only fun if you either don't have personal demons or have figured out a way to ignore them. Happily, aversion to being alone isn't one of mine, but Worry and Doubt are real spoilers. My strategy, basically, is to stick my fingers in my ears and plunge ahead: Hoping for the Best, I guess you'd call it. Of course this can also get you into trouble, but what the hell.

Leaning southwest along the Jefferson, then Beaverhead Rivers, the road passes a succession of farms and ranches scattered with reasonable, but not great, distance between them. Homesteaders snapped up this kind of land—river valleys with lots of water and grass. But south of Dillon where the mountains squeeze back in, homesteads thin out until the world is one brown range spilling emptily up the slopes, and I am sailing through it, suspended.

Since the option is available, I plan to base my hunt out of a motel; November days are too short to make camping alone much fun. I sing along south another forty miles and pull off at Lima—like the bean, not Peru. The woman at the desk shakes her head. No vacancies. "It's hunting season," she patiently explains to this pipit in tennis shoes. I wonder what she thinks I'm doing looking for a motel room in the teeny-bean town of Lima at two in the afternoon.

"Try the bar. They might have something left."

I drive the few blocks across town to the Club Bar and Motel and step through the windowless door into a smoky blue fog. A couple of guys are playing pool and another sits at the bar. The bartender, a small, older woman, is on the phone but keeps an eye on me as I approach and wait for her to finish.

"Yeah?" she says, hanging up the phone.

"Do you have any rooms?"

"For how many." The question is flat.

"One."

"How many?" she repeats, squinting into my face.

The clacking pool balls fall silent.

"One."

"One? How long?"

"Two nights, one . . . " I was going to say, "One if I get lucky," but think better of it, realizing how it will sound.

"Two nights. I'm hunting antelope and if I get one this evening or to-morrow early I'll only need the one night."

Oh. Hunting. That's a legitimate enough reason for a woman to be standing at a bar asking for a room. Everybody relaxes. The redheaded pool player drifts up to share what he knows about antelope: a huge herd this morning, he says, that you could about see from here, if there was a window, in the vacant lot by the cemetery.

"But you can't shoot 'em," the bartender says with glee. "You can't shoot in Lima." She is warmed up now and calling me by name.

"Come on, Susan, let's get you settled." Cigarette in hand, she leads me out the back door to a travel-trailer in the side yard. Judging by the weathered, built-on front landing, the trailer's traveling days are over, but not its useful life. After a brusquely cheerful demonstration of the foot-pump toilet and portable TV, the woman leaves me to carry on. With plenty of shooting light left, I trade tennis shoes for boots, don insulated coveralls, and prop my rifle against the passenger seat.

In other endeavors—extreme skiing, rock climbing, flying small planes—the point is to look death in the face but avoid it in the end. While death is not the point of hunting, it is an unavoidable consequence. Picking up a rifle isn't like grabbing a pair of skis; there is a soberness. My rifle is very plain, with no engraving on the metal or checkering on the shortened birch stock. It's an almost animate presence; a partner. It's my claws and teeth—*my memento mori*. I have killed two deer with this rifle, a fact that makes me deeply sad, but at the same time, proud.

Setting off on the antelope mission, I bump across the railroad tracks and head east along the Red Rock River, which curves like a necklace across the brown chest of the Centennial Valley. Above the valley's bejeweled breast, the Centennial Mountains wear a tiara of continental divide. I haven't been here since that first trip, but I recognize where I camped, where I walked—how many steps it has taken to complete this circle.

Now, from what I can tell, antelope hunting is different from deer and elk hunting in that you seem to spend more time driving around. Especially in places like this where the country is so immense. Unless you happen to be intimately familiar with the habits of one particular herd, it's futile to start out from scratch on foot. Deer and elk have only so many places to be, only so many patches of suitable habitat in which to hide. With antelope, the skyline's the limit. They stay in the open because they don't want to *hide* from you, they want to *run* from you. *Run, run, run!*

My plan is to drive the backcountry until I see antelope, then set out on foot, carefully sneak up on the biggest buck, and drop him with one, clean, reverent shot. With my sharp new knife I will dress him out respectfully and thankfully, and he will lie in this state in the back of my pickup on the way home. This is the plan.

Driving past the lakes I see trumpeter swans and mule deer. I see a dead bull elk in the back of a truck going the other way. Visions of dainty-hoofed, amber-and-white ungulates crowd my head but no earthly antelope appear, even by Antelope Peak. There are no doe-eyed, curious faces looking my way or bright rumps disappearing the other. The last light fades but my hopes do not. Tomorrow will be good. A hunter's most important accoutrement is optimism; her most important motivator, anticipation.

Back at the trailer I find an aluminum saucepan in the cupboard and put on water for tea, the blue flame quiet and cozy against the whistling night. I'm halfway tempted to go over to the bar to visit with the bartender or use the telephone, but instead, I sit at the dinette table and clean my rifle scope. Clear in mind and optics, I go to bed. At around three AM I notice my nose is cold. The whole trailer is cold—cold air is blowing out of all the vents. For some reason I think it will help to turn the thermostat down; it doesn't. The stove-top burners light so there's fuel, just no heat. I should find the furnace and try to light it but I don't think of that, so I turn off the burners and go back to bed, figuring it's not that long until six o'clock anyway. By five, it's too cold to sleep under the thin blanket so I turn the two burners back on and dress in front of the stove. The bar is locked, and there is no office, so I leave a note on the door about the heat and drive the few blocks back across town to the café for breakfast. Thirty minutes later, I'm prowling out of Lima in the dark, ready for action, a picture postcard of Annie Oakley on the dashboard for good luck.

On the map, this part of Montana is a blank space. In truth, it's a broad, rolling plain covered mostly in short-grass, sagebrush, dirt, and rocks. Trees are distant blocks of evergreen on faraway slopes. Today, the ground is nearly bare of snow.

"The moon is full, the night is clear, huntin' season is drawing near," I sing along with Jennifer Warnes as darkness eases away. Cruising with the hormones, driving, singing, looking for wildlife.

"My a-a-a-aim is pretty good, I'm as quiet as a deer in the wood."

With the wind blowing this hard, I should aim . . . from some recess I hear men's voices argue about compensation, drop, and distance; velocities, grains, ballistics, powder charge—*at two-hundred-and-fifty yards, shoot X-and-such high; at three-hundred yards shoot X-and-a-half-such high; if the animal is running, shoot* . . .

"Close your eyes, count to ten," sings Jennifer. I'm not a ballistic sort of woman. I would rather wait for a sure shot than calculate and compensate. My men friends think this is a gender thing that I'll grow out of when I come home empty-handed enough times.

Much of the land around here is public, but I stop at the Matador Ranch to ask permission anyway because I have come to like this part of the process. No one is at the house, but a boy in coveralls blows like a brown limb across the compound. When I catch up with him, he is conversational under a black knit face mask, and leads me to the barn where his father is working.

"I've seen a herd of thirty or forty off to the northeast," the man shouts congenially over the wind. "If you can find 'em, you should have 'em to yourself. This late in the season all the antelope hunters are about gone." I thank him and drive north until I find a promising-looking two-track going off to the east. Two-tracks are like hiking trails for trucks. For an hour or more, I follow the track following the contours of the land. Without trees the view goes forever; ground merges with distant mountain, with sky, with cloud, with sky—then swoops back around until I'm sitting on where I'm going. As far as I can see, no pavement, no people, no buildings, no cows even. No antelope either, here in the open, in the middle of nowhere, on the margin of Montana.

The temperature is eighteen degrees, a fact I know precisely because before I left home, Pat installed a digital thermometer in my truck so I could see when I was about to freeze to death. But the truck is warm and filled with music, and over the next rise will be my buck. But, over the next rise is a frozen creek, lying like a dangerous snake across the track.

The creek is about two truck-lengths wide and who-knows-how deep. It has taken me all morning to get this far. I can't go around and I don't want to go back. I can't see very far onto the other side—the land swells and drops, swells and drops, and right now I'm in a bit of a drop—but my antelope is over there somewhere, surely.

Setting the emergency brake, I get out to reconnoiter. Toward the middle of the creek the grayish ice looks pretty thick, but near the edge I toe through the crust and find mud. I hate to turn around. On the other hand, if I get stuck, it's conceivable no one will come by until spring. I have warm clothes and sturdy boots and can walk out if I have to, provided the ominous sky doesn't unleash a way-losing blizzard, and I don't break my leg.

With well-practiced timing, two of my more familiar personal demons begin screaming for attention. The sordid siblings, Go-For-It and Fear, have plagued me all my life, pushing me to do a thing, then scaring me silly. Fear is the worst, sometimes riding along on even the most innocent outings. Worming their ways into my brain, they vie to squeeze out any remaining rational thought. Before it's too late, I should kick their black-souled butts out of the truck and turn around.

"You hate to turn around," Go-For-It breathes in my ear.

"You'll be coyote bait," Fear moans into the other.

The music is turned off. I brought everything I thought I'd need in case of emergency, but what I need for this situation is a tow vehicle standing by. God, I do hate to turn around.

The "closed" sign drops down suddenly behind my eyes. I shift into four-wheel-low, rev the Ranger like a mad bull, and charge the creek.

Crash! Ice and water fly. The truck bucks and begins to bog down. *Eeeeyyyaaaaaaaahh.* Is the emergency brake still on? The demons chase around the cab like rabid weasels. Why didn't I think to put on the chains? My heart is ripping through my coveralls, my face is grim. With a death grip on the steering wheel, I keep the accelerator mashed to the floor and scoot wildly in the seat, trying to pull the truck forward like a chair. Now the wheels are spinning at screaming rpms but the truck only inches agonizingly ahead. Why do I do these things? When will I learn? Why can't I just *buy* my meat? I *hate* this! Seconds are hours until finally, amazingly, the truck grabs solid footing and rises, dripping, from the creek bed. As it hits hard, frozen, blessed ground, I realize I'm not breathing. Whooping, I fall out the door to stand victorious over the dark swirl of water and ice.

Hisssssssss. Sinking to my knees by the back tire, I try to focus on where this sickening sound is coming from. There's a spare, but because of the way the trailer hitch is installed, changing the tire is a complicated project that requires using vice grips in a job not meant for vice grips, and jacking the truck up and down in order to muscle out the spare by degrees. I've never done it all by myself. The demons cavort. The digital thermometer reads: 17°.

The tire still looks pumped up, so—hoping for the best—I drive on. If a record buck gets up twenty yards away I doubt I'll stop; the hormones are occupied guarding the demons.

At forty years old, I'm beginning to understand that it's nearly as easy to calm myself as it is to terrify myself, and much less taxing. So here, in the middle of nowhere on the margin of Montana, I pick my favorite music and sing along with Nancy Griffith and Tom Paxton, tip-toe-trucking down the two-track, watching ravens flip on the wind.

"I've been a-wandering through this land, just a-doin' the best I can . . . "

The sky is overcast, but clear enough to see the Centennial Mountains, so at least I know where I am in the larger sense. In the smaller sense, I don't have a clue.

At a fork in the track Fear whines, "Where *are* we?" I stuff the Annie Oakley postcard in its mouth and head southwest. The gas tank is half-full, the tire seems to be holding, and I know in which cardinal direction to go. So there.

An hour or so later, a ranch building appears in the distance below. Still singing with Nancy, I wind slowly off the plateau, out of nowhere into somewhere, amazed at how civilized a gravel road and one ranch building can look. Another hour later I roll into Lima on all four wheels. (I decide the hiss must have been water bubbling down through dried mud, although the next day I will find a nail in that tire.)

The trailer is still blowing cold air and the bar isn't open yet, so I drive to the vacant lot by the cemetery where the antelope are. My buck is standing in the middle of the milling crowd, chewing his cud. Clever creature. I'm more amused than frustrated—really—although I suppose I make a forlorn figure, parked on the edge of town by the graveyard with my hunter-orange vest, unloaded rifle, and hundred or so antelope. I'm too glad to be sitting here instead of trudging toward the Centennials. I think I'll go home.

So, I lost the antelope card. It wasn't too smart to wait until the end of the season, but at least I played the hand. I came, I tried, I learned.

I lassoed a chunk of years beginning and ending at the Montana border.

I hoped for the best.

The demons are sleeping, the hormones quiet. I gather my stuff from the trailer, leave another note, and pull away from the Club Bar with Lyle Lovett.

"Ain't it somethin' / How the way things go / Ain't it somethin' . . . "

I'm not carrying home any material measure of success, but there is more here to measure than meat. There is acceptance and grace. Most importantly, there is simply being out. Hunting. Thirty miles north of Lima, humming along, I begin to daydream about elk.

MARYBETH HOLLEMAN

The Wind on My Face

I DID NOT COME HERE TO LOOK FOR OIL. I bring no shovel, overturn no rocks, hunt no pools of sheens or sludge. I know I could find some—at home I have a jar of *Exxon Valdez* oil that a friend collected from a beach two months ago, over five years after oil drenched Prince William Sound.

I am on Perry Island simply to be where I was the year of the oil spill. To put myself back into the land, alone, understand what the spill invoked in me, feelings that resurfaced last spring as a tidal wave of events that have capsized my life.

All around me is quiet except for the rain steadily beating on my rain suit. Clouds are low, hiding in the tallest peak on the island, the one with the glaucous-winged gull colony on top. I listen closely and can only hear rain pinging off leaves and waves breaking on the beach. Beyond that beach, whitecaps tell me the water is too rough for my leaky seven-foot inflatable boat.

Five years earlier, during the week I camped in this same spot, I saw no rain. No waves. No clouds. It was unusually warm and sunny and still. Too warm, for the sun softened the oil on the rocks so that black tar stuck to our clothes and acrid fumes stung our eyes. After a few days, we all had headaches, so we moved the entire camp. Too much oil for the oil spill observer project.

Yet this place has haunted me since, as has the oil spill itself. I decided to return to see for myself how well the place had healed, and to find some way to heal myself. Now I dwell on the dilemma that arose this spring. Somehow I sense they're connected—the spill, this place, my desires. But how?

It does not surprise me that I felt increasingly unsettled weeks before the fifth anniversary of the spill. All last winter, I anticipated its arrival and looked for words to encompass all it meant, but I was only revisited by demons I thought long gone. It does not surprise me that I met Rick again that week. It does not even surprise me that I find myself in love with him, unable to give him up, even in the face of losing my marriage and my life as I've known it for fifteen years.

What does surprise me is the turmoil and the fear. And here I face both: the turmoil of a storm brewing around me, wind whipping up waves, water pouring from the dark sky; and the fear of being alone in the wilderness, on an island twenty-six miles by water from the nearest town. Why have I thrown myself back into this place alone?

But I'm not alone. As I set up camp, I hear an eerie yet familiar sound overhead, the sound of voices deep in nature. A pair of loons fly across the cove and over my campsite, flying in such synchronicity that it seems the very air binds them together. They are Pacific loons, with smooth, striped, gray-and-white necks, and silver heads holding ruby eyes. I watch their flight, my face turned up into rain, for as long as I can. Long after, I listen to their songs.

I am glad the loons have paid a visit. Their songs have always amazed and comforted me. I crave comfort now, for I am fearful of the feelings that have been haunting me since I arrived. It's only been five hours since my husband and son left me, my gear, and my little boat here. Now they're on their way to a warm, dry house, and it's all I can do to keep from wishing I was with them. As I string tarps to trees, creating a dry refuge from which to see the cove, I think of the loons. I wonder if they are the same pair my friend Nora observed five years ago.

Four months after the *Exxon Valdez* ran aground in 1989, a half dozen of us camped on three of this island's beaches. We came here simply to bear witness, to share what we saw and didn't see with those who only knew images replayed on television. Nora, one of hundreds so disturbed by news of the spill that she flew up from Delaware to help, hiked up to a lake where a pair of Pacific loons nested. She told me their nest produced no young that year. Did I just see that same pair? Did they survive the spill years?

I've got a roof over my head now, so I scout for rocks and driftwood to create a place to sit and to store my food out of the rain. My campsite is on a short spit of land, with a cove on one side and an open view of the Sound on the other. My kitchen looks out over Day Care Cove.

This is an unofficial name given to this cove by a couple who spent many summers kayaking the Sound before the spill. They named it "Day Care" because they always saw so many birds, seals, and sea otters raising their young in this safe, secluded, and nutrient-rich spot. The name doesn't fit as well these past five years; so far, I've seen only one grebe with her three young.

On the other side of the cove, the land rises steeply to the tallest mountain on the island. It is still shrouded in clouds, but I can trace in my mind its peak—a tan rock dome, segmented with crevasses that are linked with vegetation. At the mountain's base, there's a low pass where a creek meets saltwater—the source of my drinking water.

This is among the safest places to camp in Prince William Sound; there is no giardia in the water, so it's safe to drink, and there are no bears—as far as we know. I've got plenty of water and food, a dry tent, a hand-held radio . . . I know I am safe. My fear of being alone is a fear of finding out what I'm feeling.

I am in the place I love, the place that drew me to stay in Alaska one more summer, then one more year. Now I've lived here nearly a decade, and I'm still not ready to leave. Every summer my husband, Andy, and I go to the Sound and explore its glaciers and fjords and coves and mountains. It's a shockingly beautiful place, always showing me something new, but it's not an easy place.

This Sound gets an incredible amount of rain and snow, cold and dark. Even in summer, the water is dangerously frigid—if you fall in, you have about fifteen minutes before hypothermia sets in and muscles shut down. Two outer islands, Montague and Hinchinbrook, protect the Sound from the full force of Gulf of Alaska storms, but it still can have dangerously high seas. So to be here is to expect storms; to expect to need winter clothes, a survival suit, a radio to reach the Coast Guard; to expect to be uncomfortable.

The rain pours down and gray skies envelope the island. I'm tired and cold, and my attempts to build a campfire with sodden wood and railroad flares have failed, so I fix a quick dinner and retreat to my tent. I shrink down into my sleeping bag and write in my journal.

It's windy and rainy. Waves crash the shores with frightening force, everything is damp and cold, I'm having my period, complete with cramps. I am miserable.

Miserable.

Well. Is this punishment? Trial by fire? By wind and water? Or just coincidence?

There's a bird twittering madly outside my tent. No, it's a squirrel. Probably upset because it can't get to any of my food.

The wind has picked up. It howls against my tent, shaking the walls and beating them with rain and a loose rope. The tent floor billows up, and I'm glad I tied it down with ropes and stakes. I hear waves breaking on the beach, a steady roar punctuated by a thunderous crash every few seconds. The wind makes waves crash at a tidemark so high I feel it tugging at the edges of my tent. The rain dashes sideways so that, even with my rain fly and big blue tarp overhead, I still must zip shut the screened window to keep from getting wet.

The roar increases. I imagine crawling out of the tent and getting swept away to sea. Then I worry that my little boat, my life line, will get swept away. *Did I tie the line high enough on the beach? Are my knots strong enough to hold?* I venture out. Everything is just as I've left it, only wetter. The boat is still tethered; my driftwood campsite is intact; the same trees stand around me; the same boulders line the shore. The storm is not reshaping the island. I am being reshaped.

For months now, I've felt as if I'm in a wave, caught up in it, unable to control even its direction, much less its force. I can only hope to ride it rather than drown in it. I can only hope it will not dash me against a rock cliff or throw me, gasping, onto a beach. The boat that is my life has capsized, strewing all the contents around me. I don't know which pieces will sink, or make it to shore, or end up with me. These images of wind and water are the only way I'm able to explain to others how I am feeling.

I love two men. How can that be? Yet it's not even that simple. This isn't about two men; it's about how I've been changing these past five years. These men are mirrors, and in them I see two different versions of me. One shows me who I've been, the other shows me who I can be. One shows me stability and devoted love and a smooth path through a tended meadow; the other shows me passion and amazement and a trail disappearing into thick forest. Right now I have one foot on each path, each in a very different world. I am split in two, camped on an island that is exactly midpoint between where each man lives. How do I choose?

Daylight brings restlessness. Back out into the wet, I walk the beach that fronts the Sound. Waves tumble fist-size rocks as I walk the edge of the tide. Beyond this small bay I can see the long, thin line of Lone Island. Thin lines of blue sky beyond reveal snowy peaks of the Chugach Range on the mainland—ice fields gleaming white in the sun.

Looking back toward the cove, I see that my mountain is still shrouded. I think it snags the clouds and holds them; they pile up over the cove and keep me wet. Out beyond Lone Island it's sunny.

Overhead, there's a shrill cry. Two bald eagles slice the air above me, curving around the bay to alight on tall spruce across the entrance to the cove. I've seen them there several times, but not once by the eagle-nest tree. The nest tree is closer to me, on a rocky point off this beach. It's easy enough to spot; the trunk is marked with a red triangle.

The year of the spill, a biologist with the U.S. Fish and Wildlife Service helicoptered to our campsite and hiked over to that tree. I went along. In the nest, he found an unhatched eagle egg, perfect except for one small, dark spot. Oil. The parents, he explained, probably picked up crude oil on their feet from combing the beaches for food. Then they landed in the nest, and one drop of oil hit their single egg. That one drop killed the embryo.

Most eagle nests in western Prince William Sound failed that year. This year, I've yet to see an eagle by the nest. Instead, I hear crows near the eagle tree, noisily chattering and frequently bursting from the treetops to circle and chase each other. I suspect the eagles have abandoned it.

For an eagle to abandon a nest is rare. Perhaps waiting for an egg that never hatched made them lose trust in the nest. Trust. I know Prince William Sound itself didn't turn on these creatures, that the spill came instead from the inhumane acts of humanity. But how do these eagles know that? How do the loons, who as a species have survived for ninety million years, comprehend the spill? What in their collective memory can they compare it to? How do they know they can still trust their chosen lakes with their young?

At one end of the beach, I follow a path through the skunk cabbage and berry bushes to Aleut Beach. The pathway is overgrown; I step on the large, thick leaves of skunk cabbage, then up a slippery plank coated with moss. After following more remnants of the driftwood boardwalk, I stumble out of the forest onto the beach. A narrow bay, flanked by cliffs, funnels into the short, rocky beach, depositing whatever floats by. The white-and-tan boulders of Aleut Beach are coated in oil so thick that the edges of rock disappear into the ooze. A stench of oil fumes surrounds me. Waves make a muffled sound against the sludge.

I blink, look again.

Now the oil is gone, back into memory. The remaining black stains on rocks are probably black lichen; the ooze is only a woven mass of kelp swept up from last winter's storms.

I sit on a log, heart beating fast. Feeling faint, I put my head between my legs and stare at the smooth log. I remember it, remember the stains of oily boot prints on it, made by cleanup workers who likely spread more oil than they removed. Now the log is worn back down to a sun-bleached brown. *Tabula rasa*.

Two oystercatchers fly by low, veering precisely along the water line. Their sharp chatter reminds me that my presence irritates them. I wonder if they're the same pair I annoyed here five years ago. I saw them every day, no matter which beach or headland I hiked to. I began to think they were following me, but they always acted as if I were following them—staying a few yards in front of me, taking flight and circling around the beach at my least movement, then landing again just beyond me. I'm happy to see them again.

Walking back, I follow the shoreline and come upon a sea otter bobbing in the surf. His boat-shaped body floats effortlessly as he pounds a rock onto the shellfish on his belly. Turning his head, he sees me and dives for cover. Even though I see him several more times, he is never curious enough to stare back before diving. It worries me.

Before the spill, otters would look at me a long moment, then continue their lolling about or come closer to examine me. Now, otters and seals and sea lions seem less willing to stick around in a human's presence. Is it that the more cautious animals avoided oil and therefore survived? Or is it that the oil and ensuing cleanup has made these animals less curious and more fearful of us? Trust again. Perhaps the sea otter knows the spill was caused by humans and not by some unfocused wrath of his home, Prince William Sound.

I return to my lonely camp, still unsettled by my apparition. I didn't expect the oil spill's hold on me to still be so strong. Since then, I've made nearly a dozen trips in the Sound, and I've been to this very island several times; why am I reliving it now?

This is my first trip alone in the Sound. Except for a few hours here and there of solitary walks, I was always with another human. Maybe other people acted as a buffer, drowning out the voices in my head.

Those are precisely the voices I need to hear now, for I need to face the demons that are surfacing. They are tenacious. Five years, and if anything, they've grown stronger. What am I avoiding? What do they want of me? I wanted this time in the Sound to help me find some answers. But instead of a relaxing trip, a soothing sun on the beach with which to contemplate life, I get a storm and clouds and rains of discontent.

In the morning, I see a harbor seal in the bay. His silver head trolls the water, turning several times toward me so that I can catch his big, dark eyes. Then suddenly he disappears, his black snout the last thing I see. For a moment I am simply delighted to have spent a few minutes in his presence. Then I wonder: Is he one of the harbor seals left blinded when oil touched his eyes? Is that why he seemed less concerned over my presence than the sea otter, because those dark pools of eyes are useless?

Darkness overflows with dreams. I am with my son Jamie; the sun is high in a cloudless sky; we are clad in the lightest of clothes. We do errands in town, pass a simple day, yet I feel full and happy. Everything is so good, I think, *this must be the day I'll die*. Then I find myself in darkness, alone, rain still pouring down outside the tent, my sleeping bag and clothes damp around me.

Last May, I told a woman I'd just met about the changes confronting me and my inability to see the choices clearly. She told me to ask my dreams for help.

"Right before you go to sleep, think of a question you want answered," she said.

So every night I have asked myself, *Who do I need on my journey?* And every night, though my dreams are full of people, the only one with me is Jamie. Rick makes one brief appearance; Andy never appears. So I keep asking, like an owl, *Who, who, who?*

Perhaps it is right neither permeates my dreams. For so long, I have not even trusted my own heart—I've second-guessed every feeling, every thought that was at all emotional or intuitive. How can I trust my dreams? Or perhaps neither man appears because I am asking the wrong question. Not whom I shall be with, but who I shall be.

More rain. I feel like a squirrel. I sit under this tarp, my midden piling around me: spent matchsticks, coffee bags, tissue paper, pencil shavings, chocolate-bar wrappers. I want to get out, maybe putter around the shoreline in my little boat or hike some of the hills. But I can't find the energy to move far from camp. I am sodden.

The oystercatchers are on the beach in front of me. They crouch low, legs bent and heads down, creeping down the beach as if they are stalking something. Their round, black bodies are the same size and color as the beach rocks—only their orange beaks and legs give them away. They remain close together, one always a hand's-breadth in front. When the leader stops and sits, the other sits next to it, feathers touching.

Offshore, the mama grebe swims over to a spot where low tide has exposed rock covered with popweed and barnacles. Her three chicks are on the other side of the cove, still within sight, but farther from their mother than I've seen yet. It is midsummer; they will soon be on their own.

All around me are animals mated to place. Grebe chicks letting go of their mother but remaining dependent on the cove; eagles rarely moving their nest site; ravens willing to combat winter's freeze so they don't have to migrate; loons returning to the same lake year after year; Arctic terns flying twenty-five thousand miles to come back each spring to this one place, Prince William Sound.

We humans, meanwhile, flit around the globe like bats without echolocation or moths confused by a candle's flame. We are restless, unbounded, unable to commit to a place or to each other.

I hear the loons and am drawn back. Winds cleanse the beach with waves and the forests with rain. Perhaps I would be better off committing to a place for life rather than to a person. Just hunker down on this island, pour myself into this life, and release all the rest that looms over me like a rain-laden sky.

Clouds are lifting, rain has stopped, and I decide to boat across the cove and hike to the lake. Surprisingly, the cantankerous outboard starts on the third pull, and I move easily across the flat water to the stream on the far side. There I tie up the boat and stumble about on slippery rocks before finding the trailhead, which is marked by the remains of a small wooden building.

The trail through forest is barely visible, and seems more like a small animal trail than a human one. Perhaps only river otters have traveled it since the other oil observers and I last walked it five years ago.

To escape oil fumes, we walked to the lake several times. Up in the fields and forests, we could almost forget about the oil spill. We hiked until sweat ran in rivulets down our bodies, then swam in the cold, dark lake, letting fresh water cleanse us. We lay on rocks that had never been slick with oil, drying our bodies in the sun. Not until we heard a plane or helicopter overhead, or the steady drone of an outboard in the distance, were we forced back to reality.

Then we talked of the starfish convulsing in the poison of a shallow tide pool; the oily footprints of a river otter who had scampered un-wittingly through a pool of oil; the fishing boat that came to scoop up floating masses of kelp; the massive barges and dozens of boats and men in West Twin Bay who cleaned oil off the kelp; the death and destruction caused by oil and the futility and frustration of the cleanup going on all around us, on the shores of Perry Island, on the waters of the Sound.

I hear the gulls, see some flying by, and know I'm nearing the lake. Pushing through another dense pocket of shrubs, I come out on a hum-mock overlooking the lake. The lake is immense, surrounded by rock cliffs, and so deep the water looks black. On a rocky point that juts out into the lake sits a large spruce, as perfectly shaped as a Christmas tree. It is adorned with a hundred white gulls.

I stretch out on the hummock, hands behind my head. Hearing a sound like breath being expelled, I look up. A gull flies by, wings carving the air. She joins a raft of birds in the middle of the lake, cawing and cackling, flapping their wings, splashing water on their backs. I've never figured out why the gulls congregate here. There's no food for them; it's all by the sea. They don't nest here; they nest up on the mountain.

Well, why am I here? What do I want?

I want to feel the wind on my face in just this way.

I want to feel passion, always. Even if it hurts. Just to know I'm alive and in this world.

I want to know Prince William Sound, all of it. I want to hike over every inch, climb every peak, walk every beach, stand on every headland.

I want to feel this place the way these gulls do—as an extension of myself. I want the borders between this place and me to dissolve in the knowing.

I want to feel more love—pure and simple, not captured in a tangled web. A single, solid love that encompasses all.

I want to fly and sing like these gulls. To hear my wings soar through the atmosphere. To catch the perfect thermal and glide all day.

I want to be fearless.
I want to sit here and watch white birds cluster on a dark tree at water's edge.
I want to trust my heart.

It's my last day here. Still cloudy, but no rain since last night. I take one last walk through the forest to Aleut Beach and around to the rocky headland of Observation Point.

In a rain forest, it rains. But the rain doesn't just fall, land on the ground, soak into the soil. It covers everything. It clings so totally that, even after the rain stops falling from the sky, even when the sun shines all day, it still rains.

On me. As I walk through it. The trail is spongy sphagnum moss and my feet get wet. Even the planks are wet, and I slip on mossy wood. Skunk cabbage, as big as my three-year-old son and studded with diamonds of rain, slaps my legs, spraying water. Slender grasses, green orchid, purple aster, and ladies'-tresses shiver as I pass, releasing more liquid. This rain is like seed that disperses by attaching to a passing animal's fur, so easily does it cling to my body. Droplets seem to jump out onto me, as if dry is simply an abstract concept here, as if an equilibrium of wet on all things must be maintained.

Onward. I scramble up a hill, grabbing onto roots. Now salmonberry and blueberry wave wetly against my hips. Spruce and hemlock saplings rub my shoulders and pat my back with damp needles. A passing breeze coats my hair and face in the lifeblood of this forest.

If I stay here long enough, will the hair on my arms grow moss? Will tendrils of old-man's-beard hang around my face? Will my feet sink even deeper into black soil until I am rooted in place?

I reach a bluff overlooking Aleut Beach. I take in the scene through the branches of a hemlock perched on a bluff's edge—rocky beach, cliffs, ocean, distant islands. It is beautiful. That is all. This is the first time

I've been able to simply see the beauty of this place without my vision being clouded by memory, suspicion, doubt, fear.

My eyes move from landscape to the pattern of twisted branches that make up this hemlock. I pull out my notebook and sketch the tree, every branch, every angle. I try to be exact, but there are so many twists that my sketch falls off the page's edge. This tree has led a life textured by wind and rain, contorted into a shape made more beautiful by strife.

How do we choose what to lose? How does this tree give up the security of a forest with trees all around to live on the edge where wind tests its strength? I know this tree came from a seed that simply fell here, carried by the forces that now shape it. Prince William Sound's wildlife didn't choose to lose so much to an oil slick; it simply happened. The spill has forever changed it, but it survived. Events are absorbed and become a part of who we are. To attempt to get over them is as futile as to keep living them.

As this tree holds past storms in every bend, so the Sound holds the spill. So do I hold my past. I can't choose to lose that which is already a part of me. I can only trust my heart as the tree trusts the bluff to hold it, as the loons trust the lakes they nest upon. They are all acts of faith. All I can do is take my chances with life and hope I weather them as gracefully as this hemlock.

My last evening on the island. I take my wine and sit on an upended stump on the beach. Smooth, gray roots curve to fit my thighs and reach to frame a picture of Prince William Sound. Gray-blue waters connect it all: to my left, a tan outcropping of rock covered with popweed, barnacles, and black lichen; beyond and to my right, a rocky headland crowned with tall, dark spruce; off in the distance, a green slice of island floating in watery clouds. All around I hear voices: gull, crow, eagle, grebe; waves, trees, rock, wind.

Words to a favorite song come to me, and I begin singing aloud. After a few moments, I notice the gulls and crows, eagles and oystercatchers, are silent. I keep singing. A crow alights on the top of a spruce near me. I keep singing. I sing an album full of songs, songs of love and loss, the bitter-sweet blues. All the while, the crow sits and the birds listen. After days of me trudging around silently and listening to their songs, they finally get to hear from me. I add my voice to the songs of place, and trust Prince William Sound will contain it.

LORI HOBKIRK

Cycling the *Koru*

WHEN THE PORTER WHEELED MY BIKE BOX THROUGH THE OVERSIZED BAG-GAGE CLAIM DOOR IN THE AUCKLAND AIRPORT, A SMALL, TANNED, BROWN-HAIRED WOMAN PICKED IT UP AND CARRIED IT AWAY. I followed to see where she was taking *my* bicycle. Moments later, the porter wheeled out another bike box, which turned out to be mine after all. We both began assembling our bikes and gear in the baggage claim area, and talked about our trips, and how neither of us knew where we were going after leaving the Auckland airport. Nor did we have maps, except those in our guidebooks. And it was Saturday. In fact, it was a three-day weekend in New Zealand, so the best maps—which could be bought from the Lands and Survey Department—wouldn't be available until Tuesday. *Great planning*, I kept telling myself. Kathy and I decided to stick together while in Auckland; then we would go our separate ways. She wanted to tour the South Island first. I wanted to cycle north to the Bay of Islands. But all I really knew was: I was going to take my time.

I had been living in Minneapolis, Minnesota, for three years freelancing as a theater costume designer—sometimes working on four shows at once. Now, feeling burned out and somewhat lonely, I either had to make a bigger commitment to my career, the place, and its people, or do something entirely different. Should I try landing a fabulous job with a big theater company? How could I develop more meaningful relationships with my neighbors and friends in the Twin Cities? Would I ever feel at home in the cold, flat North Country? Or should I return to my Colorado home? Whenever faced with the big life questions, the best option for me was travel—for a long time, far away, and by myself. It would only be a temporary aloneness. The solitude would be a great way for me to heal the fatigue and prevent the weariness I had experienced in the din of my daily life. I admitted to spiritual poverty.

I can't say that I always dreamt of being a lone traveler. It just ended up that way. When I was a kid, my father—whose family was Scottish—put dreams into my head by announcing on Sunday mornings that we'd be catching the two o'clock flight to Scotland. I immediately excused myself from the breakfast table, packed my bags, and placed them by the front door. I planned my whole day around the idea that I would be in Scotland before bedtime. I had no reason to believe that a trip like that *wouldn't* happen, even though it never did.

To this day, I leap small buildings if I know that I have an opportunity to be somewhere else before bedtime. And I take pride in knowing that I can pack my bags and be ready for an adventure faster than anybody I know.

My original plan was to sightsee for two months in New Zealand, then fly to Adelaide, South Australia, and spend Christmas with my stepsister and her family. I would then cycle in Australia for about one month, then fly to Fiji, Hawaii, and back home. My plane ticket was good for one year, with four stops. I didn't know how long my money would last— the length of my trip was dependent on that. But once I landed in Auckland, everything changed. I felt comfortable there.

In New Zealand, I wanted to go slowly and see everything. I didn't want any appointments or deadlines. I wanted to sleep, eat, and drink outside. I wanted to stay for the whole year. I wanted to feel the terrain under my bike and the warm summer air on my face during the months that would be winter in the Land o' Lakes.

And so, on that drizzly October spring day, Kathy and I wheeled through quiet, hilly neighborhoods, not knowing where we were going, distracted by being in a new place, and feeling jet lag. The forty pounds in my panniers felt like eighty, and I wished I had trained for hauling more weight.

After the second night of camping along the beach in Waipu Cove, Kathy and I hugged goodbye. For a while after she left, I felt lonely. The feeling took me by surprise, as I was still in my aloof Minneapolis mode. After three years of wandering through the city and making only a few meaningful connections with people, I wasn't prepared to say goodbye to a woman who had become my best buddy after two days.

Dew collected inside and outside the tent that morning. I got a late start as I waited for my tent to dry, something I would do many times in the next four-and-a-half months that I ended up being in New Zealand.

That night, a woman who grew orchids for exporting to the United States invited me to camp on her property, that is, *after* her friend, Mary, stopped me on my way out of Whangerei to ask about my trip. Mary was intrigued because I was alone. She walked with me through town, then phoned ahead to her orchid-lady friend, and I cycled the remaining thirty kilometers to the woman's house. I was greeted at the gate by the entire family, all of them holding white orchids, which they attached to my handlebar bag.

That was how my trip began in New Zealand. Maybe people were sympathetic because I was alone, or because I traveled by bicycle. Maybe it was a New Zealander's nature to welcome me into their community. Everywhere I went, I met somebody who knew somebody who knew somebody else who had something to offer me: coffee and poached eggs, a place to sleep, a ride, advice, or an ice cream. I had no preconceived ideas about what it would be like to travel alone, but as I am a loner by nature, it seemed time for me to move away from that, to experience a different vantage point. I welcomed their affections.

My first purchase in New Zealand was a raincoat. Not the lightweight, anorak-type parka that I normally wore throughout my childhood during the daily afternoon rain showers in Colorado, but a blue, nonbreathable, suede-like plastic, hooded coat that came to just below my cycling shorts. It was designed to be worn in the sheep paddies during monsoon season—days when the rain came down in sheets and you couldn't see three feet ahead. It made the perfect cycling jacket, as the sleeves were long, the hood spacious, with a bill at the top to keep water out of my eyes. It cinched at my waist, and was big enough that I could wear a wool sweater underneath—which was my second New Zealand purchase.

New Zealand showed evidence of a lot of rain. Palm trees grew at the Auckland train station. Flower beds outlined driveways. The Auckland Botanical Gardens looked the same outside as they did inside, with snapdragons growing into bushes and moss collecting in cement cracks. On some roads, red bottlebrush blossoms slapped me as I cycled by, giving my face a wash with dew.

It was in an REI brochure that I read there comes a time, while bicycle touring, when a person feels at one with everything: the self, the bike, the environment, and the road. I felt it many times on my way around the East Cape of the North Island. It wasn't just the warm Pacific beaches, the cloudless sky, feeling sunburned and windburned, seeing White Island—an active volcano—off the coast in the distance, or having the road to myself for most of the days. I felt it in my cadence on the flats and the uphills, in my developing muscles, in my lungs that pumped with my feet that pumped with my heart.

I had figured that a car could travel the same distance in one hour as I traveled in one day on my bike, and the twenty-five hundred miles it took me four-and-a-half months to ride in New Zealand would have taken a car four days. I had drastically slowed the pace of my life.

"Ah, yer on a push bike, eh?" people asked when I stopped for afternoon tea and bickies (cookies), or a banana-honey-sultana sandwich I concocted, or to buy a scoop o' chips. The next question was always predictable: "And yer traveling alone?" "Yer game!" they said, "Good on ya!" and proceeded to recite road conditions, letting me know the next big mountain I would push my bike up. I quickly learned that "mountain" is a relative term. "You will know when you've reached the big one," they warned. "No others like it 'round here." Some days, the cycling seemed especially difficult. The road often went directly up and over a mountain, instead of around it, and there was always a head wind. On other days, the "big" hill was a gradual climb around a seaside cliff, with an overlook at the top, and several sheep around. But it was always peaceful and rhythmic. I never once felt bored.

Maevine and Ted Ingram caravan-camped next to me one night in Te Araroa. The next morning, after witnessing me pack up my tent and load my bike, they invited me in for coffee. We went through the usual introductions and I learned they were a retired couple on a golf-course-tour holiday. Ted carved traditional Maori weapons out of kauri wood native to the North Island. He recommended I visit the Wanganui Maori Museum. He would even take me there if I got to Bulls—their hometown between Palmerston North and Wanganui.

Ted was anxious for a captive audience. He led me outside while delivering an elaborate discourse on Maori symbolism in weaponry. The *koru* spiral, double spiral, he told me, is used as a *leitmotif* throughout most Maori art and weaponry.

"The spiral represents life," Ted explained. "People start at the top of the spiral, and with life's experiences, circle their way down. The load, the weight of our daily lives, the energy drained from it, brings us down and down, as we continue circling into the spiral." Ted spread his collection of weapons on the picnic table during his oration, gingerly unwrapping each one from newspaper: a *pokopoko* (walking stick), a fish carver, a bonker (mallet), and a hunting knife with the blade carved out of jade.

"Then," he continued, "the spiral starts circling back up without a break in the continuity. This is because the wisdom obtained from these experiences lifts people out of their doldrums, helps them 'see the light.'" With that thought, along with an egg sandwich, Ted and Maevine sent me on my way.

A few days later, I reached Gisborne. The temperatures were well into the eighties, and I spent the late afternoon chatting with people on the beach, watching schoolgirls play volleyball, relaxing my legs after cycling into a head wind all day. I ran into a fellow who said he had spotted Marilyn—a woman I met at a bed-and-breakfast—a few days ago. On a whim, I posted a note at the youth hostel for Marilyn to contact me at the Beethoven House in Wellington, in one week. The Beethoven House was a hostel-like place I had read about where the innkeeper played only Beethoven's music. Sounded cheap and intriguing.

I wasn't convinced, though, that I wanted to hook up with Marilyn as any kind of permanent cycling partner. After all, I sought solitude. Yet, I liked her spirit and laughter. And she was from Minneapolis, so she was a connection to my past. She knew places and people I had been intimate with, and we both celebrated spending a winter in a warmer climate. I also enjoyed playing my new game of crossing paths with the same people over and over again: posting a note, mailing a card, hoping for a response. I was becoming a part of two communities: the vagabond cycling family—scattered during the day and congregated for dinner around a picnic table at night, and the Kiwi community—the home away from home, the family of swans that groomed me, the ugly duckling, with their beaks, and swam round and round in greeting.

Dinner was routine, no matter with whom I ate. Everybody knew to contribute something and make room at the table for a strange face. Just outside of Gisborne, a man pulled into camp in his used Honda Civic, Bob Marley's "No Woman No Cry" playing on the radio. He pitched a tent and brought out all of his cooking gear. Soon he made his way to the campground kitchen where he washed white basmati rice under the faucet and began creating a Jamaican curried-chicken dish. The sound of chopping was heard throughout the campground. Two German motorcyclists sat on a picnic table, snacking on pretzels while discussing where they had been that day and where they would go tomorrow. I cleaned the derailleurs and oiled the cables on my bike near my tent, while contemplating what would go with a can of chicken soup.

"Has everybody eaten?" The man in the kitchen appeared in the doorway, wiping his hands with a towel. Nobody in camp answered because they didn't know who he was talking to. "Well, I'm making Jamaican chicken for everybody."

With that, we all set in motion. The German couple cleared the picnic table and contributed fried lamb chops. An Australian man made hors d'oeuvres of Ritz crackers with cheese and salami and a small pizza he pulled out of the oven. I sliced apples for dessert. We adjusted spotlights on the table that the Aussie man packed in his caravan, and Michael, the chef, dished up a feast of curried rice with sultanas and chicken breaded in a combination of allspice, tarragon, garlic, and onion. One big, happy family, we chowed down beneath swinging palm trees, the Wairoa River behind us. We argued about the German and American governments, art, education, violence, rape, television, and the Tongan culture. The

Aussie quoted Confucius every now and again. After cleaning up, I went to my tent knowing I would never see these people again, but it didn't matter. People come and go. Everybody just keeps moving.

The people I met, and the families I became a part of, loom behind every image I remember about New Zealand, and perhaps are themselves the connection to what I was supposed to learn there. We helped each other by heralding which roads to avoid, and where the good campsites were. We were there for one another.

One week after leaving Gisborne, I checked into the Beethoven House, a twelve-room Victorian mansion in Wellington. The innkeeper pondered, and admitted that my name sounded familiar, but, he said, there was no mail for me, no phone messages. *Oh well*, I thought, *hooking up with Marilyn wasn't meant to be.*

I was holed up in Wellington longer than expected, as there was a ferry strike, and that was my connection to the South Island. Since I had been in the country, there had been a bank strike, a dairy strike, a bus strike, a journalist strike, and now a ferry strike—and there was no way to find out about the ferry strike because of the journalist and radio strikes. A lot of commotion for such a small country. For days, I wandered around the windy city, the city with handrails along the sidewalks. There was a storm every day. The rain blew sideways. I sat in tearooms scribing postcards to my friends back home.

Finally the strike ended and I wheeled my bike onto the Cook Strait ferry, crossed to the South Island, and cycled directly to Nelson. Nelson is home to one of New Zealand's two Mexican restaurants. The other is in the Scottish settlement of Dunedin: the Roberto Burns Mexican Restaurant. I was hungry and craving something other than bike grub (nuts, dried fruit, and juice). Near the window sat Marilyn, chowing on an enchilada with Mexican rice. She *had* seen my note in Gisborne after all, and she *did* send a postcard to the Beethoven House—and she, too, figured she would never see me again. We had catching up to do. She had had flat tires, lots of them. Eleven in six weeks. When she left the country two months later, she counted twenty-two flats in all. We decided to camp together and wait out the rain before heading south to Christchurch, where she had entered a triathlon.

Marilyn and I biked together for the next two weeks, first to Christchurch for the triathlon, then to Queenstown for Christmas. It was the hardest cycling I did on my trip, as she pushed me to ride more miles and more days in a row than I was used to at my leisurely pace. It was a nice change, though. I thought more about cycling, and less about where I was in relation to the rest of the world. All that mattered was the road ahead, which gear I was in, and whether or not my water bottles were full.

On one of our shortest days, we cycled forty-five miles from Punakaiki, the Pancake Rocks, to Greymouth, along the west coast of the South Island, in pouring rain—and by New Zealand standards, it wasn't *that* bad. The black, stormy beaches along the Tasman Sea were a cold, wind-whipped reminder of the "southerlies" that belted the west coast of the tiny country.

One woman explained to me that you can't walk on the rocky, black-sand beaches of the icy Tasman Sea in the summer without wearing shoes. "The sand is a scorcher," she revealed. "The blackness absorbs the sun's heat like asphalt."

But there was no sun on the days I was there. Gloom wore a gray, soggy dress down to her ankles. Nevertheless, I wanted to take photos, cup my hand beneath the frigid water, even stop on top of a chilling cliff and take it all in, but I couldn't. Cold would have set into my bones. My hands were already gripped around the brake levers and wouldn't move. When we arrived in Greymouth, we decided to rent a cabin in a campground to dry out. If we got a big room, we would offer space to other cyclists as they pulled into town. The Kiwi hospitality was finding a place in our lives.

As soon as we were in our room, we had everything out of our packs and spread about. Eight beds, two people, two tents, two rain flies, sleeping bags, clothes, papers, maps—everything was out of the panniers and hanging from something. I put a footstool on top of a bunk in order to dry my shoes and socks next to the heater. Cycling gloves were Velcroed around the legs of the stools. I spread watercolor paper and dollar bills, one by one, on the floor beneath the bed. It was a good thing we never saw another cyclist.

When we reached Christchurch, we had cycled about 450 miles in a week, and I was tired. I was ready for a day off, even though a part of me was sorry to be stopping in a big city for four days. Marilyn and I worried about her triathlon because of her flat-tire factor, and she hadn't gone for a swim or a run in two months. But those were the only things we could think of to worry about. Most things just didn't matter.

The next day, my job was to be Marilyn's one-and-only fan. She was second out of the water, and I encouraged her in the transition area, but she slowed in the run, finishing fourth overall and winning seventy-five dollars. Needless to say, the bike portion was her strongest, and with no flats.

We exited Christchurch as quickly as we had blown into town on the Canterbury Plains. The ride to Tekapo via Christchurch and Geraldine was gentle. I felt lightheaded and fell far behind Marilyn, not thinking much about the cycling. We were coming into the mountains, the Southern

Alps. I rode past a pine grove and got a whiff of the pines and knew I was where I wanted to be. When I rode past another grove of trees that had the effect of "aspen," I was taken back to Colorado. I wasn't homesick, but I was thinking of things that I liked, which happened to be in Colorado.

The road continued out of Fairlie, fifteen hundred feet up Burke's Pass. I crested the hill and had to stop for the view, which overlooked the town of Tekapo, the glacial lakes, and the Southern Alps. It was like viewing the Rockies from the plains: The flats of Northern Otago and Southern Canterbury settled at the foot of the Southern Alps, which rose straight up from what seemed like nothing.

I remembered Marilyn asking me at our last lunch stop, "Why did you want to do a bicycle tour by yourself, Lori?" Why? I could only think about my desire to travel, to see the world. But, in my approach to the Southern Alps from the endless flats of the Canterbury Plains, I spoke the answer: "to learn about refining my life." I knew at that moment that I could never return to Minnesota to live. In spirit, I had already returned to another state.

When I wheeled into Tekapo, I wanted to look up a woman named Sandy Joyce, a friend of an old friend of mine—just to say that I did it, and then move on. I knew she was living with a man named Bill Sargison. I wandered into the office of Air Safaris to ask for a telephone.

"Who're you calling?" The man behind the desk was curious.

"Sandy Joyce," I replied.

"Really!" He was excited. "She's not here anymore. She's over in Fox Glacier."

"What about Bill Sargison? How can I get hold of him?"

"He used to fly planes for us, but now he's in Fox, too." The man went on to tell me that there were two people at the Tekapo airport who wanted to take a flight-seeing trip over the glaciers in fifteen minutes, and a flight couldn't go unless there were more than two passengers. He offered Marilyn and me a deal: one hour for a child's fee, less than half-price. In minutes, Marilyn and I and two other hippie-cyclists from Seattle piled into the six-seater plane.

The pilot rattled off the names of all the peaks and glaciers: Mount Spencer, Mount Tasman, Franz Josef Glacier, Hooker Glacier. He went on for an hour, while the four passengers panned the sights, never putting down our cameras, hitting each other in the head with telephoto lenses and elbows. I witnessed Mount Cook from every angle. I studied its crevasses and couloirs. Glaciers, clouds, and cornices dropped off its western slopes, over sheer rock faces, and down to the Tasman Sea, twelve thousand feet below.

"So this is why people climb mountains." Marilyn had an unobstructed view of the world, like nothing she had experienced in Minnesota. I couldn't know her thoughts, but the sight of her breath being taken away seemed familiar.

This is why I climb mountains, I thought, *to have my breath taken away and to feel an accomplishment as well.* It was my creed that if I ever needed to boost my self-esteem, I climbed a mountain. I thought back to Minnesota and tried to remember what I had climbed and drew a blank. Maybe I hadn't been taking care of myself that well. Traveling helped me gain enough objectivity to see the inaccuracies of my life I hadn't realized were there.

One week later, Marilyn and I were in Queenstown for Christmas. It seemed as if every traveler we had met in the past two-and-a-half months had congregated in that town for the holidays: the hippie-cyclists from Seattle, the Aussie man with the Ritz crackers, some people Marilyn had met months ago. Santa drove through our campground in a jeep, and threw candy at the decorated tents. Mine had a two-foot strip of tinsel taped around its door. Marilyn and I planned a gift exchange and a big feast—a simple day, but memorable. She gave me a tooth brush, a box of scone mix, and U.S. air mail stamps.

Christmas was special because it was to be our last day together. To celebrate, Marilyn proposed cycling a one-hundred-mile loop, while I wanted to be off the bike. We ended up bussing into Fiordland National Park and taking the touristy ferry ride of Milford Sound. We reasoned that we would never cycle down the dirt road, through the one-lane Homer Tunnel that dropped one thousand feet from one end to the other, just to be with hundreds of other tourists. And it was the first Christmas either of us had spent in a tropical rain forest.

I felt quiet and sad during most of the bus ride. I knew that in Marilyn I had made a lifelong friend, but I had come to New Zealand to travel alone—something I hadn't been doing. I knew that after Marilyn and I split I would meet new people. I would see things I could tell Marilyn about later—we would be in touch. Traveling would be no different than when I was by myself around the East Cape. But for some reason, I wasn't as ready to be alone as I was when I originally arrived in New Zealand. I didn't know why. The sadness was overwhelming.

I cycled by myself to Te Anau on New Year's Eve. It had been an unusually dry and warm day for that part of the country. There were no southerlies off the Tasman Sea. There had been blue sky all day, and lots of activity in the campground. Windsurfers and fishermen came in off Lake Te Anau later than usual. At eight in the evening, the sun was still two hours from setting, and I collapsed in my tent after logging the day's mileage into my journal, and reading. I wanted to take a short nap, then wander around town to bring in the new year. I stretched out on my sleeping bag, the tent walls reflecting a warm orange glow I hadn't witnessed since Colorado.

I had been cycling around New Zealand for two-and-a-half months, and the rhythm of touring had become second nature: Wake up at half past six without an alarm, shower and dress in the same ol' cycling shorts and jersey, break camp, and load the panniers—everything in its place—eat something (usually bread or a pastry in town, and coffee), and ride, ride, ride. Later, I did it all in reverse: Pull everything out of my panniers, set up camp, cook dinner, walk around with other campers and tell stories of our travels, read, write, and sleep. Some days I covered only twenty kilometers, and others, one hundred thirty. This was my life, day after day.

I ended up in Te Anau on New Year's Eve because I was headed in the direction of Stewart Island, off the southern coast of the South Island, and I wanted to be as far south as possible in the Southern Hemisphere before returning north. Or so I thought. But in the tradition of hailing in a new year—as well as taking the liberty of a lone traveler and changing my mind—Te Anau was a turning point. Some critics might say it was the rain. Others might analyze that I had made a symbolic journey into my outer limits of soul and self, and could go no further into the remote areas of my mind. I had been alone, on and off, but how much further could I go? I lay in my tent reflecting over the past months and scheming about the future: where to go, how to get there, where to park my bike on Stewart Island that had only eight kilometers of paved road, how to budget my money, and what to do at midnight in Te Anau. Since I was traveling alone, I could make these decisions in my own time. I could do whatever I wanted. Meanwhile, it started to rain.

Te Anau gets twenty-five feet of rain per year. The town is situated along the coast of Lake Te Anau, the largest lake on the South Island and the entrance to Fiordland National Park—a tropical rain forest. For some reason, I didn't think it would rain the day I was there. But what was I thinking? I had a poorly designed Jansport dome tent that nearly bit it in Palmerston North on the North Island, in a southerly that almost flattened my entire outfit. And now my seam sealer was running low, my rain re-sourcefulness thin. There were no trees to camp under, no vacant cabins in the campground or in the whole town. I lay in my tent on New Year's Eve thinking that I would go to town as soon as the rain let up, possibly seeking refuge on somebody's floor. Then, in the distance, I heard the sweet lilt of a bagpiper.

In times of distress, one retreats to safety: things from childhood, things that worked in the past. As a kid, whenever I roller-skated two blocks from home, I was always able to hear the drone and flat notes of my dad's bagpipes. I imagined he couldn't wait for my sister and me to go out and play so he could don his kilt and take himself to Scotland. That night in Te Anau, I could tell that the piper was only two blocks away.

It rained harder. Being in a tent during a monsoon is worse than being in the monsoon. Rain beats on all sides. You can't sleep, you can't hear yourself think, the music from a bagpipe gets drowned out. After three hours, I was sure it couldn't keep up. I had to pee. I had parties to attend. I wanted to toast in the new year. I wanted to be around my Kiwi friends, my cycling people. Any minute it would let up, I knew it. And with a keen ear, I listened for fewer drops to fall against my tent.

I'm always listening to what's going on outside my tent. Traveling alone has changed how I hear things. In Colorado, a splash in the lake could be a mass murderer, but it's probably a beaver. If something nears the tent door without becoming quieter, then it's a squirrel or a bear. If it sniffs or pants a lot, it's a dog. In New Zealand, a scraping in the wee hours is a possum cleaning out panniers that weren't brought in for the night. Sheep or a cow will graze between the tent and the loo. In the mornings, teka and kiwi birds come out of the rain forests to peck at the damp ground for crumbs and worms. On the North Island, honking and chortling all night at Lake Tutira is a bank of one thousand black swans in their sanctuary. And a monsoon rain will never let up. It begins with big drops plummeting onto the tent six inches apart, and continues until you can't pick out one drop from the next. It's like being among one thousand washing machines—and you don't dare open the doors while the machines are operating.

I tried to make myself useful. What else could I do while stuck alone on New Year's Eve? I cleaned the tent. I repacked all the panniers, and refolded clothes and maps. Then I tidied the place, stacking the bike bags in a corner and straightening the foam pad I sat on. I would have paced the floor if I had had the room. Then I sat back, critiquing the design of my tent and making mental notes on how it could be better at repelling rain. Mostly, I felt myself descending on the *koru* spiral, and I knew it was time to think about the loneliness I'd felt since Marilyn and I parted one week ago.

The rain had truly isolated me, not just now, but throughout the entire trip. It left me alone when I didn't want to be. It left me powerless and immobile. I pictured all the other travelers I had met downing pints in the pubs without me. Maybe a kind family had taken in Marilyn, or maybe she was in a hotel. I was homeless. I was a vagabond. I had opened the washing machine doors, and vulnerability had come flooding in. The rain challenged me to go on, to get up the next morning and accept that, yes, it would rain again. I had never felt so alone on New Year's Eve, much less on the whole trip. The world seemed dark outside my tent, though I knew people were celebrating around the world. Typically, I rejoice in knowing that I may be someplace so remote that nobody else in the world has a clue as to where I am, but not that night.

When the tent floor started to look like the land of ten thousand lakes, my main concern was to keep three things dry: my plane ticket, passport, and sleeping bag. I wrapped them tightly in their plastic bags, moved everything into the only dry corner and huddled up alongside. When the ceiling itself began to leak, this was bad news. I was very weary.

I felt trapped, and this was some kind of test—for my gear, as well as my peace of mind. I donned my raincoat and cried. I was humiliated. I had never sat inside my tent wearing a raincoat.

I never spoke of that particular night because I wasn't interested in hearing people say, "See, you shouldn't have been alone." But being with somebody would have only given me somebody to cry with. After all, what I really wanted was to be warm and dry forever, and have a new tent. It wasn't just the company or the New Year's Eve parties I wanted. I also wanted something that was impossible: to be in control of the weather. I wanted to unzip the tent door and walk into the world whenever I pleased. But that's not what going out of your comfort zone and having an adventure is all about. It's about losing control and digging deep within to find a way to cope, to find a way to ascend the double part of the *koru* spiral.

When I thought it was midnight, I toasted my water bottle and hummed "Auld Lang Syne." It was a peaceful changing of the guard—out with the old year, in with the new—in spite of the pelting rain. I made resolutions to keep going, regardless, to learn to live with the rain, to always seek out a good adventure, and to learn how to construct a good tent when I got back home. I decided that tomorrow I would move indoors and dry out. Then, I would cycle out of the rain forest, not to Stewart Island. I can change my mind, I told myself, it's okay. I can come and go from anyplace whenever I want, because I am a free spirit and have lost all track of time. I don't wear a watch. *When the weather stops you*, I thought to myself, *either get better gear, or move on.*

Faintly, about one hour later, I could hear the bagpiper again, this time playing "Amazing Grace." There are moments when all of your heart and soul are full and you think there is no room for anything else, when suddenly you stumble upon the most perfect thing. It comes at the perfect time, and in the perfect place. I listened to the music. I felt myself breathe. I remembered Marilyn's clarity while flying over the Southern Alps. *I know why I'm here*, I thought, *in Te Anau*, in the rain. It was as simple as knowing to ride on the left side of the road—something that confused me in the beginning, but quickly became second nature.

I listened for the piper to play the tune all the way through, then, as is traditional, to be joined by a few more pipes for the second round. The third time, an army of bagpipes join in. And I hoped to hear it that third time with one thousand additional pipes, then ten thousand. The rain was letting up.

The January 2nd Te Anau newspaper ran an article stating that the level of Lake Te Anau had risen fifty-one inches in the past few days, and that on New Year's Eve, twenty-four inches of rain fell in twenty-four hours. "However," it read, "this had caused no major problems."

As soon as my gear dried out, which took a few days, I cycled north to Cromwell in the heart of the Otago region. Why I chose Cromwell, I will never know. I didn't think about it, I just went, and fast, before the rains came again.

The best way to study a person is by asking, "Who are your people? Who is your family? Who are your kin?" And the answers to these questions will reveal a person's essence, a *raison d'être*, an explanation of tribal passions. If a person had walked up to my tent in Cromwell and asked me, "Lori, tell me, who are your people?" I would first return to my childhood, packing my suitcase in time to catch the afternoon flight to Scotland. Next, I would look around me at the light-skinned, dark-haired, green-eyed people of Cromwell, the people who looked like me, who welcomed the outsider, and interviewed me for the front page of their newspaper.

"Yank Visits from Colorado, America," read the headline. It might as well have said, "Young Lassie Finds Her Way Back Home." Somehow, it all made sense. I had found my own kin, without any planning or forethought. I had made my way to Cromwell like a pup coming home to dinner when the whistle blows.

Early Scottish settlers found the area ideal for horticulture, as Central Otago is the driest and hottest part of the country. A desert, in a sense. And Cromwell, a major tea-time stopover between Wanaka, Queenstown, and Alexandra, at the foot of the Remarkables mountain range and at the confluence of the Kawarau and Clutha Rivers, often gets passed by. Cyclists stop at the bakery and move on. Motorists make their last stop for petrol before driving to Queenstown. A traveler seeking an arid climate and swell people will set up camp for about three weeks—long enough to fall in love with the place—and then become stir crazy.

I picked apricots for three weeks because the weary part of me needed to settle, as well as to increase my cash flow. I wanted to leave my tent up for more than a day and eat leftovers. And I wanted to get to know the locals. When I was picking fruit, Fergie, weighing no less than 250 pounds and always wearing his "King Kiwi" baseball cap, white tank top, and red gym shorts, brought us tea and biscuits on the back of his tractor for our *smoko* (break), twice a day. This was really precious, I thought, really a treat, until I heard a rumor that the orchard next door gave their pickers cream-filled scones!

After my third day of picking, I was promoted to packing. I learned to spot an active bacteria on a one-and-seven-eighths-inch apricot in a fraction of a second. Anything like that went to the local market. The really clean fruit was shipped overseas. And even though I was indoors for the first time in three months and had a hard time adjusting to it, I slowly warmed up to my colleagues, and vice-versa.

But something in me changed. While it was my body that remembered the daily movement of cycling, it was my mind that felt at peace. I realized that my *raison d'être* wasn't just determined by *where* I was. That part I had discovered in the Southern Alps. It had to do with *who* I was with, as well. And in three weeks, without realizing it at first, I became attached to the people I worked with: Jill, the quality controller, who took me to the movies in the high school gym; her mother, Elva, overseer of packing; Suzanna, a woman from Invercargill; Carol, who led me to the town's secret water hole just up the hill from the orchard; Wendy, who taught me "Cromwell-speak" by translating, "There's a wee paddy behind the hoggett"; Bob and Sandy, friends of Jill's, who let me stay three days at their sheep station twenty miles into the Remarkables; and, of course, Fergie, who regularly took me motorboating on the Clutha after work, then to the lower pub, because he wanted this Yank to have true New Zealand experiences.

I felt that I had found in three weeks what had been missing from my life for three years in Minnesota. Temporary though it was, I was a part of a community. People around town knew my name. At the pub, they stood in line to "shoot pool with the damn Yank." They listened to my ideas and told stories about their families and lives.

Even though after three weeks I was ready to get back on my bike, leaving the orchard was hard. It would have been easier if I had known I would someday return to Cromwell. But one can never predict these things. That's when goodbyes are in order. Fergie gave me a kiss, and everybody shut down the machines and came outside to see me off. They gave me a card that read, "To one import, from all the exports," and signed their names. They waved and jumped and yelled as I rode down the driveway. They hollered until I was out of sight.

What I learned in Cromwell was: When the fruit is ripe, you have to pick it. Timing is everything. The three-week-long apricot-picking season was enough time for me to feel the love that had been missing from my life. It was the right amount of time to admit that I was, indeed, on a journey from Minnesota to Colorado, via the South Pacific—not Nebraska.

When I began my escapade in Auckland, my mission was to ignore time and drift aimlessly on unfamiliar roads. Now I realize it was impossible to succeed with that goal. I looked for familiarity everywhere, and I backtracked on roads enough that I created a past for myself. I hooked up with the same people over and over. I returned to the same places. These repetitions gave my New Zealand life substance.

If a person doesn't understand their past there is a good chance it will be repeated, but if the past is never revisited, chances of misunderstanding it are just as great. I created a life in Cromwell that would have been similar to a life in Colorado—working and cycling and being a part of a supportive community—but I had to check it out before diving back in.

On my last day in the country, I was up early in Christchurch, preparing to catch an afternoon flight to Australia. It was raining, of course, but I felt hardened to it. I treated myself to a breakfast of poached eggs on toast with two cups of coffee. Later, I plowed into a car that had cut in front of me to make a left turn, but stopped instead. The brakes on my bike were wet. I instinctively turned the bike enough to save it, and maimed my left thigh instead. The elderly woman in the car rolled down her window and asked if I was all right, and would I care for some lunch. I could only smile at her sweetness. She went with me to buy a banana-yogurt shake and, what do you know, I ran into Kathy from day number one at the Auckland airport. Four-and-a-half months later. Turned out we were on the same flight to Sydney.

"Kathy, my friend!" I cried. I was happy to see her and gave her a big hug. "Have we got stories to tell!"

SHARYN LAYFIELD

On Wind and Work

"THE WIND IN ONE'S FACE, MAKES ONE WISE."

–George Herbert

WIND. It pushes and shoves, lifts and carries away. It is a constant, unquiet presence on this mountainside where, on a day in late May, I am digging in soil that has not been cultivated for more than fifty years. The sod won't let go without a struggle, the shovel is a cheap one, and below the sod lie long-established settlements of rock nested in stone ringed with smaller stones.

Mornings I rise at dawn, put on the soil-heavy jeans with a friend's daughter's name label inside, and the plaid cotton shirt my stepson used to wear. I wrap a scarf around my hair, and lace up the work boots that came from a pile destined for the Salvation Army. I take up the shovel, whose handle is caked with dirt I only notice in the morning when my hands are clean.

I begin. Cut at the sod with quick, hard jabs, drive the shovel into earth, and hit rock. Make forays from other angles: rock. "It's a big one," I say aloud, excavating soil to expose its outline. At every turn rock and stone stop me. Finally, I catch the edge of the central rock and get under it, levering it up all around like a stuck jar lid, coaxing it, then putting my full weight on the shovel handle and hearing the wood strain, working against time and earth's suction and the bed of stones and my fear of hopelessness, until the rock rises in a wormy apocalypse. I lay the shovel aside. On hands and knees I take hold, extract the rock and drop it just beyond the hole. It takes a minute to catch my breath, sitting in the dirt with this lozenge-shaped white rock of maybe sixty pounds. Now I roll the rock to the nearest pile. And begin again. Sod, soil, rock.

I set goals for myself: this three-by-three-foot section by lunch time, that whole strip by the end of the day. I keep at it, relocating fat worms to safer soil and praying for those severed by the shovel. Blake said, "The cut worm blesses the plough," but I'm not so sure. I sing: "Keep Your Sunny Side Up," "On the Sunny Side of the Street," "Yes Sir, That's My Baby." I converse with the mourning doves, the chickadees, the starlings and jays, all at peak activity level these spring days, collecting, building, keeping contact with their mates, and listening for the distant calls of their enemies. I dream of the time when I can stop for a drink of water, a pee, something to eat. And I cry, angrily, because the wind has joined forces with the obstinate sod and the truculent rock and the swarming no-see-ums and the pain in my back, to make this task impossible. I hear myself say, "If he were here, I wouldn't have to do this," which only makes me cry harder.

But who is this he? Certainly not my ex-husband. Not my sad father, either. Who, then, is he, this combination of Yul Brynner in *The Sound and the Fury* and Captain Jean-Luc Picard of the *Starship Enterprise*? He's bald, that much seems clear; strong, protective, tenacious, capable of obsession. He is the Father with a capital F, who was with me long before the Christmas I got my first desk and began inventing stories about an island where a girl named Eve was held captive by him, her lover (knowing little about sex, I only got as far as her bathing suit top falling off in the ocean), her abductor, the one who demanded her absolute obedience and love. He could be brutal, yes, but it was only because he loved her so much; more than anyone or anything else, he loved her. Even now, standing ankle-deep in dirt, I can taste the enthralling numbness that came over me each night going to sleep in an unsafe house, as he instructed me to turn my palms up at my sides and lie very still. "And then she began to cry," an invisible narrator would whisper, and the story would begin and safety would slowly descend upon me.

Wind blasts me back to the here and now, where a forty-four-year-old woman labors on her own to make a garden on land that doesn't belong to her, not even in the way people talk about owning; land that is liable to be sold out from under her within the year. I clean off my boots before trudging upstairs to the bathroom, leaving mud on the carpets. I fill a plastic juice bottle with water, drink half, refill it, and get back to work. For the rest of the morning I try to conjure him, to hear what he has to say about this life I'm living. But of course he is not here, not anymore. If he were, maybe I wouldn't be doing all this.

Lunch is a cheese sandwich, a cup of tea, a brownie, and a smoke. For such an occasion I take off the boots downstairs and go up in my socks. I unwind the sweaty scarf, wash my hands and face, and stop to glance out the bathroom window at the garden, taking what solace there is in height and distance. *It's not so bad*, I say to myself. *It's coming along*. And, *You're never going to make it, damn fool*. I look vacantly through the mail—a feed store flyer, catalogs featuring pretty summer clothes worn by women untroubled by bugs.

It is only back in the dirt, in a section that seems to be nothing but *schistos* and clay, that it makes sense. He was an invention. I invented him, and I have left him behind. So this is why the desolation. Nothing stands anymore between me and this—what's the word? Not *loneliness*; too much longing in that. *Solitude* smacks of self satisfaction. *Isolated* sounds geographical, coming from the Latin meaning "converted into an island." Converted into an island. That's close. What's needed is a word without connotation, as in *The Only One There*. Or rather *Here*. A word without shadows. Because that's what it's like, this aloneness. There's no sweet melancholy to it, no shimmer of promise. It's not an interlude, not a retreat, and it comes with no built-in distractions. It's like the first time you got death. Maybe it's a new level of getting death, one at which you can't—or no longer want to—dissolve it in sweet melancholy or distraction. This aloneness demands something new of me: I'm supposed to feel it.

At evening I sprawl on the grass watching salmon- and yellow-lit clouds converge at the horizon, and wind-driven, smoke-colored clouds overspread them, turning into the night sky. The garden is assuming a half-moon shape, bordered by my stone monuments to labor. The soil that was dark and fresh early in the day has gone gray, and the turned area is meager. Coming upon it, you wouldn't think much work had gone into this garden, unless you knew better.

While outside wind bangs the barn door and impersonates a blizzard, I lie in bed reading Lyall Watson's *Heaven's Breath*, which tells me all about wind. In a section on ill winds, for instance, I discover that there were once witches who bottled up malicious winds, and others who sold favorable winds to those going to sea. There's a job for me in my pension-less old age. A whirlwind once frightened people in a Birmingham, England park by showering them with hundreds of frogs. (No mention is made of the frogs' state of mind after their ordeal.) Winds pick things up and move them—big things, like houses. They pluck and implode chickens, impregnate women (so they say), and carry deadly disease.

But they also carry pollen to more than ten thousand plants, sometimes over thousands of miles. And vitamins, and friendly bacteria. Some scientists think the ingredients for life were originally transported to this planet on the wind. It's clear there's much more to the wind than mischief. My wind may be trying to tell me something. In a chapter on the "Philosophy of Wind," Watson writes:

... the most common and readily accessible experience of other-
ness and togetherness, of being involved in something very big

and very strange, is that of being blown by the wind. . . . You are touched by something invisible, something that bends trees and makes strange sounds. It throws the ocean into confusion, whips up fantastic froths of cloud and carries off a desert in its arms. And yet it communicates directly and intimately with you. You can feel its effects deep inside.

I have certainly felt the presence, these past days, of something big and strange. At times the wind has seemed to blow only at me, trying to push me back into immobilization, to make me give up. I have had to hold on tight to myself, so as not to be carried away. I have been scoured of feeling, sensation, static.

In that sense, the wind has accomplished a kind of spring cleaning of the mind. The more I work in the wind, the less I think. Wind and labor quiet me, until I'm no more than a figure bent in a field in some medieval book of hours, seeing only what is before me, not needing to look up at the viewer who, turning the page, is caught for a moment by that red kerchief burrowing in dark earth. What is truly big and strange comes to me through my skin, my hands.

I fall asleep, book among the bedclothes, and see the vivid, open earth, crawling with worms, rock-studded. My muscles twitch in rhythmic memory. I dig all night and wake up early, knowing it will take one great, final push to complete the job today; endurance, and a miracle. The wind's so wild, I stuff my ears with cotton from the vitamin bottle, and add a tee shirt layer for warmth. This end of the garden seems more stone than soil, which means more bending, gathering, tossing: a slower pace. I entertain myself with a movie-of-the-mind in which the wind manages to sweep me up and over the pines, my bright scarf and shirt billowing like sails. Where to? The South Seas, I think, where Gauguin painted his famous triptych, *Where Do We Come From? What Are We? Where Are We Going?* The people in that painting seem threatened from every side, by serpentlike vines, dark figures, despair, and death. Yet they are calm, monumental; they look out at the viewer, as they must have the painter, with knowing gazes. *These are your questions,* their eyes say, *not ours.* But where DO we come from? *Blown here by the wind.* What are we? *Flotsam, with souls.* Where are we going? *Wherever the wind takes us.*

By late afternoon it looks unlikely I can finish by dark. But energy from God-knows-where and a marked decrease in the stone population renew the hope, and I work on silently, though something between my shoulder blades feels about to tear, and there is no feeling in my left foot. If and when I am done, I will have the luxury of thinking about tomorrow, when I will move on from shovel to hoe and rake, and begin hauling bucketsful of the horse, cow, and chicken manure I've been collecting.

I will plant by the end of the week, weather permitting, and know before long what grows well in wind, and what doesn't. Far ahead, still, lie the deep snows of winter on a mountain, and even farther, the new crop of rocks the earth will press up into the garden next spring, whether I am here or not. But I don't have to worry about any of that now. I just have to keep going, cultivating this spot where I have landed, and remembering I'm not the first to work this soil. As for the wind, runners know well that if it pushes you backward in one direction, it will push you forward in the other. Maybe one of these days I'll be out here in the garden and I'll smell the deep, sweet scent of tropical flowers, gathered on Gauguin's island and carried thousands of miles on an amorous wind.

ANN STALEY

Crocus sieberi

IT IS A GRAY AND WET NEW YEAR'S DAY. I am up to my elbows in soapsuds
and wine glasses when I glance from my kitchen window and see a white
page fluttering from the windshield of my Honda. I wonder about belated
political campaigns or early ones, consider that Eagle Scouts might be
about, then move with curiosity through the rain to the mysterious white-
winged thing. I smile deeply when it uncurls to reveal itself as the poem it
is, delivered by someone practicing a random act of kindness. This first-
of-the-year gesture has made me forget rain and dishes, and especially because it is a poem I already know and love, brings me delight. It also
brings me to my senses. The words focus my attention in the way the bells
of Consecration once alerted me to the words, "Be mindful of Thy creature, O Lord." For this guerilla poem is one of Wendell Berry's, and its
two-word conclusion a reminder as resonant and sonorous as bells: "Practice resurrection," I read and say to myself as I reenter my steamy morning kitchen.

I am still thinking about this little mystery a few days later when I sort
through the latest deluge of catalogs. Though it is cool and damp and
inches of rain have fallen, and although I've been thinking about resurrection, I have proceeded no further than the daring zen koan, "Love aerobics as much as scones." This seems to be my best effort of the new year
so far, until the cover of one of those glorious gardening magazines stares
me to quietude. "Beginnings," it announces in white letters superim-
posed on pale violet-colored crocus emerging green and bright from
snow. No intentional act of kindness here, but nonetheless a comple-
mentary reminder to words previously delivered. I am contemplating

now, thinking about the world beyond scones and dishes and Hondas, to the world where resurrection is a practice, where the sound of bells is replaced by wind and water and emergent green. What I realize is that my autumn months have been an unknowing preparation for my new year's benediction. I've been practicing and practicing without quite knowing it.

Although some can make transformations among the familiar, I have found that changes of scenery, even small ones, are helpful. Once, I drove ten thousand miles to accomplish an interior sort of shifting that another person might have made by contacting her lawyer; another passage required an air flight through Iceland and a ferryboat bucking its way across the North Sea. But I am older now, and if middle age means anything besides gray hair and wrinkles, it means acquiring enough wisdom to transform oneself by "traveling at home." So, I've been driving a few miles south of my food co-op, out past Modern Carpet and B and H Auto Wrecking, to a somber wetland situated near the Willamette River. Once a month, for the last five, I've gone south in that same Honda, as though the poem had already been affixed to the dash.

I found Kiger Island Slough because my teaching colleague wanted it as a field study site for our ecology class. We'd been out during the late summer's heat, waded the slough, rafted downstream, and discussed the parameters of our project. In early September, I returned alone after assigning the class (which always turns out to include me!) a series of monthly visits and writings about "a natural place you love." We were doing the Sand County thing, reading Aldo Leopold's essays and trying to write like him, and I felt that the sort of humble, everyday, and yet hidden qualities of Kiger Island and its slough would provide me with enough focus and range for exploring and reflecting. I was right on all counts, and so have returned each month, taking my notebook and colored pencils, coming home to write and think about it all. My visits and almanac have become works-in-progress, as I suppose resurrection is, small monthly tests that seem more important than the work of equating aerobics and scones. Here's one version of what's been happening out there:

September: Late sun, water-riffle sounds, green vistas. Is this willow? Is this bunch grass? A guardian set of firs stands taller and just beyond the deciduous trees. Here, on this log, I could sit happily for a long while, the mid-September sun hot on my right arm and leg, not scorching, a reminder of summer.

Rearranged, I watch the sun-shadowed movement of my pen. I stop after each word, slowly and laboriously, so it must be my ability to focus that gets these notebook lines filled. The wind is warm but with a hint of the cool nights to come. I hear one small, chirping bird, a few insect rattles, the rush of the wind through weeds and grasses. Two more hours of light, perhaps. A thankful breeze blows in across the water, ruffling pages. As I raise my head I think of a line from a poem, "Even the upper end of the river believes in the ocean." How long will it take for the water I'm seeing, hearing, to find the Pacific?

October: An impressive autumn storm has blown into the region, fifty-mile winds and heavy rainfall for the second time in a week. The sky is gray, and very little light penetrates the cloud cover— someone has turned on the dimmer. The wind scatters leaves on the road as I drive east toward the slough crossing and toward the farms and fields that are Kiger Island. Trees which still have their golden leaves appear as neon contrast to the gray of this day. As I cross the slough I am amazed by its turbid, gray-brown waters. The upstream pond has filled. This site is incredibly changed by the increased amounts of water, almost three inches. I think longingly of the sun and heat of my first visits and realize that I don't own enough rain gear to feel comfortable in such a torrent.

I drive onto the island, taking the road marked DEAD END, deciding it will be interesting to see what's out there. The land is predominantly agricultural, and I pass a Christmas tree farm, a field of beets, a lovely old apple orchard, grass-seed grasses, a sign for filberts, and many fields that have been turned. The soil is dark, rich brown, too wet now for planting and abandoned to the elements. A couple of sadly dilapidated tractors are abandoned as well, and I wonder about maintenance. This is exquisitely productive soil, close to the river, the bottomland that has been developed as the Willamette River had lost its channels.

I drive further, looking for hopeful signs and finding some: a pumpkin sitting on the front steps, a bed of marigolds that still blooms orange and yellow, a front door painted a deep green—little signs, I think, but good ones to see on this dreary, wet day.

November: This afternoon I notice a field full of geese, mottled gray against the tweedy, cropped grasses where they hunt seed, rest before another takeoff south. Water from recent rainfall stands in puddles, reflects sky. The birds' groupiness, their diligence in the field, gives me heart. I notice the water level in the slough. The banks where I walked and waded are completely submerged; the log where I sat in September is gone, swept downstream; the branches are bare with only a few brown leaves twirling in place against today's breeze. The language of water is not slow.

Trees are being harvested at the farm east of the slough, and trucks have made muddy ruts between the rows of evergreen. Some of the harvest is stacked, wrapped with twine to get safely to Christmas tree lots in California or downtown Corvallis. I think about retirees with artificial trees and hope I'll just quit the holiday traditions altogether before I forego the scent of fir that fills the living room in the days before and after the solstice. Trees and mud make me wonder about some of my students' field study conclusions. Who owns this land? Who farms it? I'd like to interview some of the people who live on the island, see the road maps. I've always liked islands for their finite borders, remember another November when I visited Skye and the Orknies off Scotland's coast. Could I be an island dweller? Am I already?

Things to be thankful for as this month begins to turn into the next one, time rushing ahead, the year moving to its darkest days: my teaching journal; and good words I discover in students' papers; and those geese who will be somewhere else tonight or tomorrow, but who will return in the spring; and light translucent, reflected; and all shades of brown, taupe, bark, umber, tan, mahogany, burnt sienna, ash, walnut, and cherry seen along the road today; and branches against the sky, the moving pattern of them; and that circle of fir marking a homestead; and all warm places where we can go to watch November winds.

December: The morning is bright, sun on its low, arcing pathway through this midwinter day. The air is so clear that the world of the slough seems crazily two-dimensional, yet I can see individual branches and bark traceries on trees far in the distance. Ansel Adams's camera could have done justice to this place, but I am alive to see it, to experience it with my eyes. I keep telling my students about "seeing," keep arranging writing prompts and texts and questions and silences so that their seeing will be deepened. Education, I have decided, is entirely about seeing or about re-seeing, vision at the heart of all I am trying to do. In fact, this crystalline day with its blustery winds, with the frost's definitive etching, I feel myself lacking words, feel only the warm pulse at my temples, in my eyes. I walk and walk. The world is sparkling and calm.

So. Here's a blessing to the muse who delivered my new year's manifesto, and to the man who wrote it, and to Annie Dillard who has seen miracles indoors and out, and to the cartoonist whose suited, wooden man sits in his recliner and says of nature, "It has no plot!" And here's a second blessing for all quiet places where waters meander and leaves rot into mold, where generations of trees migrate to sunnier spots, where dark soils are hospitable to apples and filberts and grasses and middle-age women. I'll be going back again this month, crisscrossing land I have come to know, listening to the sweet hum of wind, watching the world in its resurrection, practicing.

VERA LÚCIA MORITZ

The Moment of Understanding

SOLITUDE PUSHES PEOPLE TO THEIR ESSENTIAL DEPTHS. My time to learn this came at nineteen, when I found myself alone in the Amazon Jungle.

If the truth be told, I didn't want to be alone, but I didn't have an alternative. I was traveling up the Amazon River on a small freighter headed for Manaus. There were about a half-dozen other passengers and the crew. The boat stopped at every village and hamlet to deliver and pick up goods and people to transport upriver. Most passengers took the boat for shorter distances, traveling between villages that were two or three days apart. I was the only one booked all the way from Belém, on the Atlantic Coast, to Manaus. Actually, I was booked all the way back as well. If I had had any more money, I would have made my return trip some other way, but all other ways were more expensive. Manaus, located in the heart of the Brazilian Amazon, is not connected by any road. There is the river, and planes. Planes were expensive, hence the freighter up and back. As things turned out, it didn't matter how I traveled back.

The trip was not the great fun I had expected. It was monotonous. The boat chugged along the wide river and almost all I could hear was the loud hum of the engine. I couldn't see much jungle life from the boat, except when we stopped at the villages and I had a chance to go on shore—or more properly, into the quiet backwaters where houses were on stilts. A few days into the trip I realized I had made a big mistake, but now I didn't have any way out.

One night, about twelve days into the trip, as I tossed in my hammock, the boat engine sputtered and jerked and then it stopped altogether. I heard commotion from the crew, clanging and banging, but the noise of the engine never came back. I fell asleep again hearing the music of the jungle instead. This was a great improvement, but now we were stopped.

It was hot, still, and humid. Insects buzzed and bit. I was lonely. I missed the ocean breezes, the sights, smells, and foods of the seashore. I missed a dear friend who now was dead, my eighth-grade French teacher. She had died four months earlier. This woman was the first great love of my young life. It was she who had given me support to go forward into undertakings unusual for girls my age in Brazil, such as going to engineering school. Her death hung heavily on me.

Besides the grief of bereavement that could not be acknowledged, I had some other complicated feelings. For several years, I had been aware of my preference for women. Early on, while other girls giggled about boys, I simply dismissed them. I knew that kind of feeling was not accepted and spent my teen years thinking that only I in the whole wide world had feelings "like that." Then there was the warm glow of being near a woman. I would lie in my hammock at night and doze off imagining what the company of a woman's body might feel like, my hands moving over the soft curves of her back, only to wake up in terror, my heart pounding as if caught inside a snare drum.

I didn't know the word for *lesbian* in Portuguese, but even without a name, the fear of forever being an outcast haunted me.

It was to escape that I took all my savings and bought the tickets for this trip to the farthest-away land I could afford. I didn't then have a particular attraction for the rain forest, and haven't been back since; I went there hoping that in an exotic land my unspeakable feelings would somehow disappear. They did not. I was still feeling the same unspeakable longings to have a woman's body next to mine. And now I was marooned in some nameless spot up the Amazon River, had spent my savings, and God only knew how many days it would take for that lame crew to fix the blasted engine.

The next morning arrived. The boat's machinist declared it would take at least three days to fix the engine. I thought I would go crazy. Alone or not I had to do something. If nothing else, I couldn't stand another lunch of fried monkey.

As luck would have it, we were near a hamlet. This provided a chance to do some canoeing on my own. The other passengers stayed on the boat smoking cigars, but I went to the hamlet searching for a dugout canoe and a paddle to rent. After rejecting a couple of sorry tubs, I found a canoe of good construction, carved out of light wood and with a decent stern. It came with a great paddle, and I felt I could paddle to the ends of the world if it came to that. As I was born on an island in the South Atlantic, I felt at home with dugouts and enjoyed canoeing, although I had no experience on rivers.

So I rented the canoe and paddle for three days. The man from whom I rented was doubtful. The family gathered all around. Neighbors came to see. "Why did I want to paddle a canoe?" Because I was tired of sitting on the freighter and the engine was broken and it would be stopped for several days. "Tired of sitting?" The thought that one could be tired of sitting clearly had never occurred to them. Rest, if they ever had any, wasn't something one could have in excess. Now they were incredulous. "And what was I going to do?" Just paddle on the river. See the jungle. "But there's nothing to see!" This was the last straw. That one could get tired of resting and would think to pay good money to paddle a canoe just to see the jungle was so far beyond their comprehension that the haggling came to an abrupt end. They stood there open-mouthed, at a loss for words. In that moment of bewilderment I pushed the canoe off the muddy edge and paddled away before they could think of another question.

Earlier on I had asked about tributary rivers nearby. There were, of course, several, all of which branched here, there, and yonder. As searching for the canoe had taken the best part of the day, I spent the remainder of the afternoon paddling on the main river, up a ways on one edge and back down to the freighter on the other edge. I say edge because there was no such thing as shore: The thick growth of trees rose vertically from the water, without much of a transition zone. In this up-and-down trip I scouted for a tributary that I might take as a road into the jungle.

There weren't any maps for this area, but even if I had had one it would have been of little use, first, because I didn't know how to use a map and second, because the river flow changed the channels often.

It is a great thing to be young and inexperienced: Practical fears haven't materialized yet. Had I known then what I know today about the world, I might still be cutting sugar cane in the fields of southern Brazil, rooted to the spot where I was born. That I might get lost in the maze of channels never came to mind.

Back on the boat, I went on a mission to round up supplies. I found a quantity of boiled cassava, guava paste, water canteens, a machete, rope, and an empty lard can that looked as if it could come in handy. The cook offered a roasted leg of monkey, which I refused. He did, however, weave a basket from a palm frond in which I could stow my supplies.

The next morning, before dawn touched the forest canopy, I lowered my basket onto the canoe, which was tied to the boat, undid the knot, and started paddling. The canoe and I were no more than a peanut shell in that big quiet river about a half mile wide. I paddled upriver in the waning darkness toward the tributary I had scouted the day before. That was as much of a plan as I had, to go up a tributary and see the jungle from close by.

As day broke, there was much to be seen. Although this tributary was a sizable river in itself, the edges were close enough that I could see birds of all descriptions. Some I knew, most I did not: toucans, macaws, araras, and many smaller birds all singing and chattering. I spotted monkeys of all sizes, animal shapes I had never seen before, and all manner of plants, ferns, and orchids growing on the trunks of trees. I didn't know the names of anything I saw; this was a foreign land altogether, entirely different from my wind-blown island in southern Brazil.

I kept on paddling, more by feel than by sight, as my eyes were taking in the myriad details of the landscape. Pretty tropical flowers. Colorful birds, lots of them warbling musical songs. I could have stayed just for the listening, myself and the jungle, in a noisy sort of great peace. I paddled on quietly, the canoe gliding without a sound so as not to scare away the forest. The river became narrower and narrower, then branched off.

I took the widest branch, but even this became as narrow as a tunnel, with dense foliage all around and over. Soon there was hardly enough room to paddle, and I was beginning to think about going back when the tributary opened up into the river-equivalent of a meadow. There, on the edge of this opening, was a sight to behold. A tunnel of orchids arced over the river. Beautiful, scented Amazon orchids that were all in bloom, extravagantly beautiful, with their exquisite shapes, delicate colors, and soft curves. Soft curves. Soft, soft curves, a mesmerizing thought.

I rested the paddle across the canoe and let the boat glide until my nose touched the first orchid dangling over the river. I kissed it. The beauty of the scene overwhelmed my eyes, my nose, and my other senses until there was nothing left of me but sensuous feeling. I paddled backward to gaze at the orchids again.

Slowly, the symbolism of the situation dawned on me as I sat in awe, understanding I was on the threshold of something profound and transforming. Alone, in undisturbed solitude, feeling. I understood all the longings I had for the soft curves of a woman's body as the naked orchids rested in the sunlight filtering through the tree canopy. I had traveled so far to avoid these feelings. It was as if the Fates had made an appointment for me.

No amount of therapy would have persuaded me to so fully accept who I was as contemplating those orchids did. Nor, afterward, would there be a force in the world that could stop me from my feelings.

Much later that day I said goodbye to the orchids. They belonged in their world; I had mine to find. I reversed direction in the canoe by sitting on the bow and slowly, reflectively, paddled back. As I proceeded to turn back I realized that I didn't know where I was. There wasn't anyone else, anywhere, who did. Somehow, at that moment it didn't seem to matter. My mind was on other things. I found the way back by luck, not by diligent navigation. I could just as easily have become another chunk of protein in the tropical food chain. I returned the canoe without saying much, from which the owner concluded he had been right in telling me that there wasn't anything to see. The rest of the trip, up to Manaus and back down to Belém and the Atlantic Ocean, I spent in deep, dreamlike meditation, charting new freedoms for my life.

ALISON WATT

We Are Not Alone

A GROUP OF WOMEN ARE IN A BAR. A man comes up to them and asks, "what are you doing all alone?" The women look at him. "We're not alone, we're together."

The line of women threaded in front of me. The ten students on this Outward Bound wilderness trip ranged in age from nineteen to fifty-two, and we were struggling. Effects of the Colorado mountain heat, the tedium of having to hike a section of road to gain a new drainage, and accumulated tiredness were all showing. However, today was the day we would put each student on solo. I knew the change of pace would be welcome—two days of solitude, inactivity, and reflection. Mentally I ran through the pre-solo arrangements that Jessie, the other instructor, and I needed to make. As I thought of things done and still left to do, I absently noted that drivers of on-coming vehicles were openly curious at the spectacle of twelve women, visibly hot and tired, each outsized by a dusty backpack.

It took a while—I don't know how long—before my mind processed the sounds coming from behind. My attempt to pretend our wilderness experience was not currently happening on a road had also diverted my other senses. I realized I was hearing free-form sobs, lung-catching and compelling. Turning, I waited the few steps before Angie, the last student in the line and the only person behind me, caught up. My arms were open, and she took the offering with a single wail. I crooked her to my shoulder, one hand curling the back of her head, the other somewhere around her pack. She cried as children cry: hiccuping air into misery, her fists knuckled to her teeth, lips stretched and distorted. As I held her, I wondered if she noticed the jeers, horn-blowing, and whistles from men in passing vehicles. "Lesbos!" one screamed, tilting waist-out from his moving window. The spittle of his hatred flecked his chin, hair deranged in the stream of passage. I stuffed my need to roar, to counter, much as I had earlier stuffed my sleeping bag into the mouth of its sack.

"Assholes. Fucking assholes." Hearing Angie's vehemence, I then knew she had found a moment of composure, her anger a distraction from her unnamed misery. Of course she had heard. That kind of invective is honed for reception. My smile widened as I looked at her more closely.

"God, you look awful. There's snot everywhere."

Angie snorted a laugh, propelling a grimy string of slime away from her nose and across her front teeth. Normally, she was the first to court vulgarity, so I mocked disgust, knowing she would respond with more laughter. We busied ourselves with cleanup, smearing with the backs of our hands, pulling down the sleeve of her tee shirt, fantasizing a leave-no-trace tissue.

"So what's up?" I asked, her composure now established.

"Oh, you don't want to hear," she answered. "It's gross."

"Come on," I said, allowing a little affront in my voice. "First, you know that nothing that hurts that badly can be passed off as gross. Second, could I decide for myself what I want to hear?" She flicked a grin of contrition. Bantering came easily to us.

Her account actually was gross. She told me how, as a small child, she had been abandoned by her mother, then fostered by a preacher and his wife. From the time she was four, the preacher trespassed the privacy of both her room and her body. She said that his hand clamped over her mouth had embodied his threats, should she tell. At twelve she had run away, was found, and taken back. The abuse intensified, always at night, always with admonitions to maintain secrecy. Angie said she was unable to sleep, that she had to wait for the safety of dawn to drop her guard, and only then if he hadn't come in. At sixteen she ran away again, created a survival pit in a big city, and waited to grow up.

"But why now?" I asked. "What brought it all up today?"

She laughed, irony swinging her pitch. "It's always there," she said. "Years of therapy, a totally supportive husband, a PhD in psychology, and it's still always there. Today, though," she continued, "I'd fallen asleep waiting for the others to finish packing." She shot me a look. "You and your crack-of-fucking-dawn starts. It seems to me the earlier we get up the longer it takes. Just kidding," she added, matching my pretense of annoyance with mock submission. "But I was tired—we all are—it's been hard on us. Anyway, I was ready first, as usual," she said, hiding her pride under dropped eyelids. "I fell asleep because it was dawn and then Sonia was shaking me awake. I couldn't cope. I always have to wake up by myself, or with an alarm. She frightened me witless. Now, if you and Jessie hadn't frog-marched us over more mountains than I've seen in my whole life, none of this would have happened." She tried a laugh through a weakening voice. I encouraged her by clowning a shrug of bewilderment. I couldn't bear the idea of more tears.

"Oh, right," I said sarcastically. "Nice one. It's all *my* fault." It worked. A grin of acknowledgment and she adjusted her backpack, hitching it higher and tightening the hip belt.

"Come on," she said, "we haven't got all day."

We talked some more as we hiked on, exchanging more details of our lives. I knew Jessie and the others would be waiting for us at the point where we leave the road to begin climbing the drainage. Six days into the trip and she and I were working well together. A motorist slowed down to point out we were way behind the others. *Would he have done that if we were two men?* I rhetorically asked myself. As we drew close to the others—who were waiting exactly where I had anticipated—they tactfully engaged each other, giving Angie the space to remeld without scrutiny.

Jessie and I held back, after encouraging the students to hike on ahead. It was good to be off the road, and it would be good for them to navigate their way up the drainage. I told Jessie of Angie's outburst, and how it had shaken me.

"You know, we've been together for six days now. All sorts of stuff is coming out. Every night someone reveals another horror story. And now this from Angie." I looked at Jessie. "I mean, is this an unusually damaged group of women or what?" As we caught each other in a simultaneous head shake, we both laughed. "No, I know, I know," I said. "We're all damaged. We're women." Jessie leveled a brown-eyed gaze at me, speculative.

"Actually, d'you really think so?" she asked. "I don't feel like I have major issues."

"Maybe you don't." I grinned. "Or maybe they're lurking around somewhere. But you do know where these women are coming from. There's an empathy in you that's in every woman who's prepared to recognize our collectivity. We all speak the same language—it's just some of us have lost our tongues." I beamed at her, pleased with my insight. She threw back a yell of laughter as I tripped over a root and crashed to the ground.

"Allow *me*," she said, hauling me up by my pack.

The trail tracked a river, overhung with alpine shade. It was a relief to be out of the sun, as the heat was building despite the still-early hour. Our objective was a plateau about two-thirds of the way up the drainage, where we hoped we would find some good solo sites. I anticipated solo with pleasure. I was tired and needed a rest. Solo has always been central to Outward Bound courses: an opportunity for students to gain space from each other; to rest; to develop a relationship with their environment that group living prohibits; and to smell, taste, and swallow the raw fear that accompanies wilderness isolation.

In reality, solo is considerably safer than most students' preconceptions. Each student is designated their own solo area, with boundaries about the size of a supermarket. Straying beyond improvised perimeter lines is forbidden. Adjacent students are within whistle sound of each other, and whistle drill is learned as part of solo preparation. A solo base camp is established by the instructors, at least one of whom is there at all times. Students demonstrate their ability to find base camp before being left at their sites, and know that they will be visually checked by an instructor at least once a day. Finally, a code of signals is devised, allowing students to indicate whether or not they would like to be spoken to during an instructor's check.

"You know," I said, coming back to the moment, "it's sort of bad timing, the students going out on solo now." I had no consciousness of what I was beginning. "Angie told me she doesn't know how to tell the others about her past but feels she needs to. Molly clearly has stuff she's working on and is waiting for the right moment. Susi has, too. And Launa hasn't even begun to process what happened to her on that mountain pass." We lapsed into recollection of that horrendous day, forty-eight hours ago. Ten students, all variously needy, but Jessie and I had had to focus entirely on Launa. Her fear was so great she had tried to check out. Drifting off, she had lost all awareness of her feet, her balance, and her ability to carry her pack. I returned to my first train of thought. "They're actually bonding really well, and so willing to work on issues, I wonder if solo is going to interfere with that?"

Jessie squared up to me with another of those brown-eyed looks.

"Well?" she challenged. "There's always an alternative." There was a bright defiance to both of us. I now knew where this was going.

"Gotcha!" I laughed. "Let's have a collective solo!"

Two hours later, having arrived at the plateau, we put our idea to the students. We were sitting in the configuration of group earnestness, a circle. The women were tetchy. They had had words on their hike up: dissent over the slow pace determined by, ironically, the youngest; accusations of whining, of lack of grit, of insensitivity; and a lot of what they called "general bitching." It was hot. We were tucked into this flat table of dry pines, the river nearby, flowing full and vigorously downward. The trees smelled of musty resin, and gray jays circled above, blinking. I felt soothed, despite the tension.

"We were thinking, Jessie and I, that perhaps an individual solo isn't what you need right now," I said. "And maybe you feel that, too. Maybe this is one reason for your irritation with each other." I paused, and looked around the circle. "We want to know if you think a group solo would be more appropriate." I was surprised at the vehemence of their response—a unanimous, celebratory, "*Yes!*"

We decided to set up solo sites anyway, so that those who wanted time alone could have a personal spot. We also designated an area we called "common ground," where women who wanted to be with others could be. Daytime could then be spent alone or with others, as each woman chose. Sleeping would be separate, the women wanting to brave the edge of nighttime wilderness. Evening meals and talking circle were voted to be collective, with attendance required.

Later, Jessie and I lounged in her mid, a pyramid-shaped, open-bottomed tent. She was sketching, I was reading. I looked up to watch her moving hand, brown and strong, skin roughened and cracked by outdoor living. The sureness in her grip around the pencil, the sweetness in her drawn lines—the duality caught me. *We women are really quite wonderful*, I thought.

That night, our meal was festive. The students reported an afternoon of rest, reflection, some tears, and serious body-washing. We ate pizza, another culinary success under our belts. As dusk slipped over the mountains, we lit candles and hid them inside a ring of water bottles. The improvised lantern cast its spell. Women settled, eyes resting on the light, thoughts elsewhere. Angie, sitting on my right, was agitated. "I can't do it," she whispered. "I want to, but it feels way too scary."

I suddenly had a sickening inspiration as to how I could encourage Angie to talk.

"Tell you what." I said. "Remember what I talked to you about this morning, about *my* dilemma? I'll talk to the group—if you will." Angie cackled, her eyes sardonically approving.

"If I may say so, with my life-out-there-psychologist's-hat-on," she said, punctuating each word with underlined irony, "that was a very smart move." She laughed, freely this time. "Okay, Ms. Instructor. If you've got the guts, I have, too!"

The talk circle was opened by Susi. She fingered the necklace we had all made on the first night. We had each stated our hopes and intentions for the course, tying a symbolic knot in a piece of alpine cord. The string of knots had been joined into a necklace, its purpose to provide comfort and inspiration to the wearer. Since then, the women had been passing it among themselves, intuitively recognizing and prioritizing need. Susi had asked for the necklace earlier in the day. She had said she was feeling troubled, had feelings too big for her. Now we listened as she tried to bring us up-to-date with her early life. Another tale of abuse. Another woman's attempt to redefine herself, to erase the stamp of a male relative. She told us how, on this trip, each step she had taken on difficult mountainous terrain had become a personal triumph. She had had no idea how frightened she would be of losing her footing. "What does this mean?" she wondered. She knew it meant something, and she knew she could now work on it.

Pam was next. She was analytical, surprised at how powerful the course was for her. She laughed as she described her pre-course vision of camping at designated sites with picnic tables, day trips with day packs, campfires. She said she had had no conception of how much we would talk, how open we would be, how therapeutic the mountains.

"There's an inconsequentiality to our lives that living in the wilderness shows up," she reflected. "Mountains are real, they set their limits, they set ours. They expose us, make us vulnerable and strong at the same time." She paused, eyes lost in the lantern. "They make me feel as if it's pointless to play the charades that real life dictates," she continued, tweaking both index fingers in a parody of quotation marks around "real." "That it's a waste to be so egotistical, so precious. They make me feel raw, stripped clean, healthier." Other women nodded assent. She spoke for them, too, they said.

Then it was my turn. Shit! Why had I made that deal with Angie? I took the necklace, fingers shaking as they traveled the knots. *It's always like this*, I reminded myself, *for some reason it doesn't get easier. Actually*, my inner dialogue modified, *it's not for some reason. It's for a very good reason.*

"I haven't told you before, and I want to tell you now," I said, pitching my voice over the blood thumping in my ears. "I haven't told you because I've felt vulnerable—and also protective of you. I've wanted you to know me without labels, and without causing offense. I've wanted to be able to hold your hands over the steep bits, without rebuff. Push your butts into the rock when you're climbing, without recoil." I managed to swallow a rising giggle, not only because of mentioning butts, but because I was aware that nervousness was giving an ecclesiastical cast to my language.

Then I looked at Angie. "And I've wanted to offer hugs for your tears, without rejection." I forced myself to look around the group, to make eye contact. "I'm a lesbian."

I laughed into the silence, despite myself. Jessie's eyes were as wide as her smile. She'd had no idea I was going to do this. "And the reason I want to tell you," I continued, "is because you've all been brave. So open. So prepared to take risks. I want to honor your risks by taking my own." Everyone remained quiet for a few seconds. "Oh, yes," I added, plunging again into the stillness. "This is really important. The reason I haven't told you is *not* because I'm ashamed. On the contrary. For the last few years I've been as out as it's been appropriate to be. I've done my time internalizing everyone else's bigotry. Actually," I added, "everyone's fear. People are frightened by what they don't understand, by what they see as an unacceptable difference. They turn their fear into attack. It's easier that way." I stopped, knowing I was in danger of beginning a lecture on sexuality more fitting to my earlier life as an academic. "Anyway," I said, shifting position to indicate a change in tone, "for a while I took on people's hatred, their stigma. Then I began to be able to turn it around, to see the problem as theirs, not mine." I grinned, relaxed now. "In fact, I'm quietly proud of myself."

I clenched my hands around my knees, then drew them up chest high. It was night black outside the circle. Eleven pairs of eyes were on me, faces strangely illuminated by the bottle lantern.

"Wow," said Patsy. "I had no idea. And that's a compliment," she added. The roar of laughter surprised her. As the youngest and most naive, her comment personified her. She did break the tension though, and she knew it. "Was I one of the people you thought might be offended?" she asked. "I mean, I know I go on about going to the bathroom in private and stuff, but I don't mind. Really!" More laughter, the sort that is supportive and forgiving.

"Actually, you were one of those people," I said. I wanted to continue the honesty. "And when I talk about not wanting to offend people, what I mean is not that I think it's okay for them to be offended. It's not. But I do understand that most people's negative responses are learned. Giving people a chance to decide if they like me before getting all hung up on labels usually works pretty well." I looked at Patsy, thinking. "And you know, it's not part of my job description to come out." People laughed. "No, what I mean is, not only is it hard to do, but on some courses it simply isn't an issue. Not every group is as open as this; not every group could handle it; and not every group should. Although," I added, "when people get homophobic it's really hard." I returned my thoughts to Patsy. "You seemed more shockable, perhaps less open-minded. You made me feel nervous." She took it hard, I could tell. But she took it.

Other women made brief but sweet comments. They thanked me, applauded me, admired me. I felt good, and was glad I'd done it. I handed the necklace to Angie. "Your turn."

"Oh shit," she said, an echo of my earlier response. As she talked, she cried. She was hugged, encouraged, and she heard the women's fury. Her voice grew stronger as she realized our lack of censure, that we felt only rage at what had been done to her. She, too, was glad in the end.

The necklace continued to be passed around the circle, and so the journeys continued—date rape, paternal abandonment, anorexia, marital rape—journeys of healing through revelation. When it was Molly's turn, her face spasmed with a struggle as she took the string of knots. We leaned forward to catch her dropped voice.

"I, also, have a solo gift for you and for myself," she said. "I've been debating this all afternoon. And now I'm scared shitless. When you two suggested a group solo," she looked at Jessie and me, "I knew that was what I needed. I *knew* it was. Whether I wanted it or not was a different matter. But I feel excited as well as scared," she added, "because I'm going to do something I've never done before." She stroked her cheek with the flat of her hand, thinking.

"Despite being the oldest here, I'm way behind in lots of things—and not just on the trail," she joked. "The death of Matt, my teenage son—which I've told you about—was actually preceded by something I've kept to myself for over ten years now." She stopped, fishing a bandanna out of her pocket. "I know I'm going to need this," she said, trying her old trick of lightening seriousness. "A few months before Matt died, I'd fallen in love with a woman, and had left Matt and his father. After Matt's accident, I felt so guilty. I knew it wasn't my fault, but I felt—and still do—that it was. I've never 'come out' before," she said, with exaggerated mockery at using this phrase. Again, she looked at me. "I've never called myself a lesbian before."

I looked back, steadily, but felt responsible, uncomfortable. *What the hell have I started here?* I asked myself. To my relief, Molly continued, taking ownership.

"I know I have to do it. I know I have some serious owning up to do. My lover and I have always lived apart, even though she has often pushed me for more commitment." Molly's face crumpled, and she knocked tears away with the bandanna. "She's had cancer for a number of years now, and I'm frightened to death of losing her. But what I've always said to myself, right up until today, is that I'm frightened to be out. It's been easier to hide behind fear of social disapproval than to admit emotional frailty." She stopped, crying freely. "And you," she said, fixing on me with a laugh between her tears, "*I* knew you. I recognized your little sleights of hand, saw you field questions the way I've done for years. And I also knew you would come out. I didn't know when, as I think you didn't, but I knew that when you did, I'd have to, as well."

"So it's all my fault," I said, lightly teasing and feeling I'd come full circle since this morning. God, what an age away that felt.

One other woman came out that night, and the following night Susi did, too. She said she'd missed her opportunity the previous night as her turn with the necklace had come before mine. We all laughed.

The morning after our first solo circle, Jessie and I resolved to keep a low profile.

"I'm exhausted," I complained. "All that emotional dredging last night, it's worn me out."

"D'you think we get more lesbians on a women's course than on regular coed courses?" she asked.

"Of course we do," I replied. "In fact I'm surprised there aren't more. It seems an obvious choice to me. Although," I added, chewing worn skin off the inside of my thumb, "the straight women know what they're doing. There's something qualitatively different about a heterosexual woman who picks a women's course. She understands what it will be like. How good it will be. And she knows she can't hide behind men, and she knows that men won't hamper her PGD. Personal growth and development," I added, seeing Jessie's forehead furrow.

She shoved her nose into my face. "Don't you patronize me, you smug little dyke. I can't help being straight!"

Outside, the sounds of giggling overlaid with zealous coughing caught our attention.

"We've brought you something. Open up!" I recognized Angie's voice, and looked at Jessie. We pulled faces of horror, resenting the intrusion, the demands of work. I leaned forward, and reluctantly zipped open the tent. Ten women were sitting outside, in a circle. My heart sank, and my face must have shown it.

"Hey, don't worry! We don't want anything," laughed Betsy. "It's just you've been snoozing so long we were worried you'd get caffeine withdrawal." The others roared. Our morning coffee fixes had become the brunt of many earlier jokes. "And another thing," she said, affecting the professorial posture so much a part of her other life, "we were worried about hypoglycemia." With a dramatic sweep of her arm she unveiled one of the big cooking pots. Steaming corn bread, moistly golden, was on the grass before us.

As they poured coffee and handed round the honey, I reflected that this was the first time I'd been taken care of on a wilderness course. The women were solicitous, but also jubilant. I asked them how they were doing. It was Molly who stated it best.

"What I realized last night as we were all sitting and spewing our hearts out, was that for us, as women, being together is our solo. When else do we get that kind of space for ourselves? When else can we talk freely, honestly, and not fear interruption or ridicule? When else can we sit under the stars, and just be, not 'alone'—you know, the way men see us when we're without them—but together? We're on solo from our lives as women. And we love it."

I lay back, full with corn bread, a pleasant buzz from the coffee. And I loved it, too.

ANN BAKER

Night above Sasho

KISHTWAR IS A MEDIEVAL CITY IN THE HIGH FOOTHILLS OF THE
HIMALAYA. Taped Pakistani music screams out from the shops along the
main road. Goats nibble in the cobblestone streets that feed into the
one paved strip. The deep, open, stone-lined sewers were probably
more elegant than those of London or Paris at the time they were put
in, and do not seem inelegant now.

There is little sense that the British conquered this place. They
came, built their system of Bungalows outside town to shelter their own
hikers, and disappeared with less trace than the Asian traders who moved
their caravans through. The city has a cramped mystery, a feeling that outsiders have been passing through for millennia, being sheltered and sup-
plied for their travels. The back streets are an orderly bazaar of
single-room shops selling one thing each: fabric, metal pots, dishes,
candles, trunks, sneakers, tobacco, and rugs. Uphill stand tall stone
houses with turquoise window trim and purple cosmos leaning out of window boxes.

Like others before me, I came to Kishtwar to be sheltered and sup-
plied. I was beginning a trek heading for Lamayuru in the former kingdom
of Ladakh. Kishtwar sits against the flank of the first range of the Hi-
malayas and Lamayuru is up and over Umasi-La, the "highest pass in
trekking," as my outfitter assured me. I wanted to be in the highest mountains and to enter a culture that had been Buddhist for so long that the architecture and the language and even the stones of the place were shaped
in that belief. Kishtwar was the gate to the high mountains and Bud-
dhism was the mountain religion. In northern India, religion seems like a

matter of altitude. The Hindus live in the foothills and the great lowlands, the Muslims hold the high Valley of Kashmir, and above them, above timber line, the Buddhists have their barley fields, their *mani* walls and prayer wheels, their monasteries, called *gompas*, set along streams of glacial run-off and guarded by eroded mud *chortens*, miniature templelike structures that hold the ashes of ancient lamas.

I did not set out to cross the highest pass in trekking. My plan was to quickly reach Leh, the capital of that part of old Tibet still accessible to Westerners, and trek out from there. It was the doubtful tone of a fit, young, trekking outfitter assessing my forty-five-year-old female body's ability to walk so far and so high that generated in me a kind of competitive acquiescence. I would do it his way, I would prove that I could make it, and I would become a pilgrim in the process.

It was the combination of a high, harsh place that had nurtured a powerful spiritual and cultural life that drew me. The silk caravans came through Leh. The monasteries on peaks and high slopes around the city were furnished in gold, turquoise, and brilliantly embroidered tapestries. Their walls were painted with the best art of their time. In material terms, it is a poor place now, but it had once been rich in every way. The learned Buddhists were part of a chain of wisdom that went back thousands of years. I wanted to touch that chain.

From growing up in the American Southwest, I knew the combination of harsh landscape and ancient culture. I wanted to see one of the places from which the nomads who crossed the Bering Straits thousands of years ago set out. They were the ancestors of the people who settled in my native Arizona and farmed and grew cotton long before my father did. I was crossing back to a very old starting place that, before the silk trade, before the Buddha, was the home of people who made alliances with mountain spirits and discovered pathways out across the Earth and even across the border of Death. I had *The Tibetan Book of the Dead* in my backpack and a Navajo turquoise ring on my finger. I felt like I was going for the first time to a place where I had already been.

The trek from Kashmir was the reverse of my original plan. I would still get to Leh, *Inshallah*, God willing, as the Muslims say about every endeavor, but I would climb up instead of landing swiftly in the heart of my destination. Sheik Nazir proposed trekking up to the monastery at Padam, about a five-day climb, and then, after resting and washing socks, traveling two more weeks on trails that mountain people have traveled for centuries to the great monastery at Lamayuru at the edge of the Tibetan plain.

I was trekking without friends or other Westerners but I was not alone. Leaving Srinigar, we were a party of five: the cook/leader, two porters, the driver, and myself. The first day, traveling by car from Srinigar to Kishtwar with the three men wedged into the back seat and me up front, aloof beside the driver, I had no idea what my relationship to my companions would become. They were as strange to me as the steep hills we crept up and over and the villages that dotted the landscape.

Cha Cha was fifty-something and our leader. He was handsome and slender in his Kashmiri outfit of long, Nehru-collared shirt and pants that gathered at the ankle. He cooked and smiled and kept up a line of patter that drew everyone to him. Lasa came from a tiny village near the Pakistan border. He worked in Srinigar for cash but had land and a house in the mountains. He spoke excellent English and was very attentive to my needs. And Yousf, it seemed, came along for the ride. He was dark, with hooded eyes and a moustache. He wore a shawl around his shoulders or over his head and gave off an air of being offended by having to associate with a woman. He and I seemed to hurt each other's feelings at every turn. I felt him watching me and was sure, each time he laughed, it was about me.

We had all known each other on the houseboat in Srinigar, where I made plans for the trek, but had only superficial dealings with each other, buffered by suave and handsome Nazir, the entrepreneur who put the whole package together. Now we were on our own and awkward. We passed the Gujars, herders from the mountains, with their hennaed hair and beards, their horses packed high with small children balanced on top of everything else. The women wore bright colors and brass jewelry jingling and flashing. Even the horses wore brightly colored halters with tassels and tiny bells. I didn't make conversation with the Gujars or negotiate with them for supplies. My companions and I had to develop a language and a way of being together. That first morning I didn't know how to begin.

On our first stop, hours up into the hills, the men took me into an empty tea-room and then went outside to smoke. At my solitary table I asked for apple juice, and knowing that the bottles it came in were very small, asked for two. The look on the waiter's face told me I had blundered but I didn't know how. He went outside and consulted with the men. They all talked and gestured. I watched through the window. The waiter walked down the street and finally returned with the two bottles. I sat with a knot in my stomach wondering what was so problematic about two bottles of apple juice. It was the unbelievable luxury of ordering two that had lead him to question his hearing or my intention.

We started out again only to stop before we got out of town. The horn didn't work. The men looked worried and the driver said something about turning back. I couldn't believe it. Brakes I could understand, but a horn? A crowd gathered, someone found the right wire and we went on. Above that village, the switchbacks in the road sharpened.

The lorries roared down the narrow road at us on our side, and finally, in the dark, as herders bedded their sheep and goats in the road, I understood about the horn. Time after time, up and down those gorges we met sheep bunched between mountain wall and cliff, their shepherds camped in the dust with them, little fires between the white-painted boulders that sometimes marked the outer edge of the road. At the sound of our horn, the men drove the flock off the road, uphill, the sheep climbing the rocks and each other, then flowing back into the flat of the road as we passed. About every hour we hit the bottom of a gorge, crossed a river, and looked up in the steep darkness to the next village. The single light of its tea stall looked like some near star against the black emptiness of the mountain.

Kishtwar was a surprise after all those one-light towns. I could feel the bulk of it as we drove through. I admired the simple elegance of the long colonial Bungalow we came to for lodging, with its shuttered windows and wide lawns. Cha Cha got a room for me. Much later, a man came with a tray of rice and sauce, chapatis, and Kashmiri tea. I had shaken out my sleeping bag on one of the two beds, set my books on the table between them, and discovered that the plumbing worked and there was hot water. The thick, smoke-stained walls, the deep fireplace, the wide, shuttered windows all revealed by the bare light bulb hanging in the middle of the room felt comforting, not stark or alien, and I ate and slept, feeling at home in India for the first time.

The ancient voice of Muslim tradition penetrated my consciousness before I came awake the next morning with one clear, perfect note of the call to prayer. In Srinigar, on the houseboat, I had heard the call each morning but it had been distant, floating over water and rippled by that passage. In Kishtwar, built in that sharp valley above the Chenab

River, the note could not spread or ripple. It was bright and pointed as an arrow in the mind.

I gave up trying to predict when or how things would happen. A tall primrose hedge enclosed the fading gardens outside my room, and when breakfast did not appear, I found a table and chair there and very self-consciously began my journal entries. I was gently interrupted by a quiet man in a white shirt and brown slacks, unusual dress for the hill country. He was also a guest, a judge for the land court, a Hindu settling disputes between the Muslim landholders and the Hindu government. He traveled a circuit from Jammu, the winter capital of Kashmir and Jammu Province, and was glad to talk about his work. He had the watchful, careful manner of a man accustomed to untangling impossible situations. He said he would go to the mosque to pray before going to court and invited me along. It was a good lesson, a Hindu praying in the house of worship of those he was going to judge. I felt that I understood this man and felt a kinship with him. I seemed an easier companion for him than the plaintiffs or the defendants with whom he spent his days. My stranger status was beginning to erode.

Our driver went back to Srinigar and we went shopping. We bought vegetables, cooking fuel, and live chickens, which we tied onto our luggage, and stacked everything beside the road to wait for the last bus to Galhar. That was where the walking would begin. Our lodging was a campsite on the dirt roof of a house on the edge of town that we shared with a goat and the two household dogs. In Galhar, the fashion was for dogs to lie along the edge of the flat roofs and rain a frenzy of barking down on passersby.

We met our next transport, two men and six donkeys, the next morning. The men's clothes were dirty and patched. They looked like bandits out of an old Western film, and the donkeys were so small, they looked like toys. I sat on a rock in the fall sunlight, watching the men load full-size gear onto miniature beasts, and reading the last *New Yorker* I had brought along. I paged through jokes about the excesses of gourmet cooking equipment while the assistant donkey man patted chapatis with his rough, blackened hands and cooked them on a flat piece of tin over his little fire. Again the world shifted. This mountain place seemed familiar and the shiny-paged magazine, strange. I gave it to a little boy who had been watching me carefully since I crawled out of my tent.

When we walked out of town, we were the size of a small circus troop and were perhaps as amusing to the people who waved us off. Men, donkeys, chickens, big tent, little tent, pots, stove, fuel, and one American woman striking out boldly at the head of the line. I didn't appreciate how absurd we were until a few hours later. Two men in tweed jackets, street shoes, umbrellas, and the little cotton shoulder bags that were part of the American sixties but are still standard in India, swung past us heading downhill. "Who were they?" I asked. The donkey men knew. They were officials who had crossed Umasi-La three days ago. *Just like that? No porters, no camping equipment, no boots?* They could have walked down the street in Cambridge or Berkeley and looked perfectly appropriate. I was now clearly the exotic and they were the norm. They felt familiar to me and I felt strange to myself.

Galhar used to be the end of the motor road but it was being extended. Trucks rattled past us, and jeeps carrying crisp-looking soldiers threw up a constant dust cloud. Why had I come so far to walk in the dust? Where was the idyllic path by the pure rushing stream?

We walked by the galvanized iron hovels of the road builders, already ovens in the mid-morning sun. Men and women chipped boulders into gravel by hand, and children stood in the dust without clothes or playthings. We were forced to stop at the site of a blasting, where rubble blocked access to the thin trail beyond. Donkey trains backed up for more than a mile. Men sat and smoked. We had lunch. Yousf made a pillow of his shawl, lay down in the thick dust, and slept.

The impatient American surged up in me. *How long must we wait? Why isn't anyone taking charge?* And worse, I had to change my tampon in broad daylight on the open road. I hadn't asked for boiled water to carry so I was thirsty, filthy, frustrated, and my back ached. The charm of trekking cracked to reveal this difficult reality and I did not exhibit grace under pressure.

I demanded that we move on, seeing some others inching through the car-size rocks that blocked our way. The men shrugged and I marched off like a toddler who didn't get candy at the check-out counter. I would be helpless without them later, but right then I couldn't stand them so I attached myself to the donkey train laboring over the blast. I climbed over the chunks of cliff beside donkeys who were being hauled by halters and tails over rocks much bigger than they. Now I saw the problem but my anger was fueled by days of sitting alone and not knowing what was going on. I knew from my printed itinerary, a fragile document that still had meaning for me, that we were headed for Sasho. I imagined Sasho to be much like Galhar with shops and ice and orange soda. I said, "Sasho?" to the donkey man ahead of me and he nodded. We cut straight up off the main trail, away from the river. It was all I could do to keep up with him. An hour or so later we came to a fork. He turned right, uphill again, and pointed with a gesture of his chin down the path in the other direction. "Sasho," he said. I looked. There was a wooden hut and something that looked like a water wheel beyond that. Nothing else.

I was in a crevice cut by a narrow stream and the mountains on both sides blocked any direct sunlight. The sky was light blue above but below it was getting cold and the breeze was coming up. I walked down to the hut and wondered what I had done to myself.

The hut was the Sasho Hotel. It had a small porch with two tables, a bench running along the wall and railing, a room where a fire seemed to have been burning forever, and a dark back room with some rope beds. Sitting comfortably on the bench in the customary Kashmiri squat was a tiny, ragged man in khaki shirt and pants wearing some kind of military ribbon and medal. He addressed me in very good English. It is a cliché to say it but he seemed truly delighted to see me. He loved travelers of all sorts, spoke six or seven languages passably in order to talk to them, and soon, after he brought me several glasses of boiled water that tasted of charcoal, we were looking at my photographs of family and chatting about world news. He listened to the BBC, Voice of America, Radio Pakistan, a broadcast from the then USSR, and any Indian stations he could get.

Just about the time the sky was getting as dark as the valley the porters and donkeys came. The men had had to unload all the gear, carry it over the rocks, help the donkeys over, and then repack. Unlike me, they showed no sign of anger or frustration about that or about my having marched off without them. I was beginning to understand who they were.

That night, we stayed at another British-built Bungalow above Sasho. Painted dark green with two rooms and a wide, roofed porch, it was immense in comparison to the little hotel below. The rooms were wood-floored, with unglazed windows and heavy shutters. There were some pegs on the wall but otherwise the space was bare. I was given the bedroom with adjoining bath, a tiny dirt-floored room with a drain in the middle. The porters took the other room, and the men with the donkeys slept on the porch on burlap sacks.

Cha Cha set up his kerosene stove and heated water for my bath, Lasa killed and plucked a chicken by the spring behind the bungalow, and the donkey men unloaded the donkeys and set them out to graze on what seemed to be bare ground. I washed in the privacy of my little bathroom, did laundry and hung it on the pegs, then spread my sleeping bag on the ground cloth, and got in.

It was my birthday. Cha Cha made chocolate pudding for dessert. I ate by candlelight, alone, and was completely happy. The full moon came up into the opening above the valley. The Chenab River growled below us and donkey bells clinked outside our windows.

The day had banged me around and had waked me up. I knew so much more than I had twenty-four hours before. My body felt tired but very alive. My feet were a mess from the cheap tennis shoes I had bought in Kishtwar, but right then that didn't matter. I had what I needed. My mind was calm and alert to everything within and around me.

There is a pose in yoga called the child's pose. It is used as a resting state between the more extended and difficult poses. In it the practitioner sits on her heels and folds the body over the thighs, forehead on the floor, arms at the sides. It is a position of humility and comfort, as though such a posture will call down the protection of the universe on the being who makes herself so vulnerable. That night, above Sasho, with the mountains huge and close, it was that posture I felt within myself.

GENEEN MARIE HAUGEN

Living by Mountains

IT HAS BEEN A LONG TIME SINCE I SKIED WITHOUT A DOG OR A HUMAN COMPANION.

The thought crystallizes with the sharp pain under my kneecap, a stab that arrests my momentum. I lean on my poles, gasping, waiting for the ache to subside. A quarter mile away, downhill through aspen and pine, my house is still in sight: a safe enclosure, an invitation, but the sky is brilliant and the air too dazzling to stay indoors. At this darkest time of the year, I welcome the sun and what little warmth it offers in a climate where minus-25-degree temperatures—or colder—are common.

Lifting my knee tentatively, I shuffle up the trail, weighting the skis to make them stick on the incline. The fire beneath my kneecap flares with each lift, diminishes with each tiny uphill glide. I continue to climb, careful, questioning. The house vanishes behind me. No one knows where I'm going. My partner has driven to town, taking the dog along. Hours will pass before they return.

Mindful of my knee, mindful of angling it forward, trying not to twist sideways, I plod uphill. Waves of pain break and recede. *I will move through this*, I think, *breathe through this ache.*

I can't tell if I've become delusional, grandiose in my sense of physical endurance.

When I stop to rest, the quiet brings to mind other trips, other times I have glided alone, in silence. I think of one winter when I was fifteen years younger—fifteen years more brave or foolish—and I skied to visit friends encamped in tepees near the southern boundary of Yellowstone Park. Snow fell thick and fast the day I traveled with a sixty-pound pack full of fresh vegetables and my own camping gear to a place I had never visited, even in summer. The friends did not know I was coming. I did not know how endless a dozen miles solo in a blizzard with a heavy pack would feel. Without a topographic map, I had no way to determine where I was, exactly. Only the memory of my friends' briefly spoken directions guided me.

The avalanche shovel strapped to my pack offered thin comfort: I could always dig a snow cave if night closed in. A worse thought: At any bend I might encounter a just-awakened grizzly, hungry, with infant cubs to feed in the waning days of winter. I considered turning around a thousand times while the pack straps chewed my shoulders and the belt rubbed my hips raw, but when I guessed I had traveled more than halfway, my destination seemed closer, more reachable, than the trailhead I had started from, and I abandoned thoughts of returning. Instead, I began to wonder how I would recognize a little-used trail angling off the unplowed road. I wondered about getting lost. No snowmobile or other skis left impressions in the deepening snow: No one had traveled this way in many days.

The storm muted the tracks of river otters lining the creek banks. Shrub willow flushed with sap and turned redder against the stark white end of winter. Snow collected on limbs of lodgepole and on the road. I slid through calf-high crystals, unable to see the sun. I carried no watch, and in the absence of shadows, I could not judge time. At each expansive meadow I wondered if I had reached the lake I expected to cross eventually, but I saw no old ski trails, and could not tell if ice lay buried beneath the deepening white.

Snow drifts into a thick silence I have learned to recognize over the years, so that even when waking at night, I know a snowstorm by the muffle. I skied in that enormous, silent snowfall with only my breath and rustle of equipment to intrude. Occasionally a moose stood dark, frozen amidst the willows, but nothing seemed to move except me and the plummeting snow.

When the swollen clouds lifted, the storm thinned enough to reveal the frozen lake ahead: nearly two miles long, half a mile wide—much larger in reality than imagination. The trail around ascended slightly, but the weight on my shoulders and back made me wince at the possibility of another climb. I slid onto the ice, smooth and slick beneath the snow, hoping to cut a mile and some elevation off my travel. With the end of the trip so near, I dredged up a residual of energy and skied steadily, imagining a fire, hot tea, soft cushions within reach. I did not try to cross the lake directly, but angled along its length, gravitating for the opposite, most distant shore.

I was in the middle of the lake when an explosion like thunder shattered the dusky quiet: beneath the snow, ice I could not see shifted, groaned against the long winter, groaned against the unexpected weight of me. Too far out to turn back, too burdened with a heavy pack to swim, too tired to do anything except ski cautiously, I probed with my poles for soft spots in the ice, unwilling to think of falling through. I could not think, but only slide one foot and then the other, until I reached the shore and a faint ski trail. Tears of relief froze on my lashes as I followed old tracks to my friends.

A few days later, I crawled out of a warm tepee to collect water from another, smaller, lake. I leaned over the bank to break the skim ice but it did not crack under my fist or even under the sharp edge of the metal bucket. I stood, balanced on one foot, and kicked at the hole—and careened off the bank up to my armpits in deathly cold water.

The snowbank rose vertically out of the lake; I punched my fists into it and pulled myself up, but the bank crumbled and I plunged, backward, into the icy water once more. Nothing within reach was solid enough to climb. I yelled, hoping someone would hear. When no one came, I shouted again.

Heat fled. My heart thudded slowly. Movements faltered, and I recognized hypothermia even in thickening confusion. I tried climbing the snowbank again but fell back into the water, perfectly calm, separating from physical events, detaching from the body. Awareness began to drift, hovered above the ice and snow, peaceful, beyond alarm.

There was no logic in turning away from shore, but the body's impulse to survive is stronger than reason. I found myself stroking toward deeper water, toward unbroken ice, away from the sheer cliff of snow. In excruciating slow motion, I heaved myself belly-down on the ice like an otter. The ice shattered under my weight but I slithered over it until it hardened and held, and I crawled and slipped and dragged myself to a more gradual shore. While my clothes froze stiff, I staggered to the tepee, where smoke trailed out of the stove pipe.

My friend helped strip the garments that would not bend; I could hardly bear the rough peeling away. As blood began to circulate again, phantom needles, white-hot and sharp, pierced my extremities. For the next two days I huddled in a sleeping bag and a buffalo hide as close to the fire as I dared.

When I left that encampment later, I skied the long way, around the big lake. I knew I had been lucky, or blessed, the first crossing. Good luck is a useful companion to poor judgement, but counting on luck is like depending that a boulder placed on ice will always be there. I was twenty-eight when the ice shattered beneath me and I discovered I was no longer invincible.

Today, I am not in danger of losing my way in a storm or of falling through ice, and I've become a knowledgeable and skillful enough skier—

usually—to avoid hitting trees at high speed or daring avalanches. But unexpected injury is still possible, as the sharp twitch in my knee reminds me. Or perhaps the knee ache reminds me of the birthday looming, another foot planted inexorably in middle age. Still, I have skied out of remote places with cracked ribs and broken equipment, and I've grown cautious about getting hurt where I may not be able to evacuate myself.

The brilliant sun seduces me and I ascend the trail slowly, believing I will stop before I reach the ridge that requires a fast, steep descent, carved telemark turns between aspen and wind-blown pine. Another day, the ridge and free-heel turns would not give me a moment's thought, but today, caution surfaces with pain.

Shadows turn the snow blue and I stop to listen for branches breaking, for the telltale sound of moose or elk moving across the hillside, but I hear only the caw of a single, distant raven. In the draw, seeds of coneflowers dot the snow where finches have ridden the dead stalks, but now no small birds flit in the trees. No fresh tracks of large mammals cross the ski trail, but I know creatures are near. This land, so close to my house, is National Forest: Wild ones congregate here.

I ski on, thinking that around the bend, or over that saddle, *something will happen*, something that will make me glad I stretched beyond my knee, something unusual, extraordinary even. I have read recently of sightings of huge groups of moose, dozens, and I imagine if I just ski high enough, I will see them bunched together in a distant valley. Or perhaps a pack of coyotes, usually witnessed only solo in daylight. Maybe a newly shed moose antler will lie beside the trail, or an elk carcass, scavenged clean. Perhaps a great gray owl will sweep through the pine, huge-winged and silent.

The snow is lighter, drier than I had imagined it would be, and I know I have not chosen the right skis for the conditions, especially if I climb high enough to carve turns on the downhill. The light, waxless skis

I wear have scaled bottoms, good for wetter or more uneven conditions, best for trails—too narrow for powder, too flimsy for telemarking. The low-cut boots and old three-pin bindings were designed for gentle touring, not serious control. Whatever has twisted behind my kneecap has not unkinked yet. I measure these things in my mind, still believing I will turn around, coast easily back down the trail, before I summit.

When I ski into the shade of the hill, the temperature drops. I have been moving for over an hour, slower than usual, minding my knee. I watch the sun back-lighting the bare branches at the top of the ridge and suddenly I know I will climb all the way, break a new trail through snow that falls away from my calves like shredded styrofoam. Near the top, the buds on a young aspen have already cracked open: three months too early, a freak response to the unseasonable warmth of solstice week. I will study that tree in the coming days, watch how winter determines its fate.

I think of my own fate and wonder, as I often do, how I will die. I imagine I have a long run still coming, but backcountry travel carries its own risks, and I have no plans to pursue a tamed existence. I don't know what will send me on the journey beyond this life; it could be anything— but I prefer, even hope, for my passing to occur amidst an adventure I have loved well: on a wild river, a wind-scraped mountain.

I have received a telephone call that my much-loved aunt, Mae Matara Hakala, is dying. She has been dying for a while—on and off for years— but she keeps grabbing back onto life, making unexpected recoveries, miraculous recoveries that baffle everyone, even the doctors. This time, Mae says she will not return to the hospital, that there is nothing more any doctors can do. She herself instructed my mother to come right away, saying she did not think she would survive the two days before my mother's scheduled visit. My aunt is in her early seventies, not old, surely; but as a young woman with tuberculosis, she was the only person to survive an experimental operation that removed all of one lung and part of the other. She is barely five feet tall, perhaps one hundred pounds.

My aunt Mae has lived in Alaska for most of her married life. In the 1950s, when supplies for white outsiders were brought in by ship once a year, my aunt lived and worked in Kotzebue, a native village north of the Arctic Circle, where the only motor vehicle was an ambulance. She moved to the Kenai Peninsula before the road connected to Anchorage.

Mae accompanied my uncle John, a wildlife biologist, into the Alaskan bush, enduring—enjoying—living conditions that would challenge the most vigorous person: months of darkness and sub-zero temperatures, melting ice for water, no fresh food. In Kotzebue, the native women persuaded Mae to join them as they created a human fence to funnel reindeer into corrals for "harvest." Shouting and waving her arms, Mae held her place in line as the antlered herd thundered past. The reindeer, not native to North America, are gone now, run off with caribou decades past, and the villagers have snowmobiles, outboard motors, and alcohol. The government agency that hired my uncle to establish reindeer ranges for the village did not consider that Eskimo people are bound to the sea, not migratory like reindeer or like Laplanders who follow the herds. Of that time in Kotzebue, Mae and John have friends, memories, and, perhaps, a few regrets.

When she could still travel by air, my aunt left Alaska for a European tour. She loves books, music, and art. One room of their small house is filled with her own paintings. When she sells—or gives away—a piece, it is hard to tell if my uncle's begrudging posture is affectation or truly felt. I have received gifts of Mae's art: a children's book, a small vase made from Cook Inlet clay, and three paintings—of northern lights, of a snow-covered totem pole, of pastel mountains in winter. As her health deteriorated, Mae experimented with techniques to make painting easier.

Outside the home Mae and John built on the Kenai Peninsula, I have found enormous piles of bear and moose scat amidst the trees, and I have heard the songs of wolves. The eruption, a few years ago, of the volcano Redoubt shrouded their land with ash, shards of silica, treacherous to breathe.

Recently, on oxygen all the time, my aunt lost energy to paint.

I got the news that Mae was dying, and I felt that a phone call would be too great an intrusion on the sorrow of my uncle John and gathered family. My partner encouraged me to phone, just in case Mae had not passed. I dialed tentatively. My uncle answered with a booming hello, sounding Finnish as ever. I wondered if I had been given the wrong message. I asked how they were faring. John said Mae had perked up that day, perhaps because her best friend from childhood—my mother, John's sister—had arrived, along with Mae's own sister.

My mother came to the phone, and I asked if she knew how long Mae might live. "Hard to tell," she said. It sounded like a party in the background; the women were telling stories about their shared youth. I think how odd that my mother, a suburbanite with enthusiasm for bingo and mall-shopping, would bind me to the creative, wild woman who is my aunt through marriage, not blood.

My mother handed the phone to Mae.

I said, "I didn't want you to slip away without having a chance to say goodbye." I pictured Mae on the other end, in bed, oxygen tube assisting her frail breathing, but my aunt's normally-soft voice sounded strong, steadier than mine.

"To tell you the truth, the way I'm feeling today, I might last another year," she said.

I said, "I wanted to tell you what an inspiration you've been to me: going to the university so late in life, pursuing your art, living in that wild country."

"Oh, I didn't accomplish that much," she said. When she coughed, she covered the receiver.

"I'm grateful we had a chance to share some time together," I said.

"I regret we didn't know each other sooner." She coughed again.

I said, "I'll miss you."

"I might be here awhile yet, but if you feel a breath of wind passing, you'll know that's me."

"I'll remember that. I love you." I paused, postponing. Neither of us spoke until I said, "Goodbye."

My aunt and I startled ourselves with these intimacies. Such tender words had never passed between us, had never passed between me and any adult relation.

In my family, there is an unspoken belief in the privacy of pain, of love, of fear, of any emotion other than anger. There is an understanding that we must stand alone, not burden each other with our losses or sorrows. There is a silent agreement not to probe too deeply. When, several years ago, I told a family member that a doctor had suggested I might need lung surgery to resolve chronic pneumonia (I didn't), she segued quickly into her own recent bunion operation and never again questioned the condition of my lungs—nor did I ever inquire about her bunions.

But an imminent journey toward death challenges even the longest-standing inhibitions and habitual distance, and now I wonder why I did not gather Mae and John in my arms on my last Alaskan visit and tell them how much I cherish them. What practiced fear locks the words inside? What illusion of separateness allows me to risk my life but not my heart?

Several times, recently, I have felt a breath on my face, below my left cheekbone. My aunt still inhabits this world, but I wonder if she is already practicing for the moment she detaches from us and travels on, solo.

Perhaps the measure of our success in life is what we manage to create from the circumstance we are given. I will never know the isolating depth of Mae's pain, but only the *joie de vivre* she shaped from it.

Inspire: to breathe.

My breath is measured, in cadence with the lift and shuffle of my skis. The unbroken snow is too deep for gliding on this climb; I pause often to rest my lungs and knee. The pain has subsided, but hovers near, waiting for an opportunity to intrude again. Though the temperature drops steadily in the shade, I sweat with the exertion of ascent.

Cresting the ridge, I meet the blinding, low-angled sun. Wind has piled snow into tiny dunes that sparkle blue, red, green—colors refracted off diamonds. In the north, the snow-covered Grand Teton juts above mid-level clouds ribboning the range; past that, some seventy miles away, land rising toward the Yellowstone Plateau curves into the palm of sky. The Gros Ventres cut a jagged line in the east, while in the south and west, the Hobacks and Snake River Range buckle the horizon. The sight of so many mountains astonishes, but I have been here many times, and I am still waiting for a climax to my ski trip, a singular moment that will make me say: *This* is why I came. But there are no conventions of moose anywhere in view, no half-devoured carcasses, no unusual birds—only the faint pink of the approaching alpenglow that brings to mind Alaska, the wonder light of brief winter days.

There's still chance for a crescendo to this small adventure, though. I don't know how my knee will hold the descending turns; I don't know if I will fall, rip tendons or ligaments, and have to crawl through thick snow a long way home in the nearing dusk. I have skied on free-heel equipment for seventeen winters, but sometimes I simply *forget* how to ski; I lose the body memory of how to initiate a telemark turn, how to weight the skis. I don't know what causes the sudden reversal of ability—perhaps a lapse of body consciousness, a moment when awareness detaches from the physical self, an infusion of fear. In those moments, I have been known to crash big and bad, slide for life, cartwheel down chutes, but I have never—knock on wood—been hurt enough not to ski out on my own. Today, the knee holds my attention, but I don't know physiology well enough to understand what might snap there.

I try not to think about crawling off this ridge, injured, bleeding, in the dark, but my catastrophic imaginings have kicked into overdrive. Even the worst-case scenario I can conjure today will not stop my descent, though—I know I am playing a game, shadowboxing with my own psyche. I know I like the rush, the stimulation of scaring myself. I like approaching the margin of safety. I never intend to go beyond it, but the margin is permeable, not fixed, and passing through is the risk of getting close.

I am not yet afraid to be dead.

Once, I camped in a place I should not have been, although no signs or fences barred my way. In the night I could not sleep but knew that if I did not lie still in my bag, I might cross over to death easily. Something on the mountain diverged from ordinary circumstance and pulled me strong, and I knew if I said "yes" to it, I would just go, unremarkably, without pain. I felt no fear, lying in the gateway, just amazement at how close the other world is, how porous the barrier; and I was suddenly mindful that we constantly choose, with or without awareness, which world to inhabit. Death did not seem frightening then, but almost welcoming: the release of a small, tightly bound consciousness into the infinite, like a raindrop returning to the ocean that covers the world.

I am not afraid to be dead, but like anyone, I don't want to die too soon, or to suffer. Buddhists say that letting go of attachment is the way to freedom from suffering. I wonder if I'll ever relinquish my desire to live long and fully, without significant pain.

I will not meet death today, I think, as I pull my hat down, tuck sunglasses inside my fleece jacket, and zip the outer shell high, covering my neck. I tighten the wrist cinch on my gloves, pull the wide gauntlets over my sleeves. I do not wrap the straps of my poles around my wrists, avoiding an entrapment of equipment that can break bones if I fall badly. I slide my skis back and forth to clear any snow clumped to the bases, and then I just skate forward, as fast as I can, to pick up momentum for the first turn. Over the lip and downhill, into the shade, I drop low, remembering when I feel unsteady to bend the forward knee even deeper. I expect my knee to collapse, my ridiculously inappropriate equipment to fail but—sharp intake of breath—nothing happens.

Nothing happens, except perfect turns, easy glide between aspen, powder over my knees. My face creases into a huge smile. I carve a turn beside a pine, around an ancient fallen log. The snow hardly makes a sound as it opens for me. Mindful of my knee, but absorbed in the soft descent, I don't notice any pain. I remember a blind telemark skier I once "guided," who led me into new layers of sensation: "When you feel off-balance in a turn," he had said, "quickly slide the other ski out front. Don't wait to regain equilibrium—you might not—just move on." I float down the mountain, alternating skis, keeping my attention on the path I want to travel: between shrubs, around stumps, over snow mounds. Obstacles fly past at the edge of my awareness; I see them, but I focus on the space between: *where I want to be.*

I am thankful for skiing, and for what mountains have taught me about living.

I center my attention on the line between trees, and snake through powder to the bottom of the ridge. When I intercept the trail I had skied coming up, I stop, realizing: I did not madly crash and give myself another hair-raising story I could tell later, over and again. I chanced upon no large creatures, no skeletons, no rare birds. I had no epiphany, no singular moment.

The last light flames on the mountains. My knee aches in a tender way. In the blue shade of spruce and aspen, I hear a far-off *chick-a-dee dee-dee*.

Then: my own stillness. I realize I am holding my breath, waiting for something startling that is not going to happen. There is just this quiet, this wild joy.

I breathe the cold, suck in huge amounts of air too frigid to have a scent. Frost falls off trees, glitters in the air and lands, tickling my face. Snow settles with a soft thud beneath me. Down the trail, four enormous Douglas fir grow in steady solitude; aspen as old and large as any in this part of the country live and die without fanfare. I *know* these trees, I know the curve and draws of this land, I know the signatures of weasels and squirrels scrawled across the snow.

I will not encounter a pack of coyotes today, certainly not a bear, probably not even a single moose—but I know they are here, in their places, perhaps witnessing my passing. My skin tingles. Hair lifts slightly off the back of my neck. A brief fluttering, like a finger or a breath, barely touches my left cheek.

In this life, I have often prided myself on exploring outside my comfort zone, believing that separating from what I already know offers the most fertile ground for growth. I have often detached from places, family, friends, and lovers, imagining that in the next adventure, the next exotic place, the next remarkable person, I will expand my range, discover my wholeness. About to turn forty-three, perhaps I am a little late recognizing that quiet familiarity can invigorate senses as well as danger, overstimulation, or strangeness. Perhaps I've taken a circuitous journey only to find that risking intimacy with self and place, family and friends requires no less courage than venturing out.

From here, the trail winds through pale aspen back to the house where my partner and dog will soon be returning. I will ski down to welcome them, today's small tale already gathering on my tongue. I breathe in, inhale deeply, and set my skis in the rough track, push off, and glide toward home in a rhythm only mine.

LAURA WATERMAN

Climbing with Margaret

SHE STOPPED MOVING UPWARD. Time spun itself out so that tasks she knew took only a second, such as placing an ice ax, took hours. Stalled, she leaned out on her tools and looked up at the sky, dark and scabbed with hard stars. Her eyes moved to the soft void on her right, blank and without sound.

She let her arms hang out in her wrist loops, dropped her head forward to touch the ice. She wasn't using the rope, but it was in her pack. Her head repeated: *partners belay partners belay partners* with such tedium it made her gag.

A voice! It nearly tipped her backward and she felt wild from the adrenalin as she caught herself. Where am I? That voice sounded so high and weak. It made her laugh! She rested her head again on the raw flank of the mountain until her brow went numb. She made herself kick in her left crampon and the ice cracked like brittle bone. "Damn you, Margaret," she said.

She had arrived in Talkeetna first, as they had planned, and began repacking the food. She expected Margaret in two days. But she wasn't on the passenger van that arrived from Anchorage. She called the university where Margaret taught and someone with a voice like crushed ice told her, "Didn't you hear? Professor Simon was in an accident last night on her way to the airport. A tractor-trailer jumped the median. It took out several cars."

No, she hadn't heard. Was she . . . ? "Not dead," the voice said. "Professor Simon is in a coma. Her spine is broken. They fear brain damage."

She returned to the building where she had left their gear and walked around, touching things, bending to pick up fragments of herself. Ropes, snow pickets, carabiners, ice screws, webbing, rock gear, stoves, pots, fuel, their tent, their sleeping bags—ready for climbing. Her eyes felt parched.

She had had herself flown in anyway. After all, it was to be their fiftieth-birthday climb.

Time slid back to normal and she continued climbing. After a while, she knew Margaret had reached the alcove and was waiting there. Or perhaps she wouldn't wait, but would keep just ahead, hedged behind the dark. She heard the soft *thunk*, *thunk* of Margaret's tools, and imagined Margaret's hands gripping the shafts, relaxed in the wrist loops. She felt the power of Margaret's surging swing vibrate down her own arm.

The alcove: where the avalanche caught them last time. Not a direct hit, just a sideswipe when the snow slope slid. She was belaying under a skimpy rock overhang and had a gallery seat when a Niagara-like rush of snow and ice spewed in front of her nose and out onto the glacier, creating a mound the size of a New England hill. "Margaret! Margaret!" "Fay! Fay!" Their cries rang in the turbulent air, dense with snow dust. She had fully expected the rope to go slack and was surprised not to see Margaret whirl by, a cartwheel of arms and legs and ice chunks. "Heck, Fay, it missed me by fifty feet, easy. Just noisy, that's all. I was more concerned about you. It was big!"

The avalanche creamed their route, removing all their anchors and fixed ropes, which they discovered when they began rappelling. Not an ice screw remained. They were two-thirds of the way up the mountain.

They had lost too much to improvise with scanty gear, and after that, they had to admit they were too undone to go on.

Her eye caught the headlight of a star skidding toward her, and she clenched her tools, in a panic over being nudged into nothingness. She saw the tractor-trailer, lit up for night travel, blasting the median. She clawed to her left, crampons screeching. Her tongue turned to sawdust in her mouth, and she smelled her own bitter sweat. Cars were upturned, scattered like jackstraws. The New England hill hardened into a concrete burial mound.

"'The Alaska Range is not for sissies.' That's what some climber told me, Fay, after my slide show. Oh God!" Margaret laughed. "The Alaska Range makes me go weak in the knees faster than I can sink an ice screw."

They had hooted their way up a whole summer of routes with this line. Mouths caked dry down into their throats. Hands sweating inside gloves, feet freezing in damp socks, minds riding high on animal instinct. How they both loved it. How she still loved it.

The stars dimmed. She paused and pushed her cuff back to check the time. The liver spots on the back of her hand glowed faint as phosphorus.

She looked up. It was light enough now to see the outline of the overhang. Her heart caught. Its form had lived in her nighttime thoughts for so long. The way the rock tunneled into the snow slope, making a cave-like space tall enough to stand in if you were short, then sloping to a crawlspace at the back. Exactly the same.

She scrambled up, her crampons biting into the firm snow under the overhang. She had stood right *here* to belay Margaret. The crack she'd slotted a chock into was—she fell to her knees and crawled to the back of the alcove, reached to rub rime off the rock—here. She tore off her glove and ran her bare fingers into the rough crack. It had been five years.

"But I can stop right here," she said aloud, on her knees before the crack. The rock dug into her fingers. Margaret was ahead, on the upper snow slopes. It was getting light now.

"After all, Fay," she heard Margaret's voice, "we're perfect. You teach writing with all that woolgathering and horsing around of imagination, and I keep us solid with math and logic."

She, Fay, was an Easterner; precisely, a New Englander who taught in a college town of white clapboard buildings set on a village green. Joe taught there too. Fay arranged her classes in order to be home when her children came home. She could be counted on to make pies for church suppers. But she could see that the folks she ran into at the post office felt uncomfortable with her peeling nose and raw brow. *Rash* was the word she picked up on the supermarket line. It made her smile at her weather-browned hands.

Margaret had spent four years in a New England college, which was where they had met and first climbed together. Then she had returned to Berkeley.

"You're more rooted than I am," Fay told Margaret, "and if we didn't climb together every summer that would be the end of us." She watched Margaret's hands in the Cascades, the Alps, once in the Andes, one holding the pot steady, the other stirring the dinner, the skin taut and fine-lined as an etching. Hairline thin, white scars.

The two of them had gone climbing even when her children were small, even when Joe said two weeks was his limit. Then he changed his mind. "We love canned spaghetti, Fay. Take three."

Margaret never had kids. She hardly had a husband. "Oh, Richard?" Fay heard impatience and saw Margaret's eyes clench whenever his name came up. Then she'd laugh. "Gave him up for climbing." Margaret let go of nonessentials, going through her climbing pack in the Purcell Range, tossing out a sweater, a fistful of rock gear, half her gorp. "Hasn't been used in the last three days. Gets dumped. Too burdensome." Yet on that trip, Margaret pulled out dry mittens when Fay soaked hers.

Margaret, fitting her fingers into narrow cracks, slotting chocks as precisely as a surgeon, climbing the hard bits fast, placing her left foot, then the right, one time only. If Margaret could lead the pitch, Fay knew she could follow. They were the same size.

She hadn't called Joe after she found out. He wouldn't have asked her to come home, but just hearing his ordinary voice would have put an end to it.

Back in Talkeetna when the notion not to go through with the climb struggled to surface, she had squashed it down. Stomped on it, as her kids would say. Because if she had paused to consider her options, like a rational human, she would have given the whole thing up. Now wasn't the time to come to grips with what had happened to Margaret. So, all she had to do was keep on track, like a lioness out for a night's hunt, keeping to the scent, not letting in details that didn't pertain. She had never done anything like this. She wasn't a solo climber. But, that was the thing: She didn't consider this a solo ascent.

She crawled back from the crack and pushed up. Her knees had stiffened from kneeling too long. She stood in the alcove, took off her pack and stowed her headlamp, which she had never turned on. "That was a damn fool thing, to climb without your light, Fay." Margaret's mother-hen tone. Fay saw Margaret's fingers rake off her hat and push through tangled black hair, through that central plume of snowy-egret white.

Her right elbow ached and she pumped her arm once or twice, feeling the tendon resist. Below, a shadow welled, but far out on the earth's rim heaved countless mountains, frosted peaks in pale pink rows.

She yawned in the cloudless dawn and shut her eyes, weary but strong after a night of climbing. She stretched, arms raised, standing at the mouth of the alcove. "I'm still good at this," she said aloud to Margaret.

After the avalanche they had backed off to the Wind Rivers, the Tetons, blaming their retreat on cranky knees, stiff wrists, reluctant elbows and shoulders. But this Alaskan mountain adhered to their minds like ice to rock.

She hunched on her pack and felt the crushing weight of the rope. Separately they had run their East and West Coast hills with packs of rocks, training for the fiftieth-birthday climb. Spent hours on the phone.

As she moved to the lip of the alcove she spotted the sling looped over a horn of rime-crusted rock. She knelt again and removed her pack. Bleached to dull rust, the sling was frayed and stiff and tore away lichen when she peeled it off. She held it in her gloved hands and time spun out again. Margaret was bending to sling the rock, rigging the rappel with her largest red sling, after the avalanche, when they were together again. Fay stuffed the sling in her pack. It smelled so cold here, like the inside of a meat locker. Her knees groaned when she pushed up with her palms.

Then she backed out of the alcove. Moved onto the snow slope, and adjusted her tools for climbing. She stood a moment on her front points, looking up, scanning the high slopes for safety, for a dark speck moving. The summer was dry, the snow well consolidated. The sun bounced off the snow's surface, blocking her vision. *Thunk, thunk.* Margaret was ahead, moving for the summit. And she was following.

Margaret wasn't on the summit. She searched the sheltered side of the boulders. Margaret wasn't sprawled on the snow with the gorp bag open, hat askew, sweat beads like jewels on her upper lip, tan hand offering the canteen. "Drink, Fay, to another strong mountain!"

She let the wind push and tug and rattle her clothing. Her ungloved hand sprang out to ridges, vanishing into farther ridges, kaleidoscopic in the glittering light. She had never felt so alive.

Margaret must be behind, still on the route. In the darkness it was easy to pass her by. "That's logical, Fay." Margaret's soothing voice in the wind steadied her.

Her eyes smarted and she bit her knuckles. Her teeth chattered even though she was soaked in sunlight. That summer in the Cascades when every summit had been in clouds, Margaret had said, "What the hell, Fay, who said we climb for just the views?"

They had planned to rappel and downclimb the route anyway. She couldn't possibly miss that snowy-egret crest on the way down. She would have to guard against knocking off loose rocks, chunks of snow and ice, with Margaret below her now.

On the sixth rappel—she counted to keep her mind alert—the biner gate the rope passed through wavered. She watched it open and shut, open and shut, from the tension, like a wagging finger. She had forgotten to lock it. She hated rappelling.

She watched the rope slide around in the curve of the biner, gaining on the gate, backing off. She felt a white heat in her head that made the biner glisten a foot tall, remembering when Margaret fell down that snow slope in the Selkirks with nothing in. An easy slope. Fay had been taking in the view, paying out rope in a dreamy way. Then, out of the edge of her eye, she had caught Margaret shooting by, like a sack of laundry. She had dug in her boots and braced herself, more as a way to pass the time than anything else. Her anchor hadn't been up to this. Then her vision had cleared and she could distinguish each snow crystal on her gloves as she let run a deliberate length of rope. Slowly, she clamped down the belay.

"You hauled me out of the rinse/spin cycle," Margaret had hooted, safe, back in their tent, their thin voices shrill and high, six candles blazing.

The high, bright light dimmed. The glacier was in shadow when her feet touched it and there was a cold wind. The last light flicked over the summit. By now the wind up there had blown away her footprints.

She started walking toward the tent, feeling cold. Her jacket smelled of wet, metallic cold. She could see—yes!—a hand waving out of the tent door, jerking like red flagging in the bitter glacial wind.

Climbing! "As close as we'll come to flying," Margaret said after every climb. "Just like you New Englanders say every fall, 'I've never seen the foliage *this* beautiful!'"

"We mean it, always," Fay said.

"So do I," Margaret answered. They were in the tent on a mountain, drinking tea with sugar, cold fingers wrapped around warm cups and grinning like kids on Saturday.

A great darkness welled up, obscuring the glacier, ensnaring her feet. She was closer now, and saw steam from the cook pot wafting out the tent door.

Professor Simon is in a coma, the crushed-ice voice had said. Coma: a dark, hard land where move after move is at the limit of ability. Then an endless drop.

She was worn now. The ache in her knees made her stop in her tracks, and she pressed gloved hands to the sides of her face. She felt her eyes swell, then a stream was moving down her cheeks, over her chin, soaking her gloves. She was safe, but a panic rode in her throat. She began to run, smearing tears with her wet gloves, blinking back darkness, lurching toward the flapping tent.

KAREN WARREN

November Sojourn

At the Marcy Dam trail junction, I casually sipped from my water bottle as I eavesdropped on the conversation between the Adirondack ranger and two hikers. I had watched with curiosity as the ranger approached the two men dressed in flannel, jeans, and lightweight hiking boots on that wintry November day. My years of leading outdoor trips had raised a red flag when I saw how they were prepared for a demanding cold-weather hike. "Cotton kills," I had told countless students over the years. I was glad to see that the ranger was going to do his job.

"Where you headed?" Roy, the backcountry ranger, asked the two hikers.

"Thought we'd do Marcy," one replied. Mount Marcy, at 5,344 feet, is the centerpiece of the High Peaks region of the Adirondacks and, while not a technical climb, demands a keen eye to changing weather conditions during this time of the year. *Great*, I thought to myself, *no daypacks, no water, no margin for error.*

"Good day for it," said Roy, falling into that coffee-shop repartee reserved for locals. "The weather is supposed to hold."

"Yup, heard it from the waitress down at the Noonmark," the taller one continued. As they amiably chatted, I wondered if I'd be involved in a rescue sometime during the weekend.

What brings me out in the late November chill each year? Sometimes it's an urge to cheat the icy rain of western Massachusetts by finding the sacred grail of new teleskiing snow in northern Vermont or the White

Mountains. Other years it's end-of-semester burnout; too many day trips, too many student evaluations to write, too many phone calls to return. After facilitating countless consensus decisions at trailheads, put-ins, and campfires, I'm so used to advocating for participants' needs that I'm numb to my own. A consensus of one forces me to decide what I want.

Most times I want to pause to take stock of my life from a perspective that only comes when I'm alone in the woods. One year, spurred on by my partner, I went out with the very specific reason of figuring out if I wanted a child in my life. Here was the adventuring woman, who five years earlier had disdained the permanency of a credit card and a car loan, now trying to decide about a child. I choked so hard it took another year and another November sojourn before I had the courage to broach the subject again.

Something entices me to make the pilgrimage each year. The sweet memory of graceful teleturns I left in the spring snow comes to me as I sit in meetings. The image of austere peaks, with their cutting wind and vast whiteness, sticks in my imagination weeks before as I read papers or organize the skis in the equipment room. Or the lure of losing myself by bushwhacking in my own backyard, the Berkshires, finds me with the first November gray. Rarely do I plan beforehand where I'll go. Intuition tells me what outdoor gear to toss into my truck on the morning of departure, including a huge stuff sack of topos to cover all the possibilities my whim might consider.

That November, snowshoes and skis littered the truck bed uselessly. I had come to the Adirondacks to ski but the fine dusting of white on the ground was even too thin for my "rock" skis. A new plan was needed; I perched on the tailgate and studied the map.

Some people's dreams of outdoor adventure begin with stories of intriguing places, others with breathtaking color photos of wilderness scenes. Me, I'm a map dreamer. I can fantasize adventure in the dense, brown, spaghetti contour lines of any topographical sheet. Pulse quickening, my eyes dart to the most remote peaks on the quad, searching for the ridgeline route up.

Mount Marcy commanded the center of the map. While I told myself I wasn't into peak-bagging, Marcy is the highest of the range and solitary summit stands have always held a certain romance. It was an easy decision.

These were some of the thoughts I had that morning in the Adirondacks as I screwed the top on my Nalgene bottle and watched Roy finish his banter with the two ill-prepared hikers. His parting words were a caution. "There's probably some ice up there on top," yet overall his tone had been more conversational than admonishing. I was a little surprised he wasn't more assertive about the potential dangers they faced. Maybe he didn't see that as his job.

Roy turned his attention to me. He eyed me suspiciously, giving me the once-over before uttering a word. He reminded me of a field mouse sniffing furtively around my pack to determine its contents.

"Where you headed?" It seemed this was Roy's primary conversation starter.

"I thought I'd hike up to Indian Falls and camp," I said, never quite knowing how much information to give when I'm out alone. Since he was a backcountry ranger I figured he might be useful as an emergency backup so I divulged more than usual.

"What's in your pack?" he quizzed me curtly.

Oh no, I thought. *Here it comes; that condescending tone reserved for women outdoors that I have heard too many times in my twenty years of instructing in the field.* It takes different forms, but the theme's the same each time. Once it was the Canyonlands ranger who, when I asked him to tell me the way into Virginia Park, spread my map out before my male student co-leader and traced the route for him. Oftentimes it's an outfitter on the phone whose tone says I first have to convince him I'm qualified to lead the river trip before he'll even talk shuttle prices.

"Camping gear," I said matter-of-factly, yet steeling myself for the next question, now uncomfortable about the intrusion. Didn't he see my layers of nylon and polypropylene, my broken-in Sorrels, my worn backpack? My gear didn't look as if I'd just taken the tags off. Didn't I look as if I belonged in the woods? Was his scrutiny because I was a woman or an outsider or alone? Or all three?

"How long are you out? Are you planning to hike up Marcy? You can't do Marcy without crampons, instep crampons at a minimum. Do you have instep crampons?"

"No," I replied, feeling myself beginning to lose my voice amid the barrage of questions. I resisted the urge to tell him not to worry, that I was perfectly capable of taking care of myself out there. I resisted because to prove my competence meant he had the right to question it. I resisted because at that moment I began to wonder if I was capable. All the doubts that I've heard and assimilated came welling to the surface.

"You can't do Marcy without instep crampons," Roy repeated.

"I'm not sure I'm climbing Marcy," I said. "I'll have to see how it goes."

"I was up there yesterday; the last two hundred yards are a sheet of ice. You'll need instep crampons to keep from slipping off." Did he think I hadn't heard him?

"Okay," I said. Then, trying to divert him from instep crampons, I asked, "Are there any other shelters in the High Peaks area?" and gestured to a three-sided log lean-to by the lake. I wondered because I was considering bringing students to the Adirondacks later that winter, and shelters make a good base camp for beginning winter campers.

Big mistake.

"They've taken the shelters out of the Indian Falls area. Too much overuse." He paused. "Do you have a tent?"

"No. I mean, I'm not carrying one." Tired of the inquisition, I wasn't about to tell him I preferred a nylon tarp for its light weight and the closeness to the snow it gave me.

"Well, these are the only shelters on your route."

"That's good to know. Probably should be going," I said, shouldering my backpack. "Nice to meet you," I lied.

"Same here. Be careful out there," Roy said as I walked away. Careful of what? Sexist rangers?

It would take me halfway to Indian Falls before I stopped processing my interaction with Roy. As I trudged up the trail, I probed my anger at his assumptions, making sure it was still raw to the touch. When anger no longer worked, I tried denial. I kept letting Roy off the hook—he was just doing his job, he was of the old school and couldn't be expected to treat women the way contemporaries treat me. Finally, I settled on doubt. Perhaps I should have been more communicative about my ability. Maybe I did need crampons; so why was I going any farther without them? What I experienced was the age-old polarity for women: the vacillation between doubting and believing.

The antics of a chickadee darting in and out of the balsam fir boughs finally brought me back to the present. I began to notice that the snow had deepened, that it was a full-fledged winter at this higher altitude. I moved from the noise inside me to the immense silence outside. The crystal cascading stream, the snow-clotted firs, the solitude reminded me why I love to winter camp.

Winter is my best time of reflection; the season demands introspection. Clear silent air, clear spirit voice. There is some magic in the silent winter that untangles my feelings and thoughts and brings me to my center. Perhaps it is a transcendence where I move from myself to the broader, comprehensive cycles of the earth. When exposed to those cycles, I witness a truth, an inspiration that helps me understand my own life. I have little to compare it to. In yoga, the meditative breath allows me to nourish my spine, the center of my body; in Quaker meeting, the shared silence gathers my energy of introspection and translates it through a community voice. Each has elements but neither compares. In the winter woods, my kinesthetic body joins my aesthetic spirit to create an apex of communion with self and the natural community.

Winter aloneness sparks my exuberance. I dance with Orion and my Seven Sisters, two-step with Cassiopeia across the darkened treeline. I leap and pirouette with twinkling power-points of stars composed in winter shapes. I search for the best of myself when I'm out alone in the winter.

When I'm with others on trips we fall into an easy camaraderie based on a necessary interdependence. The wilderness allows a magnanimousness about the foibles of others that just doesn't happen in the superficial world of appointment calendars and speedy goodbyes while walking away backward. It is precisely that relationship I have experienced with others that I try to find for myself when I do a solo trip. I search to like myself in the way I love those with whom I share a cup of tea around the campfire, a Class III run in a loaded canoe, or a glimpse of mountain goat babies on the open ridge.

I arrived at Indian Falls at dusk. I set up camp and cooked dinner, nestling down comfortably into my aloneness. I used my ensolite to scoop out a sleeping depression in the snow and pitched my tarp over it. I hollowed out a candleholder in the walls of my snow nest, later marveling at the intense light given off by one candle. Periodic thoughts of my morning encounter were contained by my delight at being out again in winter's sparse environment.

The deliberateness of winter camping astounds me—so organized and recipe-like. At night I am the Julia Child of the tarp as I carefully measure out each ingredient that will insure my warmth. I prepare the sleeping bag, rolling out a thick slab of down, letting it rise until double in bulk. I correct the positioning of my ensolite so I can't slip off during the night. Blending dry socks with down booties, then folding in an extra wool shirt around my feet, I stuff my legs into the bag next to the water bottle I want to keep from freezing. On nights when I'm a culinary master, I spice the water bottle with hot water to blanch my feet as I fall asleep. Zip to my waist. Rotating my upper layers so the sweat-soaked one is not next to my skin, I whisk my pile shirt around my waist to keep my midsection and kidneys at a low rolling boil. Coat the foot of my sleeping bag with my parka. Wedge my boots under my body so they won't freeze but not too much that they make a sleep-discouraging lump under my knees. Please, no icky lumps. Zip to my chin. Reserve gorp close by to stoke my metabolism to a simmer at two am. Mixing equal parts pulled drawstring and tightened hat, I add a weather-stripping garnish to the hole with my scarf or neck gaiter. Preheating my body with isometric exercises, I sift into sleep anticipating a night of *The Joy of Cooking* warmth.

Over breakfast the next morning, I decided I had to attempt Marcy. Like a compass needle to magnetic north, the mountain pulled me. I had to know if Roy was right. Yet I would only go as far as I felt safe. Nothing heroic.

As I slowly slogged up the approach to Marcy I thought about what I teach my outdoor leadership class about risk management. Accidents in the outdoors rarely happen without some accumulation of risks or mistakes. Card-stacking, I call it. A card is piled up for each risk factor that predicates an accident. A card for improper equipment, one for fatigue, another for dehydration, maybe another for being out alone and so on. By itself, each factor doesn't cause an accident but when piled high, the stack eventually collapses. The risks become a calamity. The trick, I advise the students, is to continually unstack the pile so it can't topple.

The trick for me on solo adventures is to remember my own advice. I couldn't let my encounter with Roy impede my judgment, neither trying for the summit to prove him wrong nor turning back because of the doubt he cast on my experience. In the card game of risk management I'm convinced that if ego is the joker, then intuition is my ace in the hole. I would go with what I knew to be right for me.

As I neared treeline, I wondered what Roy had been so cautious about. The way up had been steep but it had been easy enough to kick steps into the snow. Then I poked my body out of the trees, popping abruptly above treeline. I was taken aback by the power of the wind. It howled fiercely, polishing the mountain top to an icy glare. The sides of the mountain dropped off steeply. A wrong step could create a fatal fall. Falling into the great abyss, I often tell my students.

I could make out the summit cairn. I was tempted to go for the top, wanting to finish, to prove it could be done. I had trudged for too many hours to be this close and not complete the climb. I figured there were probably places behind the rocks littering the cone where the wind hadn't buffed a slippery surface. I might be able to connect these protected pockets to make my way to the top. But with nothing to hold on to, I would risk the wind blowing me across the slickness, out of control. I mentally ran through a few more possibilities but they all added up to an equation of wind and ice and steepness. The cards were stacked too high.

Marcy's grand view was not to be for me this time. I scanned the summit once more and turned back. As I descended, I wondered if I could tell people when I returned home that I had climbed Mount Marcy. A peak-bagger would scoff, while a Taoist might say that simply being with the mountain was what was important. For me, it was a question without an answer.

When I first saw the shining, bare cap of Marcy gleaming like a full moon in the winter light I knew Roy had been only partially right. He was correct about the icy top, but not about the crampons. I had found it wasn't instep crampons I needed. More important was to be out there alone, believing in myself, trusting my intuition, finding my center. Strapping on instep crampons could make me no safer or surer than I was at that moment.

ALICE EVANS

At My Own Speed

How many times had I set out to climb a mountain with my husband, only to find myself climbing the mountain alone?

The truth is, that suited me just fine. We had such different ideas about why we were climbing the mountain. He always wanted, or needed, to get to the top as fast as he could. The peak was not only goal, but necessity.

Usually, I didn't care if I reached the top. I liked to get there, but I didn't have to. I wanted, or needed, to stop along the way and look at rocks. Flowers. Gnarled junipers. Darting rodents. Glacial lakes. Clouds. I wanted, or needed, to stop and take out a book of poetry. Snap photographs. Jot notes in my journal.

Sometimes, perhaps often, I felt judgmental toward my husband and his abandonment. Always the forced march, never the act of discovery. His wildness was expressed through fast, hard movement. I couldn't keep up with him. His heart-lung capacity far exceeded my own.

And so I didn't try to hold him back, past a certain point. He would wait for me, periodically. We would speak for a few moments. Maybe share a snack. Then he would move on ahead. And I would climb alone, at my own speed.

Such was the existential state of our marriage. Each of us climbing the same mountain, traveling the same path, but going it alone.

Then came a day when we began climbing different mountains. Separately. Perhaps the change had something to do with raising a child, a child who would often climb with us, but who would just as often refuse to go along.

We had gone to the Oregon Caves National Monument for Labor Day weekend, a journey that was becoming a tradition. South on the interstate to Grants Pass, then southwest on Redwood Highway, then southeast on the long, steep road that led us deep into the Siskyou Mountains. At the head of the steep valley, where the road ended, stood a six-story lodge planked with enormous slabs of cedar. A dozen yards from the lodge door, a bear-sized crack in the marble cliff opened into miles of cave.

The morning after our arrival, we left our warm nest in the wood-lined lodge and toured the cave. Our daughter, Ursula, stayed right with the guide as he called out low bridges, pointed out favorite formations, and warned us not to touch the marble walls, lest we leave destructive body grease.

After the half-mile hike underground, I was ready to hike through the complex ecosystem of the Siskyous, one of the continent's oldest mountain ranges. Ten-year-old Ursula refused. "Well, maybe after a good lunch," I coaxed. "Well, maybe," she conceded.

Into the coffee shop. Fir counters. Mirror-lined walls. Revolving seats. Order up milkshake. Chili. Saltines and pickles. Hamburgers. Fries. Candy bars. Now, are we ready?

Ursula refused to climb the mountain.

Okay, negotiation. I haven't busted free all summer, while you, Jon, have taken any number of weekend hikes up Cascade peaks. It's my turn. You stay with Ursula. I'll climb the mountain alone. Be back in time for supper, before six, before the coffee shop closes. Too expensive to eat in the dining room a second night. Too much food.

I climbed up to our fourth-floor room, collected my backpack, and packed in three bottles of water. Packed in Barry Lopez's new collection of short stories, *Field Notes*, which I was reviewing for a local arts weekly.

Goodbye. I'm on my way up Mount Elijah. Mad as hell but on my way. Nobody wants to go with me. I'll go alone. Damned if I'll spend all day sitting by the pool watching trout. Damned if I'll spend my whole summer serving other people at the bookstore while no one serves me. Huh! Who serves *me*? Now, here I am in the woods, and no one to walk with. Well, isn't that usually the way it is? Haven't I usually gone alone into wilderness, when it comes right down to it? Nobody's taking these steps for me. Nobody's making these butt muscles move. Nobody but me.

I'm heading up Mount Elijah. I'm going so fast I can't even see the plants except as flashes of color, variegated leaves, nodding stems. I acknowledge the dark humus of rotting logs, the heart-shaped fungus like spectators lining the path, cheering me on, as I charge up the mountain. Jon couldn't climb this fast if he wanted to. Ursula, that little sass who dances by me fast as feathers, faster than Jon even, she couldn't keep up with this pace. No way. I'm on my mountain. I'm going up my mountain. Haven't I always loved the Siskyous? Haven't I always said the Siskyous remind me of the Appalachians, the mountains of my childhood? Haven't I always said I take power from these mountains, they feed me?

All right, I'm at the Big Tree. One-point-eight miles and I'm already here. Thirty minutes, at five thousand feet. I must be in shape. Usually I'd be gasping for breath. I'm not even breathing hard. I'll stop here and put my arms around the largest Douglas fir in Oregon and kiss its thick bark. Tree big as a redwood. Old as a redwood. Maybe fifteen hundred years. Big Tree says, *Move, move on up the mountain, you can do it, you can be big.*

I'm a-going, Big Tree. I'm passing two men, panic flashing through my body. I'm always afraid to meet men deep in the woods, all alone. *Breeze on by them*, Big Tree says. *Be friendly but don't stop. Keep on going, go by so fast they don't have a chance to realize you're alone, and by the time they do, you're way on by, they'll never catch you, not the way you're moving.*

Moving faster than the clouds, you are, faster than the Earth, with Big Tree pushing you. Moving on up, one more mile, two more miles, past the boundaries of the National Monument, into the Siskyou National Forest. Nobody's going to be coming up here, not today. Just you, honey. All alone.

The theme for the park this year is biodiversity, Big Tree. Big Tree, do you hear me? Are you still with me? Last night the ranger was talking about how old the area is, how unusually complex the interconnections between plants and animals. Rare plants, here. The last stand for some. I'm so glad they're preaching this at last. Twenty years ago, when I studied ecology, hardly anyone spoke this language. Now, the visitors to the park are being educated. Maybe there's hope, Big Tree. Keep on going. Up the mountain. Maybe there's hope.

What about the book review I planned to work on this weekend? Time to stop. Read another story. I love the words of Barry Lopez. This one, called "The Runner," is about a brother who suddenly wants to reconnect with his sister. She turns out to have a special relationship with the Grand Canyon, deeply spiritual, magical even. She discovers lost Anasazi trails and caves that contain their pottery. She runs the pathways of the deer and the Anasazi, and leaps the Colorado River at will.

Well, I am off again, the book in my backpack, the words in my mind, Big Tree behind me, pushing me on. Goodbye, Big Tree, goodbye.

I'm not running, but I am moving, hard and fast, up to the top of the ridge, then along it, then again along the steep section of path that begins the ascent up Mount Elijah. I have already decided I will turn back at 4:00. Otherwise, we'll end up eating in the dining room again. But I've come this far. It's what, another twenty minutes to the top? Make it thirty. Forty-five? I'll do it in fifteen. Something's behind me. Something's urging me to move.

Moving this hard, I'm sweating hard, too. But I don't want to stop. I've broken out into the sunlight. I'm free of the trees. I'm starting to get a clear view of mountains. And clear-cuts. Mountains. And clouds. Clouds, and clear-cuts. I take the pack from my back as I move. I unzip the pack as I move. I take out the flask as I move. I unscrew the cap as I move. I drink the water as I move, hard and fast, hard and fast, up the mountain.

What is that pounding in the distance? I thought I had this mountain all to myself. What is that pounding? Drumming. Voices. Chanting. A group of people, already there, on Mount Elijah, drumming and chanting. It's 4:25. It's taken me three hours to climb, what?—five miles up this mountain. I'm five minutes from the top, and if I go up there, if I sit and rest and take it all in, I'll have an hour and twenty minutes, maybe, to get to the bottom of the mountain before the coffee shop closes.

And what's up ahead there? Who's that drumming? I feel something pulling me now, when all along I thought I was being pushed. Now, a pulling. I'm moving these last few hundred yards, over ancient stone. Lichen-colored stone. Past gnarly madrone, toward the people who are drumming, chanting, on top of Mount Elijah.

I see them. They see me. A white-haired man, hair spilling over his shoulders, beard dragging across the top of his drum. A woman dressed in animal skins. Two small children in animal skins. Another man, younger, with dark hair spilling to his waist, likewise dressed in animal skins. Lord be. They see me. I see them. We behold one another. The man stops drumming. He wraps the drum in a leather bag. The others move toward me.

They are leaving the mountain. We are changing places. They are giving me the mountain. They have held the mountain long enough, and now it's my turn. The young man asks me to name the mountains we can see around us. "Mount Shasta, to the south." He knows that already. "The Trinity Alps." He knows that too. "The Marble Mountains?" Yes, he nods. "Over there, the Kalmiopsis Wilderness." "No, that's over there," he says. Why is he asking? He knows more than I do. "Yes," he says. "It's one hundred, maybe two hundred miles south to the next major road." I nod. He walks away.

The children are thirsty. They ask their mother for something to drink. "We have nothing," she says. I take out one of my two remaining flasks and hand it to her. "Take this," I say. "I have plenty." "Thank you," she says. The children smile. I walk toward the absolute peak.

The older man has finished putting away his drum. He points to two black forms moving through the clearing on a distant slope. "We thought they might be bears," he says. "Or range cattle. But we think they're bears." "Yes," I say. "I think you're right. They're bears." He smiles and picks up his drum. He moves on down the mountain.

I have forgotten about time. I sit where he was sitting. I watch the bears. I peruse the distant peaks. Mt. Shasta shining in the sunlight. The Trinity Alps have lost their snow, so late in the year. The Marble Mountains, no snow now. And all around me, near me, the peaks of the Siskyous, their ancient stones, their soft covering of rare plants. Clear-cuts abrading their slopes. I have forgotten about time. There is only now on this mountain. The sun dropping toward the not-so-distant sea. The drumming, still in my mind, my heart, beating, beating. Big Tree. Big Tree. A woman, running the trails of the deer and Anasazi, leaping the Colorado River. I could live here. This could be my place.

The wind blows across my face, the scent of kinnikinnick. The wind blows in my ears, I have been here forever. The wind blows through my hair, a woman alone in the wilderness. The wind blows hard against my back and I am running down the mountain, the urge to move throbbing in my blood. I am released. The mountain says, *Go now, go, the day is late, you have been here forever and now you must go.*

And so I run, stepping lightly over rocks. I run, now like a deer, now like a bear. I am running, running down the slopes of Mt. Elijah. This is where I almost turned back, I am running. This is where I stopped to pee, I am running. This is where I thought a mountain lion was watching me, I am running. This is where the trail leaves the ridge top and enters the National Monument. I am running, running past the spot where I stopped to read "The Runner." I am running, approaching the fallen fir. I am running, scrambling over the top. I am running, being pushed, being pulled, a cord of light passing through me and connecting me to the top and bottom of the mountain. I am running, like Carlos Casteneda and Don Juan, those radiant beings. I am running, from one place to another, the forms and smells and colors flashing by. I am running through the clearing where I watched the hawk. I am running down the slopes of Mount Elijah, and I can hear the voices of people at the lodge, I can hear the drumming on the mountain, I can hear the beating of my heart. And I am running past the cave entrance, past the pool of trout and into the coffee shop where the clock reads 5:55. And Jon and Ursula are sitting at the counter, waiting to order, and I am running into time.

TRICIA PEARSALL

Altitude Adjustment

HUMMINGBIRDS WAKE UP BEFORE COWS. Mother Nature is definitely in control. There is no sadness in solitude. Powdered-eggs-and-jerky omelet is yummy. Lightning does whatever it wants to. Yellow-bellied marmots are downright nosy. A man sitting in a saddle is cockier than when standing on the ground.

> *Got a gun?*
> *You got guts, lady.*
> *Cute haircut!*
> *Oh, God be with you.*
> *I wouldn't let no wife nor daughter of mine out on this trail alone!*

Just a few salvos I receive as I trudge the steep ascent entering the boulder-strewn, almost cartoon-gardened canyon formed by Williams Creek. Looks like the solo backpacking wilderness trip is becoming an annual event. Last year, it was just me for eight days in the Glacier Peak Wilderness of Washington's Cascade Range. Then, it was more the challenge: "I can do it, by myself, and this is how!" This year, well, like Thoreau said, "I went to the woods because I wished to live deliberately, to front only the essential facts of life, and see if I could not learn what it had to teach, and not, when I come to die, discover that I had not lived"—or dreamed to live! Well, that's a piece of this insatiable desire to hit the trail, and another part is to escape into the strenuous regimen and overwhelming beauty of the lonely, high western wilderness, to transfer my ruminating and digesting space from inside a dwelling to totally out of shelter.

My desire to go is also fueled by the impulsive ache to smell alpine meadows, to climb above treeline and dance among the peaks, to see original beauty, and to be affronted by credible danger—the kind that Mother Nature dishes out, not that of some "in-your-face kid" whose attitude and anger are assuaged by his very own personalized assault weapon. I live in the city, smack dab in the middle of the city.

For many summers, my husband and I and two hesitant, but polite, passive, and probably bribed male children spent annual vacations backpacking in western wildernesses. In fact, we started the kids packing in the mountains of Virginia before they were six weeks old. When I broached the idea of a family excursion this year, I received solid encouragement and support for my solo expedition. More and more we all seem to madly pursue diverging paths, intensely delving into self-interests, be they rock concerts, rock climbing, memorizing television cartoons, or creating twentieth-century showers out of nineteenth-century plumbing. My divergence, alone to the mountains, I label an altitude adjustment, chucking impossible schedules and increasingly demanding financial obligations, fleeing the inanities of the daily media feed, stopping to shake out the fuzzies, separating the essentials from the ever-surfacing, ever-present, and well-spun chaff. It's reflecting on the friend who died of breast cancer in the spring and fear for the five more who were recently diagnosed. It's regaining humor about disjointed but perhaps well-intentioned families.

It's getting acclimatized to being a half-pasture or out-to-pasture mom, adjusting to what life will be after my sons soon take off. Ever since I was sent the mother-gift, the one moms receive when we first hear the wail of our offspring, that "ton of bricks" of unfathomed responsibility and commitment to nurture, my sons have occupied my last thought at bedtime and my first in the morning. It's a frightening feeling, this mother-gift. I will mourn the absence of my sons' physical presence, celebrate their independence and adventures, and get over it and on with it, but it'll take a little adjustment, maybe more than one altitude adjustment. And now they flash to the world on their own, away to life.

The intensity of the act of going alone, of having all the colors of a field of high mountain flowers pierce my eyes alone, of being the only ears recording the pica squeals and moving boulders, means conversations are remembered; nothing is diffused in the melee of companionship. I am the sole receiver of and contributor to the experience and each instance must be remembered and logged. Space, outdoor space, allows this without any burden of guilt and for me, the need for space, slow motion, and consideration far outweighs the immediate need for sharing experience or the often lonely exhaustion of such an endeavor. It's about quietude, solace, not miles hiked or mountains climbed. The Continental Divide mountains are the luxury vehicle.

I did actually extend a few overtures for companionship, only to be rebuffed by more enticing offers, such as bell-choir rehearsal, trips to Omaha, practicing law, camp, fear, illness—any excuse. Opportunity doesn't knock often for an older-than–baby boomer. Opportunities are created. I can't wait. Who knows? Next year I may need body-part replacements. New multi-lens glasses grace my nose, and my mood swings are like bungie jumping off the New River Gorge Bridge. Some folks might suggest I go with a group, but I find the wilderness experience a very personal one, not easily shared with adult strangers. I don't relish inventing polite, stilted, idle chatter or having some superior woodswomen eyeing my mistakes or intruding on an operatic impulse.

The trail begins at the end of a fifty-mile grass plain in the Weminuche Wilderness in southern Colorado, near the border of New Mexico. Much of this grass plain was inhabited by herds of sheep and cattle, but most of the used-to-be ranches are now developments fueled by Californians and Texans who have more money than taste. Imagine a huge, maybe twenty-thousand-square-foot, baby-blue Victorian wanna-be going up in the middle of a vast, flat plain. Not a tree in sight. Just other giant, neon, house-trees, future forests of America!

Climbing steeply in fits and starts, the ascent is broken by plateaus of lush meadows and stream crossings still following the creek valley. At around ten thousand feet I break into an amphitheater of aspens, at last above the dry ponderosa forests, which are the kind of tinder that is presently helping to spread a devastating fire forty miles to the east. Aspen trees are one of the signature pleasures of these Continental Divide mountains. A light wind moves their stiff, silvery-green leaves, releasing the sensual sounds of a syncopated rain stick. In certain special places, the bark of aspen trees is a guest register for the many mountain travelers who have passed by their trunks. Aspen art is a "log" revealing the names and dates of nineteenth-century miners and sheepherders, as well as the flurry of backpackers from the 1960s to the present. On these particular trees, I can make out a few dates and initials higher up the trunks from the 1950s, maybe the 1940s, but most of the sgraffito-like inscriptions date from the 1970s and 1980s. God, my vision is the pits, though; part of this half-century transition thing. These new lens-wonders do provide clarity at a distance, but I still want to push open a window to see the real world.

I am dehydrated and exhausted, and have only hiked a few miles. It's the altitude, and once again, I am not in shape. Of course, this could be blamed on having arrived only yesterday from the humid, sea-level East Coast, but my body looks like a gravity experiment gone amuck, even though I run about four miles every other day. To combat dehydration, I must drink at least three to four quarts of treated liquid per day. This results in having to extricate my warm, tired body from the deep folds of Moby Grape, my purple sleeping bag, to pee in the middle of the night. As I squat over carefully scooped earth, I look up to the most spectacular sky I have ever seen, galaxies beyond the Milky Way; not one inch of unused dark sky.

Last night, I logged twelve-and-a-half hours of much needed sleep, only waking when a few small fragments of these volcanic mountains came tumbling down to a lower resting place. Ah, gravity and shifting earth. I also heard a large tree snap in the dry wind. Today's climb is putting me up near the treeline. I seem to be experiencing a greater energy loss than anticipated, probably due to a slight infection, which has accompanied me from home. My pack weight, though, seems amazingly well-distributed and not unreasonable. Thank you, modern technology, for these newfangled energy bars. They certainly aren't on any gourmet menu, but they do work. The only pangs of loneliness come when I discover small rubber animals, home tokens, placed by family members within little crevices throughout my pack. It's mostly the beauty of the high alpine blooms and views that feel partially lost for not being shared.

I have only encountered five people so far and two were forest service personnel scouting campsites. No fire is allowed for any reason during this dry stretch. I finally reach what I think is a perfect spot high over a snow-fed creek looking into a glacial cirque on the Continental Divide. I am very tired and only realize the next day that the perfect spot has often been occupied by irreverent horse packers, evidenced by spent ropes, tackle, sardine cans, human waste, toilet paper, and elk parts left behind. There is absolutely no reason for this abuse or careless abandon of an otherwise idyllic location. Given the opportunity, man will upset any precarious balance.

A wind shift in the mid-afternoon brings a strong, frosty breeze forecasting the regular cycle of July thunderstorms. After a night of chills, fever, and a horrid headache, I decide to lay over a day and count hummingbirds. Somebody left the sun in the closet, anyway. Sitting in a meadow below the tips of Indian paintbrush, nestled under thousands of white, yellow, blue, purple, and orange wildflowers, I have the perfect vantage point for watching these crazy birds chase each other in a game resembling a frenetic *ménage à trois*. The entire meadow whirs; there are thousands, well, maybe hundreds, of these small, hyper, flying machines. When I look straight up, the clouds move in two separate directions. Amazing. The pleasure of this "lay-about" day is complemented by the Christmas aroma of spruce and fir, and the discovery of a tall waterfall with bathing pool, a ptarmigan or grouse family, a wheezing deer, and a few invasive gray jays and Albert squirrels. And the greatest antidote to any less-than-energized day is food. Tonight, nut curry over couscous.

This crystal clear, blue-sky morning I am headed up to the Continental Divide Trail and south. Grits, cheese, and salsa! A swim in the creek and up we go! This is why I keep backpacking. Inhaling this pleasure of the high mountains is spiritual armor for the return to family and urban inanities. A moment to revel, not to share. This is why I go alone. The climb out of the trees, out of the glacial cirques, along the snow-melt, boggy lakes, through the low ground cover growing on these gravelly peaks. This is the top of the world, the summit, where the water running west empties into the Pacific Ocean and east to the Atlantic Ocean— well, sort of. The view down into the valley on the other side, to which there is no trail, reveals two large herds of grazing elk. This is the ultimate brain Drano.

On the crest, following age-old cairns, a lone horseman passes with a train of four horses, a dog, and rifle at his side.

"Where you headed?" I ask.

"Till it rains."

Looking up, a massive collection of dark, mean clouds are gathering over the northern peaks. I climb higher along the ridge and observe another storm mass to the south playing around the eastern valleys. Hey, it's only eleven in the morning. Don't sandwich me between these two weather beasts. On foot, I am keeping pace with the horseman, his plodding gait an imposed beacon, a mirage to follow. I'm hiking too fast.

I start yelling at the storms. "Screw off! Go away! Leave me alone!" I allow the horseman to fade into the mountain and climb around a mini-knife edge, a very precipitous peak. In front of me are huge cirques carved by fairly recent glaciers, snow ledges, and the instantly recognized phenomenon of monadnocks, graphically illustrating dry geological texts. Amazing rock upthrusts and valleys. It's too much to digest.

Every time I stop to wallow in the vista, focus the camera, or rearrange the pack, lightning and thunder kick me in the seat of the pants. Get moving! As I head down into a small valley punctuated by two glacial lakes, the huge rock faces behind me seem to have just been vomited from the earth, on fire, full of iron, sulfur, and other seductive minerals. I walk out over a precipice to view a sheer drop to the thirty-mile valley below. I want to stop, savor, understand. Spit! Boom! Holy S—! Close, so close! *"Stay off ridges, out of caves, and away from open meadows! Find shelter among dense, small trees in low areas."*

Across the snow fields; down the precipice; running, I finally reach a line of small bushes. I pass a lake and views, but no protection at all. The storms are closing fast, and I am running faster. My family would never believe this. Slow Mom, running with boots and pack down steep rocks and gullies and not losing it, but scared stupid! Finally a lone tree, a lightning rod. Lightning like crazy! I feel a tingling sensation in my elbows. Now, three trees. Oh, where is the group of trees considered safe? It's raining, blowing, lightning. I see it exit the dark clouds. Hit the ground. Not far away. Then much closer. Finally, more trees. A group of midget trees in a field of larger ones, and I slide into home plate, huddling for an hour or more. Every time I raise my head, I see another long snake of orange fire seeking earth between the trees. I start to count the seconds and hear an explosion before I get to one.

The night is white as the full moon rises between the down-sloping arms of the fir trees. What if all these trees were tall buildings? Does an urban backpacker see the moon with the same fixation when it plays hide-and-seek with city rooftops?

I wake up this morning with that dreaded, all-too-familiar feminine feeling, the feeling that my entire inner body is being shed in the form of heavy bulbous clots of menstrual blood. Grabbing every piece of cloth I can find within easy reach, I stuff them between my legs and make a mad dash out of my sleeping bag, out of my bivy sack, and run barefoot for the environmentally correct hole. At least get it in the right place, lest every bear within a fifty-mile radius smells the scent. I've read that the scent of a woman menstruating attracts bears, and I believe most anything I read about bears, and about snakes and about crabs for that matter. Of course if a bear did smell my scent, it would probably detect an end-of-the-line menstruating female and go on picking berries. My sleep had been seasoned with cramping, but I thought I was dreaming. After all, it has only been two weeks since the last onslaught. Well, here I am, at almost eleven thousand feet, discharging heavy menses with only three Bounty Paper Towels—Select-a-Size.

In an effort to pair down bulk and weight in my backpack, I neglected to include "feminine protection." Well, who'd a' thought? Oh, how I just love this transition to the "golden years"—sex without worry, to estrogen or not to estrogen, calcium, oh calcium. I've been in female denial since I was thirteen, anyway, and I am only months from fifty. I still hate/resent the uncertainty and power of the female organs, that part of my body I do not commune with easily. Another hammer on the nail into feminine endurance. Imagine men putting up with this shit. I am well-prepared for all phases of this expedition, except for this, for which I am woefully unprepared, angry, and frustrated.

All day, I hike down out of the mountains to a grassy plateau. Miles of grassland extend beyond to a large lake. Somewhere near the lake, cattle are grazing. From the sound of it, one must be a bull. As I fall asleep, I watch the sun expose the over-twelve-thousand-foot peak above my head, giving a turquoise backdrop to the sky behind delicate orange clouds. They part to expose the planets, the galaxies of the setting sky lost to a full moon rise.

I don't know myself very well. I need fifty more years. This trip, it's just rain in the desert, fast, furious, intense, over shortly and barely enough to dampen the roots—but it's all there is until next season, all over for this year. Back to urban dangers, back to routine, back to the urban kitchen, back to solo urban ventures.

He wants to go around the corner, out, for supper? I don't mind cooking at all, in fact I'd rather. We can't afford to go out, anyway. He begs me to suit myself and saunters into the air-conditioned front room, taking his vodka tonic and newspapers with him.

I hurry back to the hot kitchen with relief. Reaching for the wooden cutting board, I begin to pare the garlic and onions into tiny cubes, the basic elements of the additive, the more-than-staple which will turn the beans, the soaked black beans, into a desirable, delectable, almost superlative offering for just another daily supper. Onion essence wafts upward to my nose and eyes. I am shedding tears, sobbing, at last allowed, without rebuke or even slight humiliation, to wash out the emotions of a day. This has been not just another roller-coaster day of fractured focus, but my son's graduation day, filled with a special blend of raging pride in my child's coming of age and achievements never dreamed or expected. Choking in view of others would be confirmation of assumed weakness. It is easier to be robbed of such earned emotions.

The rhythm of dicing the green chilies soothes the difficult, exhausting realization that the role of nurturer, of stimulant, of stalwart has terminated with the maturity revealed in the child today. Gently swirling the onions, garlic, and chilies in the olive oil, breathing in the expanding odors of the heated cumin and cilantro, I move toward a wakening inside me that must be seized lest I become a library of written moments. I pick up the wooden spoon to toss pork into the mixture and turn to see a silver wolf sitting inside the back door, brought by the currents of a past so extraordinary as not to accept a future of less.

I bend down to pick up the corn, to strip its sheath to its kernels while the wolf comes to rest the fur of its full torso next to my legs. The warmth of its strength gives me comfort in expelling the tears of realization, in adjusting to an empty change. I smile, accepting the tranquil pace of shucking each naked ear of corn, which I place in a large pot of water on the stove.

As I quarter small tomatoes, I am overcome with a sense of good fortune to encounter this silver wolf, to inhale yet again the fields, streams, and woodlands from whence it has come. Mixing the tomatoes with the meat, I let the stew simmer while the rice steams. The wolf paces in circles at the foot of the stove, brushing the hem of my dress at each turn. I lean over to turn down the heat under the corn. As I walk away to fetch the dinner plates, the wolf leaps toward me, readjusting his path as he escapes through the open window, through the billowing gauze curtains. I smile calmly, serenely, reaching up to retrieve the china.

Alone Again

I NEVER WENT ANYWHERE WHEN I WAS A CHILD, ALL BECAUSE OF A PIG HOUSE MY MOTHER HAD BURNED DOWN. She'd grown up on an Idaho homestead without running water or electricity, and her Italian mother had been too busy grinding pork for homemade sausages, plucking chickens, and performing the million other tasks of the pioneer to keep an eye on her nine children. One day while playing with matches in a fit of boredom, my mother and her cousins burned down the pig house. This could have been a tragedy, fire spreading rapidly over the dry fields and wooden buildings of the farm. That didn't happen. Still, that red pig house, its long troughs filled with table scraps, shaped my whole childhood.

"We ran wild," my mother recalls with horror. "I made sure you kids were *watched*." To this day she claims her greatest mistake was allowing me, third oldest of seven children, to escape to Yellowstone Park for a summer job. When I boarded that Greyhound bus I was seventeen, a skinny girl with a high school diploma and plastic suitcase. Never had I been more than thirty miles from the border towns of Eastern Washington and Idaho.

"You'd be a different person today if you hadn't gone to Yellowstone," my mother claims. She means I'd be a household saint, not a travel writer. But I believe wanderlust is in the blood, as natural to certain people as water cascading over cliffs, the tumbling of tumbleweeds across desert sand.

Until this escape, my life had been like a toy train stuck on a single track. I grew up with three brothers and three sisters in a pretty pink ranch house in Spokane, Washington, a landlocked city of stone and pine on the edge of a vast lake country. After Sunday Mass, we piled the family into two cars and drove across the state line to the Idaho farm where my mother grew up. Down the road on a lake was the log cabin in which we lived every summer. We never went anywhere else, because my mother saw no need. Our life was a closed circle of family.

"You can go, but don't go too far," Italians tell their offspring, whether they are toddlers or grown-ups with kids of their own. "Stay near your folks. They are the only people you can trust."

In Italy, these rules confine children to the range of the village bell. In America, we had to stay within range of my mother's police whistle. In summer, that gave us the run of the farm where the pig house burned down; the nearby lake and the meadows above it; woods with makeshift tepees and wild strawberries; fields of clover and wild peas. Not to mention the joyful company of countless cousins.

In Spokane, we felt our chains. The pine woods above our new housing development offered mysterious caves and tantalizing boulders to climb. Kim Momb, later to stand atop Mount Everest, trained on the black lava cliffs that rise from the river valley. But this paradise was forbidden to me.

"Those are *city* woods," my parents warned. City woods were overrun with perverts and hermits and vandals who pushed stolen cars off cliffs. The fact that nobody ever spotted these desperados did not bother my folks one bit.

So we children braked our bikes at the edge of the woods, trembling with fear and desire. The price of disobedience was high—what our parents called "a good licking." Although convinced they had radar that could track our every move, we often defied them with mad dashes into the woods.

The odd thing was that the neighborhood kids, who found our old-fashioned clothes and copious rules bizarre, never ratted on us for following them into the forbidden realms. Forging ahead of us through the brush, they were bold adventurers braving untamed lands. What they took for granted, we found magical: fields of yellow bells and violets, breathless games of hide-and-seek, the mesmerizing scents of syringa and wild roses. We hunted blue-tailed lizards, fled from spiteful porcupines, waded barefoot across murky ponds floating with water lilies. We shot our Flexible Flyer sleds down snowy slopes we called "Suicide" and "Danger."

"Where have you been?" my mother asked whenever we failed to respond speedily to the police whistle. "I've been calling and calling."

"Just riding our bikes."

Somehow she managed not to see the pine needles in our hair. Once, I convinced her that the wood tick she had to remove from my scalp had fallen from a maple tree at school. My best excuse, although I was afraid to use it often, was that I *had* to go into the woods to retrieve our Brittany spaniel—a spotted rebel named Penny who hated girls and wouldn't come when I called.

The few lickings we got for our forest explorations made us philosophical about crime. "Damn it, it was fun," we said once the pain wore off, vowing to do it again and again.

While my mother kept us home, Dad fed our wanderlust. I've always suspected he would have been a rolling stone if he hadn't gotten hitched. At bedtime, he dazzled us with stories about his days in the Merchant Marines. He knew how rain fell in the South Seas, what Shanghai looked like before "the Commies" took over. He filled our house with adventure books, detective stories, sci-fi thrillers. He read us everything from *The*

Iliad and *The Odyssey* to Tom Sawyer and *The Jungle Tales of Tarzan*. We believed, boys and girls alike, that we could stride the world in seven-league boots, ride magic carpets, and climb beanstalks to castles in the sky.

These dreams eventually took me places my father did not wish me to go. Yet he himself came from a restless clan, German and Irish. His German grandmother had a pass on the Chicago–Milwaukee Railroad—courtesy of her husband, who worked there—and she rode the rails all her life. Sometimes she took her kids, other times she boarded them out with family members. Although based in Spokane, she spoke casually of St. Louis, Minneapolis, and Chicago—golden cities glittering out of my reach like names on a movie marquee. I never saw a jet rise over Tower Mountain nor heard the whistle of a west-bound freight, hell-bent for the coast, without imagining myself aboard.

"How could she?!" my mother complained about that vagabond grandma. "How could she dump her children on her relatives and gallivant around the country that way?"

How could she not? Alone, my great-grandmother could reinvent herself. I liked to think she went by a different name on the train—something daring like Carlotta Delmonico—and changed her age and hair color, and said she'd gone to finishing school in Paris. How I longed to possess that train pass, that life. They were as beguiling to me as the silver passenger trains that still roll across the dusty flatlands, high deserts, and blue mountains of the West.

Like that German grandmother, I am famous for mad dashes, for suddenly deciding I must breathe the air in another state or country. I believe in following these impulses even when they're dangerous. When I was twenty-six and two weeks shy of getting married, I boarded a dented Chevy Nova and hightailed it from my parents' home in Spokane all the way to Eugene, Oregon. Some one thousand miles round-trip. My excuse for fleeing was that I'd left belongings in Eugene, where I'd just wrapped up graduate school. But the truth was, I feared that brief journey down the aisle, the sudden loss of freedom. Afterward, my new husband and I planned to live on the East Coast for several years. I wanted to be alone when I said goodbye to the West, which I had loved longer than any lover.

Listening to my mother's travel advice—"You must get a good start!"—for the first and last time, I left Spokane hideously early that spring morning and shot south. Crossing wheat fields and deserts and lava outpourings, I caught I-84 and turned west. This road, following the Columbia River along the Washington–Oregon border, is famed for its high cliffs, deep gorge, and bold, blue water. It unfolds like a book of postcards, the same beauty mile after mile. Quickly, I got bored. I should have known I was in trouble when I began simultaneously driving and reading a road map. Sunlight drifted into the car, wrapping around me like a soft blanket. I slipped luxuriously into sleep.

Then something jolted me awake. The Nova was on the gravel shoulder, headed straight for the ditch. Slamming on the brakes, I threw it into a tailspin. Round and round the car spun on that broad highway. The spinning took forever. I thought: *This is it. I'm going to die.* I saw flashes of my life—cramming for finals, pulling my wedding together, flying east into uncertainty. Life was nothing but struggle. It was a relief to let go.

Then the car stopped spinning. I grabbed the wheel. I steered to the roadside and stopped. When a highway patrolman knocked on the car window, I thought I was hallucinating. He told me he'd been parked at a rest stop. "I was sure you were going to flip," he said, as though that would have grieved him. "You know how lucky you were that nobody else was on the road?"

I tried to pour black coffee from my plaid thermos, but my hands shook. I couldn't look that patrolman in the eyes. I felt so lost.

Like a wrangler getting back on a horse after a spill, I rode the Nova all the way to Eugene, a lovely red-brick college town of greenery and mist. For two blissful years I had studied writing there while carrying on a long-distance romance with Mark, a law student in Spokane. I kept my two lives so separate that nobody in Eugene knew Mark and I were about to tie the knot. But that night, I bunked with a grad-school friend named Jill and, over a bottle of wine, managed to spill my secret. She said she understood. "Sometimes it's hard to talk about the things that mean the most to us."

The next afternoon, I followed the McKenzie River east out of Eugene and cut across Three Sisters Wilderness and its haunting stretch of snow-draped volcanoes. Then I swept into the high desert of central Oregon, a land of lava spires, dry washes, and fossil beds. Shying away from I-84, the highway of my near crash, I drove the back roads all day and into the night. I was determined not to think. With no one to talk to and a busted radio, there was nothing to hear but the wind blowing across the desert and the occasional clatter of a passing truck. There was nothing but the grip of the wheel, the earth rushing by, the sweet scent of the blueberries bought for my mother at a roadside stand.

A half-moon dangled over the darkened town of Milton-Freewater as I tried to cross the border into Washington. By this time, I had been on the road more than six hours. A highway patrolman turned on his siren and stopped me in a whirl of red light. He said he'd clocked the Nova at 104 miles per hour. I hadn't felt that speed. I tried to tell him about my long journey and the bewitching names on the Oregon map that had spurred me on: Three-Fingered Jack, Bear Wallow Creek, Crooked River Gorge. I had been in perpetual motion, the Nova a rocket ship flying through space.

The patrolman smiled. I had the feeling he was a long-distance addict himself, an explorer of the back roads. He said lots of people speed up near the border without realizing it, because their minds tell them they're almost home.

"Not me. I always slow down when I'm near home."

He laughed. "Well, I have to write you a ticket, but I'm going to say you were doing eighty. That way it won't cost you so much."

The second he took off, I felt my weariness. It was all I could do to limp across the state line into Walla Walla, where I had friends. Major travelers themselves, Glen and Janice were unfazed when I showed up on their doorstep in the dark, almost unable to talk. All night long I lay in the upper bedroom of their half-furnished Victorian, wheels churning in my head.

The next day, I kept putting off my departure, expressing a sudden desire to see Whitman College, the site of the Whitman Massacre, and even the state penitentiary. It was dinnertime before I saddled up, thinking that the last 160 miles would be a snap. A ribbon of highway spun north across the rolling hills of the Palouse, one of the world's richest wheat lands, and into Spokane. The problem was that the Palouse, like the Columbia Gorge, has a monotonous beauty. Three years of college in nearby Pullman had been enough for me. Now I veered northwest toward the farming town of Lind. A woman from up there had told me the place was so tiny that I could write "Meredith. Lind, Washington" on a postcard and she'd get it.

I cruised for hours on automatic pilot, choosing well-marked back roads that skirted lush wheat farms and rolled over neat little bridges. Then the sun started to dip. The land turned dry. Somehow I slipped onto an unmarked road, then another. Coming over a ridge I dropped into a flatland so desolate that it made me stop the car.

All around me was untracked desert. A low horizon over dark earth.

No trees or rivers or fences or power poles. I was lost on the moon. Checking the gas gauge I figured I had enough for maybe thirty miles. But which way was north? How far back was the nearest town? I couldn't remember.

I got out, shaky on my feet after riding the range for so long. Beams of light broke through the gloom, tracing silver veins on the dull sand. I breathed in the familiar scents of warm rocks and musky plants. Never had I been anywhere so quiet, so beautifully still. There was no one to say, *How could you have been so stupid? What the hell were you thinking?*

I heard a roaring in my ears. Suddenly my mind cleared for the first time in weeks. It was simple. The road only went two ways and I wasn't about to turn back. That didn't suit my personality. Gripping the car keys, I promised myself that if I drove over the next ridge and the land was just as desolate, I would stop the car and scream. I'd scream and scream. Then I would keep driving.

Over the next ridge was another trackless flatland. But on the far horizon I saw a glow. I followed that glow for maybe twenty miles until the lights of a town sparkled ahead. Ritzville, about sixty miles from home. "A pit stop on the interstate," I would have called it a few days before. But that windy spring night I was enchanted by Ritzville's brightly lit gas stations and burger stands, curtained houses, and boxy taverns with flashing beer signs.

Pulling into a station, I filled up the tank. Then I stopped at a painted shack for a double burger and french fries. Dipping into the greasy paper sack, which gave off an intoxicating fragrance, I hungered for the road. Even though I'd been gone only a few days, I felt wiser and more joyful than before. I knew now that I was capable of getting myself into terrible jams, but also of wangling my way out of them. Nothing could stop me from roaming, not even a gold wedding band.

All these years later, I still love to climb into a car for no reason and drive hundreds of miles.

"What are you looking for?" asks my husband, Mark, who grew up in New York, where nobody calls driving thirty miles for Marlboros "just a hop, skip, and jump." Like many vagabonds, I married a person who never wants to leave town.

"I'm not looking for anything," I tell him. "I just want to go."

Depending always on the kindness of strangers, I've been everywhere I dreamed of when I was a landlocked little girl—and I've only begun to wander. I've seen the sun set on Mount Kilimanjaro in Africa, hopped a plane to Jordan after the Gulf War, watched the moon rise over the olive groves of Calabria, where my grandparents once tilled the rocky land. Like my father, I've seen Asia. I've seen how rain falls like the wrath of God on the South Seas, then stops as suddenly as it begins. Blue skies reappear over the coral lagoons of Bora Bora, coloring the water, and white boats ride the waves once more.

Even though I'm a grown woman with a child of my own, my mother still frets every time I step out the door.

"Something might happen," she says.

"That's the whole idea."

"Can't you go with someone?"

"No."

"At least take your husband."

"No."

I'd rather set off on my own, even when I feel scared and lonely. Something might happen: I might meet a stranger, jump ship, climb an unnamed mountain, lose myself on a winding trail. I might forget who I am and where I came from.

Who knows? I might even run away from home.

CHRISTINE WEEBER

An Unladylike Journey

I

ON SUNDAY, I DRIVE AWAY FROM THE GREEN PASTURES OF MY MICHI-
GAN YOUTH. I wade through Chicago traffic and then roll through Illinois.
Trees grow sparse as the plains of Iowa fill the space with long fields of
corn and slow-paced cows. Here, the sky holds up the land. Trees and
houses rest in a blue haze as if the heavens had melted and dripped onto
them. I awaken.

I feel like Georgia O'Keefe, heading west alone in my car. Like her,
I am desert-bound and in search of outlets for my passion. But I go with
pen instead of paintbrush, and bound for Idaho, not New Mexico.

I lunch in the only restaurant in Brooklyn, Iowa. People stare as I walk
in. I must look like a peacock wearing my breezy, multicolored skirt. I sit
with my feet on the booth across from me and eat heartily. I bask in my
aloneness. It's nice to have only a notebook and the twenty or so flies
that cling to the window beside me. I feel as if I shouldn't be breaking so
many rules at once. Will I be disqualified from the game of womanhood?

Feeling uncomfortable, I leave after my last bite. A single young
woman alone on the road with windblown hair and Birkenstocks is an
anomaly. The surprised and wary stares must have been what O'Keefe saw,
too. Not much has changed in some parts since she stormed through
the country in her car.

Large sun eaten by clouds. We got this land by force. I pass Mon-
tezuma.

I pay a middle-aged man for my first camping spot. While setting up
my Eureka tent in the dark, I am nervous and scared. The quiet and

solitude warm me, but when it gets fully dark, it seems the silence could drown me out, erase me, and suck me up. I go to the small pool for a swim. I see my shadow: flattened, wet hair and round shoulders; I feel whole; I occupy my skin. The fear of the darkness swallowing me dissipates as I move in the water.

Yet, my restless fear succeeds in stealing what might have been a great night of sleep. I keep imagining someone unzipping the tent to attack me. The wind persistently licks my tent, making the flaps hit me and the zippers clank. I need to relax and become less afraid of my aloneness, my vulnerability. I can't be "caught" before someone even tries to catch me.

On the road, I pass a run-down, deserted chapel with the words "God is with you" peeling off the side of the building. Peter Gabriel's *Passion* rolls on my tape deck. Where is the face of the God I've been taught to see? I feel the touch of dirt and wind, the whirl of space through time. I feel my body under the heat of the sun through my windows. But the paint peels off. Is it the same God that still stirs around and within me?

I drive through country my grandpa and grandma rode through to get to their worn piece of land in South Dakota. Grandpa, an orphan from Friesland. Grandma, from the Netherlands, with a degree in education. Married: March 8, 1921. Moved from Iowa to South Dakota because farms were selling cheap after the Depression. They had nine kids and a nickel-and-chrome pot-bellied stove. They traveled across the plains in flatbeds pulled by horses. In 1939 or 1940, Grandpa paid twenty-five dollars per acre for his farm. The place had worn and blackened buildings with wooden floors that curled from the treeless heat and drought. But three lovely lilac bushes had survived, and the government gave away free trees that my grandpa planted every year, fighting the forces of dry heat and clay dirt. Today the place is owned by my cousins and blooms with high, green trees, strong and arching.

When my mom was eighteen, the schools were hard up for teachers because few people wanted to go back to Platte after going away to school at age thirteen. My mother felt restless and displaced living in the flat space with small-town tension. She felt unknown by parents who had twelve children to care for, a farm to work, and a weighty religious tradition to carry forth. She settled in Michigan after graduating from college and never went back, except to visit.

I, too, pass these plains to head to the mountain country beyond. I do not travel at a horse's pace with nine children and a stove, but my dreams also ferment with hope mixed with fear. My pockets gape from lack of money. I head westward in search of a place of my own. I have a vision of going to graduate school and becoming a professor of literature. My dreams are as hard to grasp in the everyday heat of my trip as those of my grandpa and grandma were as they rode in search of their own farm, cattle, food, and machinery. I move in search of people who can join me in carving out a community of equality and openness and trust. I long for people who understand how marginalized I feel; people who will teach me about women philosophers, writers, and activists; people who will feed my hunger for the feminine in God, myself, and the earth. I want to leave my white, Western, male-oriented education in the past and cultivate a new garden, where gender issues are faced and discussed, where I can change the oil in my car *and* bake cookies. In this way, I try to continue my family's legacy of strength: the quiet, peaceful, spiritual stamina of hard people carved by the scold of Mother Nature and fed on the gifts of her breasts. Overhead, the soft clouds amalgamate together without boundaries.

I strain to picture herds of buffalo slamming across these plains. I remember my mom telling me that she was told they sounded like thunder. A pillar of dust hovered over the herd and identified them as buffalo. They had no regard for fences but they never stampeded houses.

Three Native Americans squashed into the front seat of a Ford truck from Oklahoma pass me. The guy driving has a carved face, stern and focused.

I am glad to be driving down Interstate 80 alone. I have time and space to sift through conversations and events and just remember. A line from "The Waking," by Theodore Roethke, a Michigan poet, runs through my head. "What falls away is always. And is near." My recent breakup sits next to me in the crowded passenger seat like a silent, heaving animal, sick and wounded. I avert my gaze, but the memories flood my eyes, anyway. Mark and I had planned to travel together but we couldn't make it this far side by side. He went to the East; I go to the West. How could so much have happened that I only now have time to absorb? And the little I sift through is only a small percent of all that I think, feel, and remember. People hide/conceal/contain caverns of thoughts, emotions, motives, beliefs that are as deep and twisting, dark and inviting as the Mammoth Caves in Kentucky.

Such complexities about people are part of what drives me into solitude. Only in the physical removal of myself from the place I grew up in and the people I know, do I *feel* their presence, like seeing the roundness of a light bulb only after looking away from it. I think I have taken my family and friends for granted. They have been too close for too long. As a girl, I felt overshadowed by others. Now I travel to fill my own space and shake off the motto: "Others first, then yourself." I travel solo to pay attention to myself and, in the emptiness, see and appreciate and miss those I love.

I brim over with watchfulness and tension as I watch a storm brew on the horizon. As the sun sets, I debate whether I want to continue to Uncle Merle and Aunt Jean's in Fort Collins, Colorado. I am tired and I listen to my body—I stop. Ten hours of driving alone in dry heat has earned me a rest. I take Route 61 up to Lake McConaughy north of Ogallala, Nebraska.

While driving along dark, foreign curves in the campground, I suddenly become stuck in sand. Bonfires waver at the lake's edge. I fear the loud party and the large, drunken men I see. I try turning my tires to catch a new route out of the sand but the soft surface gives way, leaving me buried deeper than before. I ask the nearest family to help. He has a bad back. She's pregnant. They cast me back into my solitary darkness.

Another car turns off the road and gets stuck. The woman has high heels and speaks only Polish. The man speaks broken English. I tell her to push with me to release the car. Doesn't budge. Heels were man's invention, not woman's. We finally get their car out with me behind the wheel. They help me shake my car free. I set up my tent in the lot next to them, using the beams of my headlights. A lid of clouds hides the stars. Darkness breathes thickly through here. I hear waves and wonder how close the lake is. I imagine it as large as Lake Michigan. Wide, encompassing heat lightning covers my tent. It crackles—long rumble, then rain. I'm scared. But it's such an adventure! I hate/love this. I dared myself to come this far down Route 61 and now I can't escape. I feel shaky and I can't sleep as the storm presses closer. My alertness rivets me.

Horrific storm. Scary. I pray. I crouch my body in the middle of the tent in case the poles are hit by lightning. My arms encircle my knees to shield myself. The bush next to my tent scrapes against the nylon roof. Rain pours heavily and doesn't let up. It hurts my eyes to watch the lightning. After it fades, it is dark so suddenly that I wonder if everything got blitzed. I am afraid to touch the tent. I feel too scared to run to my car for security. I imagine the lake being shallow like the Great Salt Lake and flooding high enough to sweep me away in the waves. I feel naked—naked and unmasked in the piercingly bright bolts of light.

I wake up to sun and blue sky and dogs barking. It's seven o'clock. The adrenaline kicks in when I remember that today I will see the Rocky Mountains again. I am in love and I will see my lovers' etched faces soon!

On the way to the bathroom, I pass a sweet and calming scent. I don't know what it is. The breeze is cool, the sun hot, and the small lake is surrounded by sand. It's nothing like my Lake Michigan. It's not salty like the Great Salt Lake, either. But this lake has been overly people-handled and is surrounded by Jet Skis and trash. I cannot walk on the landing dock because of the broken glass and fishing hooks that are strewn across it. The hung-over glaze of a guy who looks the same age as me—twenty-four—tells the tale of empty money, lonely power, and the control and abuse that has fucked this Mother Earth.

On the road again, I pass the Nebraska fields that stretch long and flat like those in Iowa. The increased number of hills and valleys alerts me to the upcoming Rockies. The gauge on my 1987 Honda Civic just turned over—my first thousand miles—I'm in Colorado! Farmland merges into space filled with sagebrush and juniper. In this landscape, it now feels natural to be by myself.

I climb in elevation, aiming for the Great Divide. The exits here have gates that close when winter storms cover the road. Huge lake to my right. Lone cow beside a silo. Dirt roads lead to the horizon. I pass a fence that has a shoe on every post. Fifty pairs of tennis shoes, leather boots, and sandals. Cows melt into the dirt like gumdrops. I can't wait to run along the curves of Mother Earth and feel her sharp edges and slopes. I can see the dark, etched line of the Rockies! I am free! My ass is back in the WEST!

Visiting my aunt and uncle slices my sense of space like mincing a garlic clove for a stir-fry. Following a fishing trip the day after I arrive, we drive out of the mountains together and I keep my mouth shut about wanting to run up and down the sides of the mountains like a bighorn sheep, gripping my toes into the rock and dancing like a character in a play—like Puck.

After leaving their house, I head into Wyoming where the mountains droop like giant elephant feet into the earth. Antelope graze. I feel tired. On the way back from Oregon in December 1993, snow covered these hills when I took this same stretch of highway going to Michigan. At the rest stop at Fort Steele, there's a bridge across the Platte River. A nearby fort protected travelers from Native Americans and bandits. The last standing building in the area is the magazine where the explosives were held. Made of brick in 1881. Native Americans came through here from the Great Basin, heading east looking for buffalo. Fur traders hunted in this area, then went back East to sell their goods. Pioneers slowly passed through to get to the Pacific Northwest. History based on violence and exploitation and disease, travel and money and business.

By 1900, all the buffalo and antelope and sheep were gone from the area. Before that time, they covered these hills thickly. In 1927, the Game and Wildlife Management planted a new batch of these animals and the population has slowly increased.

I feel the isolation pressing from the large sky. No houses here, just wind and clouds like cotton balls. I wonder when and if condos and pools will invade these forces of nature. Yuppievilles. I eat a quiet lunch in a park surrounded by playful Native American children. I'm glad for this peace between us.

The wind is incessant. On a hill sits a cemetery of soldiers and civilians from the 1800s through 1926. Around 1906 they logged in the Medicine Bow Mountains and sent the logs to this area via the Platte River. The remains of the lumber mill stand like rotten teeth, jutting out of the dust. As I slowly cross the hard, dry dirt of the cemetery, I am humbled by the work and death that preceded my presence here. I walk where those men walked but what I see is desolate and nearly barren. Their fear and greed birthed a hauntingly still silence. What kind of drive motivated these people? Does mine echo it?

I ride over the Great Divide.

II

A crescent of a moon smirks behind pine trees and amid dark clouds. The sun sets after shedding its last light onto the clouds and casting them pink. I'm camped at Canyon Rim Campground at the southern end of Flaming Gorge National Recreation Area. Ponderosa pine surround me despite the fact that I'm in the high desert at seventy-four hundred feet.

My lesson of the day: Set up camp in daylight and cook, eat, walk, and meet neighbors. Tonight I did that and I feel much safer as I bed down in my sleeping bag.

In the morning, I trek to the cliff edges to peer one thousand feet down at the dammed/damned Green River. I see the picture Edward Abbey painted in *Desert Solitaire*. Boats chortle and circle Flaming Gorge Reservoir like tiny ants that are drunk and have forgotten they must search for food.

The life and character of this (once) river has been dammed/damned only because of social pressure. The Department of the Interior has posted a mission statement:

> As the nation's principal conservation agency, the Department of the Interior has a responsibility for most of our nationally owned public lands and natural and cultural resources. [*What a lot of responsibility.*] This includes fostering wise use of our land and water resources, protecting our fish and wildlife [*so rich people can have a "challenging" sport*], preserving the environmental and cultural values of our national parks and historical places, and providing for the enjoyment of life through outdoor recreation [*because recreation will bring in money*]. The Department assesses our energy and mineral resources and works to assure that their development is in the best interests of all our people. [*When did I get to*

vote?] The Department also promotes the goals of the Take Pride in America campaign by encouraging stewardship and citizen responsibility for the public lands and promoting citizen participation in their care [*abuse?*]. The Department also has a major responsibility for American-Indian Reservation communities and for those people who live in island territories under U.S. administration." [*Why, are they children?*]

A handful of rich white people has ruined this entire three million–acre territory. Did those who built the dam realize that once the water stopped moving, the area would stagnate? Such stagnation is what typical American tourists feed on. Once the waters were drugged and sedated and under human control, did the Department of the Interior think humans would lessen their recreational polluting? Did they really believe that, down the road, people would use fewer gas-powered, noisy boats and instead use canoes?

Now only two boats are in view but I can hear them from where I sit on the edge of the cliffs. Why must I listen to the noise of some drunken bastards sporting on a gaseous boat? Why have those before me stolen the buffalo and sheep and antelope, then dammed this river? I never asked for the electricity or safety or recreation that has resulted. I'd rather have it dangerous and wild and less "fun." Why do I stand here, part of a new generation, and look out on a beautiful gorge of red rock that no longer will be carved and etched by the run of water? Those before me have forced me to be content with this gorge the way it is because all the natural and dangerous forces that made it and the Grand Canyon have been tamed by money-hungry politicians and builders.

I don't want to be content with a pacified Green River. I don't want to hear anything in the wind but the sound of crows and chipmunks, the bleating of sheep, the snort and rustle of buffalo, and the roar of uncontrolled white water. Give me wilderness. Give me free land. I will not head to Alaska to fulfill my hunger for these. I will stay planted here and demand that the land be released. America and the Department of the Interior have not only dammed the Green River in order to milk its energy for electricity, they have damned all of us. They have coerced us into believing we can only be consumers promoting the American money machine. They milk our breasts for money. For today. For the NOW.

But I am the Tomorrow. I am left with the red sunset, red from pollution. I am left with the water calmed by a dam and foamy with spilled beer suds. I am given the rocky shore strewn with cans and McDonald's bags. (I am nearly sedated—but I will revolt.)

I look through a fence into a red, rock-layered gorge. I am in a cage built by those who have thought they were making me secure and happy. But my security is my cage. They "interpreted my needs" incorrectly. I seek wilderness and slamming buffalo herds. Power that is in its own domain, uncontrolled—but lived with/beside and respected. I hear the voice of the river. If it were free, I would bow to its waves, not sell them.

I am so angry, I leave. What do I compromise in driving away to continue my journey?

III

Seventy miles from Pocatello, my destination. I eat lunch on a hill above a mile-wide valley that used to be a lake. I've passed curvy mountains and many men in big trucks.

I've gotten this far all by myself!

Fifty miles from Pocatello, a storm covers and darkens the mountains. Raindrops and wind and lightning. Eighteen miles to go. I flip my

Joni Mitchell tape. Six miles and it's pouring. I had planned on camping but I don't need another night like the one near Ogallala. I stop at Poppa Paul's to eat and again face the straight-mouthed stares of locals. As I get lost trying to find a motel, I see a double rainbow. I'm too worn out to appreciate it. Shit. My back hurts and the injured muscles in my shoulder scream and here is the first double rainbow I've ever seen. Like in Roethke's poem, "Meditation at Oyster River": "Its spray holding a double rainbow in early morning, / small enough to be taken in, embraced, by two arms—." In the midst of my pain and frustration, things connect.

No motels have vacancies due to a week-long Native American festival and popular baseball game. I load myself into the overstuffed car again and head eighty miles west to Burley to settle into the last open room I can find. The car is on empty so I go fifty miles per hour hoping to find a gas station. I pass through a reservation. No gas stations. I have horrible images of running out of gas in the flat darkness and being stranded alongside the long, empty stretch of highway. I pass Massacre Rocks State Park. Great name.

I feel intimidated by the large, reticent man who owns the hotel. Only one lock works on the door to my room so I pile all the moveable furniture against the door. Blood speckles spot the wall beside the bed. I crash onto the bed but I can't sleep. I call my mom and tell her my troubles. She encourages me and warns me to stay safe. During the night, I am invaded by nightmares about being shot, raped, cut with glass. In my dreams, I even plan an escape: Crash through the window and dive for the car. My mind is intense and wandering. I wake up sweaty but safe and the weather is peaceful.

I shower and exercise and fill the cooler with ice. I feel scared and lonely despite my self-made schedule of activities. Talking to Mom last night felt good. She soothed my fears about Pocatello. I still wonder, though. Only through experiencing the town and the school will I know if it is the place for me. I have a gut feeling that it isn't. But I've left my friends, boyfriend, family, and hometown to live there. I don't want to fail. Will people understand my feminist/womanist ideas? Will I be challenged academically and personally? Will I make friends? Will I be able to have a dog? I can only drive to Pocatello and find out slowly.

IV

I took this trip alone because Mark and I broke up and I couldn't find anyone heading to Idaho. As the miles passed, it became a rite of passage, an initiation into an adulthood carved by tools of my choice. It started a process of moving toward my own future—a simultaneously fearful and fearless act. Every woman would benefit from a solitary trip like this. The fear of would-be rapists or murderers still exists for me, but it is offset by the trust I have in my own ability to defend myself.

The semester spent in Pocatello involved deep loneliness and isolation. I was at a school that didn't suit or challenge me. My gut reaction had been true. Over the course of a few critical weeks in Pocatello, I decided to let go of my detailed plan and narrow time limit regarding my degree. I decided to quit graduate school.

Feeling like a failure, I moved to Boulder, Colorado with my new friend Sarah, a six-month-old basset/beagle mix. I arrived penniless, lonely, and desperate, having left behind a semester's workload of classes, a teaching assistantship, my own apartment, and a small handful of new friends.

I feel like a cut stone or mineral. Quartz. Pocatello cut and sliced me, refined me, hardened me. The windswept, sage-covered hills of isolation umbrellaed me with silence; this silence I carry within.

V

The night I stayed at Flaming Gorge, a bug and a moth flew into my candle and died. They were submerged in wax until I burned the candle down again in Pocatello. I let them stay half-stuck in the scented wax, for memory's sake. Shreds of them still speckle the bottom of the round candle on my bookshelf.

In Boulder, the Flatirons postcard my view in the west as I eat breakfast on my back porch. In an hour, I wade into a rushing, white glacial stream. I've learned how to cast this yellow fly line in order to lay the fly on the water's skin. I come to these waters often. Since I am a beginner, I hook leaves and twigs, and I lose lots of flies. I don't catch many fish when I go; I scare them with my wound-up line, my wading in, or my looming stare. But I have learned about time and persistence. I am drawn to the water. I continue to cast my line in hopes a fish will curl upward, hooked, ready to be my dinner.

VI

I remain a woman on a solo journey, although communing with people I love through letters, phone calls, and nights out on the town. But the death of Mark on September 14, 1995, has washed me with sorrow. My tears add to the current of my soul, speeding it up. In my weakness the waters surge forward carrying memories of him and me and numerous dreams. A strong river carries many things.

The sense of community I search for isn't arrived upon or discovered, but nurtured and grown. I trickle into the valleys of my friends; I ask them to trickle my way. I follow my passion like a rainbow trout, driven and arched, glistening in natural light, rising to a fly.

The strength and voice I've claimed since I left Michigan aren't always explicit, but sometimes in odd moments I feel my drive/passion/self pulsate. In those moments, I am an untamed river rushing in rhythm. The dam has exploded and not been replaced. Some of the cliff edges wash downstream. Other ones push against me, held firm by rock or hardened clay. I learn where to go as I move against these, and I carve.

P. K. PRICE

Navigational Information for Solo Flights in the Desert

I AM A SOLITARY DESERT-GOER, A SOLO RIVER-WATCHER, A WOMAN WHO
WALKS THE FOREST WITHOUT COMPANION. I first went to the desert thinking I knew the name of God. But once there, I realized I knew only parts
of a name: golden marmot, red-tailed hawk, mule deer, river ouzel, mer-
ganser, owl, red-shafted flicker, slick rock, river swallows, trout, sage,
alders, lupine, juniper. I return to the desert to gather more parts of the
name whispered by the voices. There is danger in going there alone.
There is more danger in not going.

I have spent seasons in the wild: autumn in the slick rock, spring
near Kennebec Pass, summer on the Dolores River, winter in the snow
shadow of Taos Mountain. Each journey is unique. In solitude, I add or
shed layers, either lose myself or find myself or do both and not know the
difference. I have learned to follow the path of personal reality. Openings
appear: doors into the desert's heart, real and illusory. To walk through requires courage. I might not return unchanged. I might not return at all.
Bones in the desert testify to this. It does not seem important any longer.
An opening in the wilderness is a challenge and an invitation: to shed
layers, to gain strength and savvy, to dance unencumbered under a desert
moon, to lie on a boulder like a lizard, to bathe in the intimacy of constellations. To learn my name and my true transit. To hear my voice echoed
from the silence of the Persiad Showers.

I go to the Four Corners area of the Colorado Plateau. There, where
the earth plays spectacular on my senses, the weight of ages still hangs

silently, alive in the cobalt-blue air. Its very mass compresses time now, time then, and time to be down upon itself so that in the lack of linearity one finds a sharpness of perspective, the point where the curve between the sides of time is catenary. At this point of balance is the place where I gather stories and stuff them in my shirt to take home with me.

Solitude is not for the unprepared. And only for those who will not plan. I offer a bit of navigational information, a few traveling tips, for women. For I travel and breathe and live the desert as a woman and the desert has taken me in that way. Neither these tips nor any navigational information I offer constitute a map, just an image upon the soul. You will make your own list.

1. *About Getting Away*

When you first go to the wilderness alone, it is best to have a purpose. This will be both a knife and a defense for the first challenges that you will encounter: family, friends, and interior inertial reluctances. Our culture acknowledges, understands, and respects "the purpose," "the task," "the goal." Unless you have one of these, a reason, it will be difficult to leave: Expect this and you will probably actually succeed in getting away. You may choose any reasonable purpose that you feel you can sell to your family, your friends, and yourself. It is best to choose a solitary activity. If you are a painter, writer, or botanist, this is good. For example, if you are a painter, you can say: "See here, I must do several landscapes, numerous botanical sketches, various bird drawings, and I need to complete at least twenty-five to thirty of these as a collection for my next show. I'll have to go alone to get that much work done." You have just fooled them and yourself: You seem to have defined a goal. This makes your journey appear logical. The task, tangible.

A writer can do the same thing. "See here, I must finish the last 267 pages of my novel and write the six to seven magazine articles that I've outlined and sent to publishers." Easy sell.

Set the goal at such a level that you will clearly be working very hard to achieve it. This discourages those who might want to come along. They know that they might quickly become bored.

This goal will be very useful to you for structuring your travel, choosing your destination, and leaving everyone behind with a comfortable conviction that you are a person with a purpose. This purpose will also be the knife that you will use to cut the weeds that have grown up around your ankles and rooted your boots to the ground. It will be your defense against comments from yourself and others questioning your sanity.

2. *About Tents and Setting Up Camp*

For the first few days you are out there, your goal will be an anchor, a map, your name, the image of yourself in the water, and the reflection of your shadow cast off the underbelly of the moon. You will need this structure. Your first few days alone, you will encounter high winds, fear, rains that will sweep you off the ground, panic, the breathing of rivers, the blindness of no-moon, new neighbors: lion, bear, otter, eagle, deer, coyote, fox, regiments of ground squirrels in full parade dress. They will ask your name and your purpose. You will know it. This will seem as it should be for a while.

At first, you will think that setting up your tent is part of the process of being out there. It will be another skin. That will seem good. Comforting. A boundary in a limitless space. A place where you can separate yourself from the line of the horizon that stretches so far that only the curvature of earth can stop the distances from running away from you. The curvature is a visual reminder of the protection of the circle if you worry about getting lost. If you walk the circumference, being careful not to deviate even a fraction of degree in latitude or longitude, eventually you will return to the point of origin. If you are like me, you will take a side step to look at a copper-green rock, a flicker feather beneath a wild gourd. You will be off course. Your plans are now altered. You will spiral instead of circumscribe.

It is important to start within a circle. Set camp there. In an enclosure of boulders, of junipers, of sage. There are many places like this in the desert. They are pre-prepared, set-aside places to be used when you are alone. They protect the desert from you and you from the desert. *Even if you believe this, stay alert.* You will find that it seems as if you are not actually alone in these places. As if there are people you cannot see—pack rat, prairie dog, raven—who guard these places. Set camp carefully. Your camp is your kiva and in the center, if you stay long enough with the proper intent, you will eventually find the *sipapu:* your place of emergence into the next, upper world.

3. *About Getting Lost*

Be prepared for the turn you take on a walk up the side canyon that leads you to the ancient juniper. You will sit down to rest. The sun will seduce you. You might get drowsy. You might sleep. A few minutes later you will open your eyes and realize that your water bottle is gone. While you have drifted, a crow has snatched your notebook, the desert breeze has taken your name, a ground squirrel has carried off your pen, paper, and your maps. You will turn around again and again in circles, looking for your boot tracks in the sand: north to east to south to west. You will not be able to tell from which direction you came.

You will be alone. You will be immediately tempted to search for your sketchbook, driven to find your notebook and pen, frantic to find your comforting USGS topographical maps. Your throat will be suddenly parched. The pain of attempting to speak words into the silence through cracked, dry lips will be too much. You cannot cry out for help. You cannot run for shelter. You are alone.

Be still.

I started to panic when this happened to me. I ran. I clawed my way up a talus slope trying to reach higher ground where I could see. Instead, my boot turned under me in the scree, my fingernails broke off grasping for handholds. I rolled and slid down the side of the canyon wall, scraping and cutting my arms, legs, and face on slick rock and boulders. I lay on the canyon floor for a long time. I bled. The sun dried my blood into a red patina, then darker until my body resembled the slick rock: skin painted by streaks of desert varnish. I realized a crushing sense of vulnerability. The stirring of a feeling that this desert is alive. That it might drive me away. That I must be careful. I was as close and as far from the desert's heart then as I ever would be again.

This is why I say: Be still. Though I know you will try to run also. Perhaps you will not fall. Not be painted by the desert with your own blood. Perhaps you will reach the top of the mesa. It will not matter. The sun will be in mid-sky. It will not reveal direction to you. You will still be lost. You will still be alone.

If you have run or wandered, return to the place where you first dozed off and sit down again. This time: Wait. It is helpful at this point to listen. It is also useful to look around. You might find it comforting to count the pebbles under your right boot. Notice their colors. Do not put them in your pocket or you will never find your way back to your tent. The pebbles will grow into boulders and you will not be able to move.

This is how you listen: Slow your breathing down until the desert wind enters your lungs, and like a bellows, takes in air and expels it for you. This way your breathing will not be so loud that you cannot hear the dry melody of rice grass all around you. Soon the juniper will begin to sigh. Counterpoint and slightly syncopated and percussive will be the scraping of branches against each other even when there is no wind. This is desert music.

You may not have noticed, but look now. The delicate heart-shaped leaves of the squaw bush have begun to turn persimmon and plum colors. The sky has collected snow-mist from a distant mountain range and has marbleized them into streamers of pearl-white swirling across the azurine blue above you. Look down again. Small buds cover the tips of the sage. Female sage surrounds you. Breathe in the fragrance of their pungent leaves. Look over there to your left, you will see a male plant of epiphedra, Mormon tea. Behind the boulder where you sit, you will see the female plant: stalks and nodules so different in form and nature that you will know the female plant in a moment. These things are subtle. Some people try but can never discern which is female and which is male. You will know. Even with your eyes closed. Run your hands gently over each plant and touch it in greeting. If you begin to relax, prop yourself up against the boulder and close your eyes. The wind will breathe for you while you rest. The rice grass and sage music will continue.

When you awake, your water bottle will be next to you. Drink deeply. Your map, sketchbook, paper, and pen will be there also. You will see your boot tracks. You can follow them out now. The sun has slipped over your shoulder like a silk dress, leaving you bare and vulnerable. Drink deeply. It is time to return to your camp and await the night.

4. *Night, Moon, and Rain*

It is best to plan to enter the desert so that you will pass your first night at new moon. Go into the night without light. Go blindly. It is the only way you will learn to walk carefully. To see without glasses. To sleep without getting dizzy as the constellations turn soundlessly above your tent.

I will tell you that it will not be easy at first. One night this happened to me.

It was not many hours before dawn. I awoke startled by the sound of small animals skittering outside my tent. Thousands of them, judging by the hoopla and noise they created. Rain fell on the tent in a continuous downpour. I suspected sleet as the sound was loud and the night cold. *What animals would be so active at night in a sleet storm?* I asked into the darkness. In the tempestuous cold wind, my tent flapped and sighed and tried to pull itself out of its stakes. I did not move. Cold, my body rigid, I listened for hours until I saw the gray of dawn from the East. Though the animals continued their scurry and the sleet continued to fall, I hesitantly looked out the front flap of my tent.

There were no animals. No rain. No sleet. Instead, the cottonwoods under which I had set my camp were dropping their leaves. The brittle, dry, gold leaves filled the air. Falling on my tent, on the ground, falling down against themselves in the trees, falling through branches, rustling and crowding against each other, piling and swirling in the eddies of the cold morning wind. I slipped on my jeans and sweater and walked in cottonwood leaves up to my ankles.

In my journal that morning I recorded the following phenological report: "October 27, 1987. 35° this morning, clear sky. windy, received 4" of cottonwood rain last night."

Make a place in your journal for your list of possibilities. Add cottonwood rainstorms. Leave many pages open. Your list will grow as the desert gets to know you.

One of the things I added to my list was moon thievery. The moon has one perfect night in her cycle. Being much smaller and of much less importance, I have decided that I, too, will expect no more than one night of fullness each cycle. Thus, I can wax and wane without whining, and wait for those few hours when I can illuminate the darkness for my own pleasure.

I say this because I learned it in the desert. I entered the desert at new moon and watched each night as the moon gathered more light each day. I ran with her in apogee and circled close in perigee. I watched her illumine herself, casting herself in the lead night role by stealing what sun she could hold.

I decided to do the same. During the day I laid out on a boulder. Took off my boots, socks, clothing. Unencumbered, I let the sun touch my skin. I washed my hair and let the sun dry it. The wind whipped it into long, lazy curls. Each strand took on a bit more sun each day until my hair was patinaed with gold. My skin burnished. At night sitting beneath the waxing moon, my skin held the warmth of the sun for hours. This is how I learned to catch and carry sun on my body and in my hair.

At full moon, against the faint persimmon moonlight reflected off the slick rock, once again I took off my clothes. Light fell around me. The wind began to sway the juniper branches. The shadows of boulders reached out to stroke me. I broke off sprigs of sage, crumbled them in my hands, and rubbed sage over my body. I broke off several sprigs of juniper and plaited them in my hair. From my leather pouch I chose several pheasant feathers and wove them in with the juniper sprigs. I scooped up a handful of sienna-red earth and drew on my body: sun above one breast, moon above the other. Zigzag lightning on my arms. Spirals on my belly. I let the wind lead and I danced until moon-set. Slowly each day thereafter, I let my skin fade until at new moon, it was time again to begin catching sun.

5. *Rivers*

There will come to you a time when you must find water in the desert. You will wander. Pick up the trail of mule deer and follow it. You may walk for hours. If night catches you on the trail, look for the place where deer slept the night before. Curl up in deer-nest but do not sleep. First imagine that your skin is deer hide covered in tawny, brown, taupe, and white fur. This way you will stay warm throughout the night. Do not be alarmed if at midmoonrise you awake, and sleeping mule deer surround you. Wait until dawn when they rise. Then follow them to the river. It is important to know that you must bathe when you reach the river. The water will be cold. Your heart will stop beating. This is necessary. Stay with the river. Swim. Roll on your side. Rest on the bank. Dig deeply into the riverbed with your toes. Immerse yourself completely. Wash your hair and your clothes. Dry yourself by lying on a boulder in the sun. Your heart will eventually start beating again. But your blood will run slowly. It will be riverine and smell faintly of seep willow. You will feel the paws of lion on the bank upstream, drinking from the river at dusk. You can find mint and watercress in a side stream feeding into the river. Eat them. You might find one lone chokecherry bush in a copse of oak and alders. Crush the berries and rub them into your hair. Then sleep.

It usually takes at least one night to know whether you have bathed in a female river or a male river. Between midmoonrise and dawn you will awaken. There will be a sound coming from the river. It will be deafening and inaudible. It will resonate in your belly. It is the river. It begins at the headwaters and by the time you awake the entire river will be chanting. Over and over in the darkness you will hear the repetitive melody. Try to follow. Your lips and voice cannot do it. You must learn to river-chant with your body. Words may come. I thought I heard them. I do not know what they meant. It was an old, old song. It is by this song that the river will reveal itself, male or female, and its history. The names of each animal, each bird, each desert-goer who has drunk from its waters, sat upon its banks, will be in the chant. Wait by the river night after night until you hear your name. Lie by the river quietly. Bathe each day and let the sun dry your skin and hair. One night you will hear your name in the river-chant. You can leave the following morning.

The river-chant is meant to be sung at night. It is the name of the river. To know the name of a river from its running-water chant is to know all that we can ever know about rivers. Such knowledge will seem significant. But it is very little. Leave a sprig of sage and a *paho* stick by the river when you go.

6. *How to Approach a Juniper Tree*

When you have been in the desert alone for several weeks, you will notice that your actions will begin to take on patterns: each done with attentive deliberation at a certain time and in a certain manner. You may have thought of yourself as considerate and courteous when you entered the desert. Think again of the meaning of mindfulness. There is more to learn. Desert ritual and ceremony will teach you how to walk, to breathe, to eat, to sleep. There is a proper way to do everything. The desert will teach you this: desert manners. Even the certain way in which to approach a juniper tree. There are variations. They depend upon the tree, the soil in which he or she has set its root-feet, and the time of year.

This is what I learned. Walk toward the tree but get no closer than five or six feet. You will know when to stop.

Then, wait. Do not speak. Wait until you know that the juniper is willing to have you approach. This is the most difficult step. A juniper tree will always keep you waiting. This is a certainty. You will wait sometimes for hours. Once I sat all day and into the night until the moon rose over the mesa. It was only then that I felt juniper turning to face me, openly acknowledging my presence. I felt frightened for a moment. Silhouetted against the light of the moon, the tree transformed herself. She was the eldest in the company of her companions. She was in charge of receiving.

She was a singer. The wind carried her dry, dark green, pungent voice on its eddies. A sound light as owl feathers fell around me like gossamer.

She was a dancer. She stopped the wind at her command and began to move sensually. From her trunk through every branch, limb, sprig, and leaf, she began a gentle stretching at first. Reaching outward in all directions and upwards to the Pleiades. She stretched for what seemed like hours. I waited. Then she began her dance on the windless, moon-glazed mesa. A slow, undulating meander. Rhythmic. The movement of circles and spirals on moonlit canvas. With countless juniper sprig brushes, she painted her dance upon the night and my eyes to remain like the memory of something unutterably lovely, someone's touch exquisitely tender on my face.

I drew in my breath. Hours passed. The moon set. Only then did she stop her dance and her whisper-song painting. She was still then, and silent in the gray dawn. She waited for me. It was acceptable to approach. Acceptable to speak to her. She had spoken first, as is appropriate for an elder. She had seen me wait: desert manners.

I took two steps toward her. Sat down. So long had I waited. No audible words came. Yet with each breath I heard my body say, *thank you.*

7. *About Going Home*

Avoid going home at all costs. It is too dangerous. Stay out there. Stay with the desert wherever you go. Even if you must remove your body and cart it back to the city. Leave the river in your blood, the bloodstains from being lost on your legs, the copper sun of full moon on your skin, the reverence for juniper in your litany. Remember your manners.

You must be careful when you return to the city. There is no safety for womanness there. You will have to go about your way veiled in order to protect yourself. You will be stronger and more vulnerable than when you left.

It is best to remember not to speak of some things you have seen and done while alone in the desert. People will misunderstand what you say. It is difficult to explain. If you try, your listener will miss the point. Perhaps be inattentive or interrupt your story. This person and many others you thought you knew will not know about desert manners.

Remember each place where you put your foot down on the desert. Remember the feel of the river in your hair, sun on your bare skin. Walk freely and rhythmically. Walk sensually with the knowledge of juniper dance-paintings in your body. See your reflection against the underbelly of the moon. Never in a mirror. Return to the desert each night. To dream and dream.

KATHLEEN GASPERINI

Princess of the Tides

THERE'S A STRETCH OF MOUNTAINS AND OCEAN ALONG THE NORTHERN COAST OF CALIFORNIA THAT IS RUGGED AND UNDEFINED. It is a lonely place, where sailboats seldom cruise or people rarely venture to picnic. Although the beaches look so near and tempting, they are difficult to reach. Trails that lead down the bluff are often hidden, rocky, switchbacking through coastal brush for fifteen hundred feet at a time. The cold, dark water, which attracts whales, white sharks, seals, and dolphins, fends off timid tourists. Only a small community of surfers dare play in these waters. Disguised in black wet suits, they often look like seals from the bluff along the scenic highway. The sharks below the surface tend to agree and attack surfers, dragging them by the leg out to sea. Tourists who cruise along this highway every summer thrive on such tales but rarely stop long enough to see or understand any more than that it's not a place for them to swim.

One summer, for me, this area wasn't a shark-infested, lonely place. Rather, it was a place of independence—where hope was gained and the tides were turned during a time when I felt I wouldn't live to see the end of my student loan payments. (That would be the year 2000, far too distant when I could barely cope with every day.) Generation X had been beaten into my head and the more I tried to shrug the label, the more I realized that maybe I was among the lost in a lost generation.

I had come from a place where career came second to marriage and women came second to everything else. Too often I felt trapped, caught between my mother's generation and the guilt of having a career rather than a family, and between actually wanting a family and still having my career. It's the curse of Generation X women. And like the rest of them, I had gotten lost trying to figure out where I belonged and was wallowing in the land of the in-between.

I came to Big Sur to find strength and maybe a bit of myself, because after the last year, I couldn't hear myself anymore. Or maybe it had taken longer than a year? Even that I couldn't tell. Too much had happened: a divorce, pneumonia, and being fired from a job I later realized I had hated anyway.

What I did know was that the voices I was hearing weren't mine. They were my ex-husband's, our mutual friends (many of whom no longer spoke to me), and the voices of a job and society that suddenly seemed to take on a parental tone: "Wha, wha, wha," like a Peanuts cartoon. "Divorce? But he's perfect. . . . " "What about kids?" "You write more than you talk these days," "You write so you won't have to talk," blah, blah, blah. It was partially true: If I spoke, I was considered too feminist, too self-centered, too outspoken. But worse, if I wrote, he read it.

So I became a poet—in Kiswahili. I had studied at the University of Nairobi for a year and was fluent in the language of East Africa. When I returned, everyone said it was a silly language to have learned: "Why not French or Spanish or something useful?" Well, to their surprise it was useful because no one I knew could understand it but me. Poems became my thoughts translated into phrases—little stories that took little time (so no one could say I wrote too much and conversed too little); stories that reminded me of what I was thinking at the time I was writing.

Specific themes came gushing out of my Kiswahili poems—usually the ocean or men or feminism—such as:

> she lives there,
> among the kelp beds and starfish,
> with the whales and dolphins.

the Princess of the tides makes her home
among the dead ships of men—
a beauty in the rusting beasts
left to her to play with forever . . .

I could be a man-hater or a lover, a whore or a painter, a mermaid or a man. And no one could understand. I loved it.

Then, I hated it. I began to question myself. To feel free, why did I have to write in Kiswahili? To save time (and for whom? may I ask), why poems? Who was society to make me this way? And for goddess' sake, who was I to accept it? I couldn't figure out where I fit in to the whole mess. But more importantly, I couldn't understand how my life had become so bleak, dead, and unforgiving so quickly. (Or maybe it wasn't so quickly?)

The bottom of my stomach had dropped out and I couldn't eat anymore. In the mornings, I awoke from dreams filled with free falls off cliffs into the ocean. I'd had these dreams before. Only last time I was flying just before hitting the water. Now, I couldn't. The ocean had become a black hole—the very hole that was in my stomach—the hole I was falling into.

I came to Big Sur to see if I could fly above the ocean again. In this same place, Robert Louis Stevenson had, as did Ansel Adams in his photographs, Henry Miller in his words, and many other less-known artists, writers, and philosophers in their various disciplines. It was a place, as Miller once put it, that defies comparison, ". . . a region where extremes meet, a region where one is always conscious of weather, of space, of grandeur, and of eloquent silence. It is the face of the earth as the Creator intended it to look." I'd have to agree—She knew what She was doing with this place.

The community of surfers here were naturalists—"Indians of the ocean," they called themselves—guarding their trails down to the beach, picking up litter, planting trees here and there, and following the tides of the sea throughout the year. They were men in love with the land and ocean, moon and stars.

As for the women, most of us discovered the area as I had—through our surfer boyfriends. But I came back one day without him. I wanted to write and live the life of a bohemian in a place where books, natural ginseng root, and pure honey would help fuel my independence. I thought the purer I could make my life—physically and mentally—the better I'd be able to deal with my emotions, which had somehow become far too ragged for a twenty-eight-year-old.

Here, no one cared about the mental world, careers, societal differences. I could write in English—long stories that would keep me in my room for days at a time. But time was different here: The tides gave you time; the people, only perspective. The moon controlled your moods, the ocean and weather followed. For the first time since I was twenty, I went off the pill (the last controlling device from my past) and looked at the moon or watched the tides and knew the exact stage of my monthly cycles. Moon drag is a powerful thing.

That summer, I grew to love bodyboarding, a sport that, like surfing, takes catching an ocean wave. Bodyboards look like big kickboards, yet they're big enough for your whole upper body to lay upon. A leash from the board attaches to your ankle, allowing you the freedom to duck under a wave, if necessary, without losing your board. But the best part about bodyboarding is the intimacy you achieve with a wave: unlike surfing, you don't stand. You lie on your board and skim the water, arcing on the rails (sides) of your board to turn, carving just inches above the surface. Some call it "a woman's sport" because it takes leg power rather than upper body strength to bodyboard a wave. And it's one of those sports (like rock climbing) that women can do as well or better than men because it has more to do with balance and finesse than strength and force.

Over the months, I had learned the sport well, and with my bodyboard, discovered a new activity at which I was actually fairly adept. In the past, everything athletic I had ever tried was with my husband: skiing, snowboarding, biking, camping. But not bodyboarding: It was my own.

For this reason, I loved it and went often with my new friends. They showed me their favorite break—a place where you had to know the swell intimately in order to avoid getting shredded on rocks and becoming yet another "shipwreck," as they called it, along the already-haunted shore. It was a rounder part of the wave break that was rarely ridden by surfers. Nicknames, such as "Girls' Break," stuck because that's where most of us rode with bodyboards. It was more conducive to catching a wave and riding on a bodyboard: The swell produced big, high rollers that peaked slowly, then ran out long and smooth for a fast, powerful ride. Leg power and a pair of fins were all the muscle you needed to catch Girls'.

One afternoon in late summer, I became the mermaid in my poem at this break. It was the last session of the day and my girlfriends had decided to boulder around the rocky beach in search of jade booty. I'm not sure why I stayed out, but the wave was so smooth and powerful, and I was feeling in such prime form that I figured I'd catch another set or two. While eight guys vied for rides far to my left, taking turns on a big swell that broke aggressively just before a splattering of jagged rocks, I bodyboarded alone along my smooth surf.

The solitude was soothing. I could hear my heart pumping and feel my lungs fill with oxygen as I ducked under another wave and popped up on the other side. I lay there on my board, kicking aimlessly as I waited for the next break, and watched my friends, now far up the cliff, who were bending over and staring at the ground, picking up rocks here and there on their way to the car. From my perspective, the view looked like the 1-2-3 Jell-O I used to eat as a kid. A pale blue sky followed by green mountains made up the top layer. Frothy white water along the narrow, white-sand beach was the layer of whipped cream in-between, and the deep, blue-black ocean I floated in quivered and rocked like the most flavorful part of the three-layered dessert.

So much had happened since the days of Mom's Jell-O: I had grown up, learned life was not always black and white, and discovered myself along with nature. It always seemed that I learned more about myself the more I ventured into the forest or hiked along a beach or up a mountain. But for me, it was always the ocean that I found most attractive. Perhaps it's the enigma of waves that pull me to the sea whenever I feel lost. Unlike a mountain, they are a powerful force that's ever-changing—a piece of nature that defies analysis. And I was sick of being analyzed by a world of ancient beliefs.

Moving to the coast on my own was planned. But bodyboarding by myself was not. Yet, I quickly got over my discomfort at being a tiny thing in the huge sea and imagined myself the mermaid in my Kiswahili poem, swimming and communing with the waves and ocean kingdom below. As I turned to the horizon to look for the next set, I felt something rub against my legs and catch my fin. My heart leaped to my throat as I turned my board around, sure that a great white was about to have me for dinner, and my friends would find my board the next day washed ashore with a big shark bite in it, like the pictures we'd seen in the newspaper. Another brush against my left leg convinced me that I was now among a school of hungry sharks. Just as I was about to scream "Jaws!" the head of a dolphin popped up three feet in front of my board. His shiny, metallic skin sparkled in the late afternoon sun. Then, just as suddenly, he disappeared. The relief made me howl with such laughter, I almost fell off my board. I looked up the beach and to my left and realized no one had heard my nervous laughter. The sounds drowned in the crashing waves. I was alone in that sound.

When a few more dolphins brushed against my legs, I reached out to touch them in return. And they let me. I stroked the underside of one with my hand and rubbed another with my leg. I dove under, knowing that my leash would keep my board from floating in, and watched the dolphins spin and perform back flips. With my legs together and arms overhead, I did the same, kicking my fins together and flipping over and over as they did. As my hair flowed behind and curved in a circle, one dolphin kept poking his head in my hair, playing with the tangles and circling with me.

It was an impressive show, and I felt privileged to be part of their performance. I popped back up just in time to see yet another perfect wave coming my way. To stay or ride became my only concern and I chose the latter. With my upper body back on my board, I kicked hard with my fins and paddled with my arms until I caught the crest of the wave. As I steered left and rode down the falls, I caught the shadows of my dolphin friends catching the same wave. Three dolphins and I, riding a wave that had made its way from some unknown storm out in the Pacific, swelling right then, so perfectly, only for us to ride. We rode high, then dipped low, gaining speed in the trough, the dolphins alongside me, carving the same pattern.

With each wave came a greater sense of confidence. I was alone in human terms, but not in the ocean kingdom. I became a part of their family, like a sea creature, like a mermaid—more dolphin than human; more connected than solo. Only the parameters had changed, and I wanted to stay here forever. I caught more waves, each one better than the next as the dolphins and I grew more comfortable with each other's styles, touching on occasion as we carved down the faces. At one point, I no longer had to paddle—I just reached out and grabbed hold of one of my friends' dorsal fins and was pulled into the wave's crest without the effort of my legs or fins. He gave me a ride that was bigger than the wave. Inside I was screaming with excitement, soaring along the water like a dream. The dolphins were teaching me to catch surf as they did (for the record: one powerful kick of the tail, head tucked, and glide with the current, dorsal fin for steering, barely slicing the surface). *Feel the swell and hear the water crescendo rather than think about it*, they seemed to say. I followed their lead, kicking with the momentum of the swell, and releasing down the face of each curl of blue-green water.

Girls' Break with its smooth curl and amiable ride was really Dolphins' Break, and they let me in. I wasn't lost here. Or anywhere. I was home in the ocean, sharing waves and skimming across without wings. I was strong inside simply from being here in this special moment at this time, with these sea creatures. After all, what was it that I had overcome to find the independence to conquer a new sport, then ride a wave all the way from Bali, by myself, with dolphins? It was a moment of hope—a moment that made more moments like this seem possible.

If only the rides could last forever, I thought, but the sun was sinking and my human friends were surely up at the road, waiting for me by the car. I rode through the white water and walked onto the beach, hoping that this wouldn't be my last and only ride with the dolphins. Maybe the tides would bring them back again. As I turned around, I saw the glimmer of a smooth head, curved like a question mark, as it popped up for a brief second as if to say goodbye. Then it disappeared back into the ocean.

For some reason, I knew I wouldn't tell anyone what I had just experienced. I didn't want to. It was a solo session intended for my ocean friends and me. The dolphins showed me another way to ride—without muscle strength or thought, but with sound and feel. A metaphor for life? Perhaps. Or perhaps it was a reminder of senses I'd forgotten. I no longer needed wings to avoid falling into the ocean. *Use what's inside*, the dolphins had said, *and you can ride the swell of a lifetime*. But to explain that to my friends would defeat the whole purpose—like Kiswahili poetry, it wouldn't make sense to them. So I didn't.

I packed up my fins and towel in my backpack, and with my board under my arm, headed up the rocky trail, switchbacking higher and higher under the light of a rising half-moon.

VALERIE VAN BROCKLIN

Flying to Wild Places

AUTUMN IS PAINTING ITS WAY DOWN THE CHUGACH MOUNTAINS ON THE EAST SIDE OF ANCHORAGE, ALASKA, WITH JACKSON POLLOCK SPLASHES OF RED AND YELLOW ON THE TUNDRA ABOVE TREELINE. What a day to fly—sky so blue it gives you an ice cream headache. I take off from Lake Hood in *Bug,* our Alaska bush plane, shortly before my husband, Karl, takes off in our Cessna 185 from Merrill Field Airport across town. Due to weight limitations, Karl carries two of our friends while I haul fly fishing gear, provisions, and our retriever, Tao. We're headed to a cabin about seventy-five air miles southeast of Denali, North America's tallest mountain. Like so much of Alaska, this place is accessible only by air. The only company we'll have on the gin-clear stream are lunker rainbow trout and brown bears.

In a few moments, Karl passes me in the faster plane, and I watch him disappear ahead. My arteries hum with flying delight. Between scanning the instrument panel and the horizon, I read stories of deep trees and watery mirrors below me.

Minutes later, my reverie explodes as the vibrant, vital droning of the plane's engine ruptures into a hesitant jerk, and then . . . near silence . . . just the propeller's blades slicing the air as quietly as a windmill's. My hair stands on end, stomach and heart clench and freeze as if I'd heard a shotgun shell—not mine—being chambered in my bedroom in the dark of night.

I hit the microphone switch and try to inhale some composure. "Four-niner-Juliet, I've lost power." I don't even know if Karl is still in range. Karl's strained but firm voice rips the deafening silence, "Tell me exactly what's happening." As I do, *Bug* begins unequivocally to descend. I search for a spot to put her down.

The radio crackles, "Are you close enough to a lake?" My eyes lock on to a pond. "I've got a small one. I'm not sure I can make it. I'm going to try." I trim the plane's pitch for maximum glide range then try to restart the engine. No go. *Bug* descends irrevocably. Karl's entreaties fracture the stillness, "What's happening? Can you hear me? Val! Do you read?" to which I can only respond sharply, "I'm busy now!" And I am.

All of my neurons are riveted to flying the airplane to the ground. When I realize I'm not going to make the small lake, notch by notch I pull in full flaps, readjust the pitch, and slow to a hair's breadth of stalling. Then I dig my brain cells in against the rest of my body's screaming instinct to pull the nose of the plane up, away from the ground, as it rushes faster and faster at me. If I give in to that compulsion, the plane will stall—and become a rock instead of a glider. I hunker down into years of hangar talk to guide me purposely downward, remembering to wait . . . wait . . . wait . . . until just two or three feet above the ground before finally pulling the nose back.

I crashed. The dog and I survived without a scratch—thanks to *Bug*'s slow stall speed and the floats' absorption of much of the impact. But *Bug* was broken: Her left wing folded back against her fuselage and her struts collapsed, causing her to rest on banged-up floats. I radioed Karl my GPS position, and the dog and I were airlifted out by an obliging Alaskan pilot with a plane that could operate in and out of the small nearby lake.

We retrieved *Bug* and rebuilt her. The first time I flew her solo again, I almost threw up. I'd spent the rebuilding months seeing—whenever I closed my eyes—a narrow tunnel of landscape coming up at me, a dead spruce dislocating the left wing, Plexiglas from overhead raining down in sparkles. But once Karl, a licensed aircraft mechanic, had meticulously inspected and test-flown *Bug*, there was nothing left but for me to fly her myself. As I preflighted the airplane, I had to keep swallowing the fear that tasted like a dirty nickel in the back of my throat. I don't remember take off. In the air, I had atrial fibrillation each time the engine dropped one r.p.m. After I landed, my legs were shaking so badly on the rudder pedals, I had to wait before I could get out of the plane.

I never considered not flying. It isn't courage that keeps me going. It's appetite. I can't give up the wild places flying takes me—outside the plane and inside myself. Sure, I could get to the outside places from the passenger seat, but not to the inside ones, the places where desire and regret, chaos and passion, and the fear of settling are sharp-edged bits of colored glass in my heart's kaleidoscope.

Maya Lin, designer of the Vietnam Veterans Memorial, says "To fly, we have to have resistance." If the air doesn't resist, doesn't push up against my airplane's angled wing while the wing pushes down, my plane wouldn't fly. Fear is *my* resistance. I try to push it down and it pushes me up. I fly solo against the resistance of fear—the fear of a premature coffin of middle-aged settling and the competing fear of crashing again. And in pushing against such fears, I am lifted.

On this morning, just over a year after the crash, as I get ready to fly to the Duck Shack for a few days of hunting alone, I don't get defensive when Karl repeatedly tries to armor me in details. Today, each time he appears from the bedroom or office, he comes with a bit of advice. I smile each time he says, in this new way, that he loves me.

"You'll be light so you might as well top off the tanks."

"I figured I would."

"There's a spare battery in the shed. Why don't you take it? I don't expect you'll need it, but you'll have it just in case."

"Good idea, hon. Thanks."

"Take the satellite phone. Call and let me know as soon as you're at the Duck Shack safe. If I'm not here, leave a message."

"I will, love."

I understand his concern. Flying in Alaska is different. No roads lead to where I'm going. I'll be flying over wilderness that a plane could go down in and never be found. We both know of pilots with a lot more experience than I have who have disappeared in this harsh landscape. But I don't push bad weather or heavy loads or low fuel—all frequent causes of downed planes.

"Have a good time," Karl finally says on his way to play golf. We hug and murmur "be safe" and "I love you" into each others' necks.

Then he's gone. I know tonight, in the lantern-lit Duck Shack, I'll miss him with a pinched heart. But now I'm a kid out of school for the summer. The dog and I scamper to the car and drive out to Lake Hood, where I pull on hip waders, radio the fuel truck to come and top off the tanks, and preflight the airplane.

I start *Bug* up and radio Lake Hood Tower for permission to taxi for a west departure. When I'm cleared for takeoff, I pull the stick all the way back and push in full throttle. As *Bug* gathers speed, I watch the horizon for the second nod of the nose up and then ease the stick forward. Like a boat, the plane levels out on the step and gains more speed. After the length of two football fields, the floats break from the water's grasp and we're climbing. I laugh out loud, the relief and gladness of finally flying bubbles over.

Nearing the Duck Shack, I fly low to scout the tide line. There aren't many birds, only a few of them on the north pothole. I skim onto the water and taxi up to the shore within forty yards of the Duck Shack—a sixteen-by-twenty plywood shell on stilts with a leaning front porch and steps. Inside are bunk beds, a table, folding chairs, a kerosene stove for heat, a two-burner propane stove for cooking, and Coleman lanterns.

No sink, bathroom, running water, or electricity. But since location determines the value of real estate, the Duck Shuck is my favorite place on earth.

I tie *Bug* down and unload while Tao races back and forth between the plane and the Duck Shack. Then I call Karl and leave a message. After changing into chest waders and zipping Tao into his camouflage neoprene vest, we're ready to walk out to the north pothole. There are only a couple of hours before dark, but I'm too eager and restless to wait until the morning.

It's rained hard recently, and the water is high. Even the trails are flooded. After a half hour of hard walking, I sit down on my folding camp stool in high brush near the decoys, my feet in six inches of water. I try to make Tao stay in the high grass where he'll be dry, but he keeps slinking out to squat shivering in the cold water next to me.

I spot a lone wigeon flying in the distance and whisper fervently, "Come on, come on, turn." It does, and sets its wings to glide into the decoys. All space and time compress into the pinprick moment of *Mark!*— my heart's cry when I see the curved wings slicing the sky, speeding toward me. From my eye to the gunsight to the wing, I emit an invisible laser beam. I stand firm, fire, and miss on the first shot. The wigeon flares and kicks in thrust. My second shot fires, and the bird drops.

It's a long swim for Tao. I reload, and wade out behind him, in case the wigeon is only wounded and takes off; but it floats lifeless where it hit the water. Tao retrieves the bird and is huffing from the cold by the time he reaches me. In the silky, echoing grass of the flats, I kneel, stroke the bloodied feathers smooth, and silently pray, "Thank you, wigeon, for all your grace." There is joy and sorrow after the shotgun's blast. I exalt the mathematically pure intersection of sight and flight that I touched for one brief heartbeat *and* I grieve the beauty stilled. I hold the contradiction in my heart. Here, now, I am of two wild places: an outer wilderness I have entered as predator animal and an inner realm of questions, voices . . . contradictions that no other wild creature shares.

Tao and I have come out of the far side of the pond. I see a log perfect to sit on, with a stump at the end that will suit Tao, too. I look back at the decoys, now at the far edge of my range. There won't be as many shots here but at least the dog will be in a dry spot. I sit down, pat the stump next to me so Tao knows to jump on it, and rub him under his vest until my hands and his sides are warm. We settle in. His eyes are locked on the decoys. This is business for him. I look around so as to mark birds coming from any direction. It is still for a long time. I curl my toes in and out to try and keep them warm. I blow into my hunting mittens.

Just as I am about to slip into that timeless, quiet place where stillness meets a beating heart, I hear honking, then the breathy rustle of wings. Seven trumpeter swans sail in, splash, and glide up to the decoys. Tao locks on alert and I firmly whisper, "Stay." I count two snowy white adults and five gray cygnets. Settling in, an adult skims the surface with its bill clacking like castanets after seeds floating on top. The swans take turns sticking their heads under water, folding their long necks back to rest their heads under a white-blanketed wing, and acting like sentries. Continually, two or more honk back and forth in 1:2 time. When they paddle with their big webbed feet, their rears waggle with the comic self-importance of a matronly Garden Club president walking to the podium to assume office with a gavel's rap. We watch them from not twenty yards away.

Tao whimpers as ducks fly in. I don't shoot, even when the ducks are well clear of the swans. I don't want the swans to leave. This, too, is hunting—this syringe of concentration that transfuses me with nature's details. Shadows lengthen, spiders crawl, and the air grows colder. I venture scratches, shifts, stretches. No response from the swans. I murmur "Good boy," and scratch under Tao's chin.

Nothing. I'm getting cramped and decide to take the next clear shot at any ducks. Some teals come by fast and high. Stiff, I stand too slowly, and shoot. I am behind the birds, and they whistle away. I pause to listen for the basketball-slapping sound of swan wings as they lift to fly away. They're unfazed.

Tao and I watch the swans until the pink of sunset on snow-capped mountains cools to gray. At last, I stand and we start round the pond. Only when we've circled back to the decoys side do the swans begin to rise. They start out across the water's surface in a frenetic flapping of over-size wings and feet, a feathered version of Keystone Cops, ungainly and seemingly impossible to get airborne. When they do, I watch a symphony of grace in the sky.

When we hunt together, Karl always beats me back to the Duck Shack to welcome me with a Coleman lantern in the window and smoke curling out of the stovepipe. I begin missing him as Tao and I walk to the empty shack under the darkening sky. I hang the wigeon between nail heads on the edge of the front porch and soon have the kerosene stove fired up, the lanterns lit, and Tao fed. Only then do I peel out of my wet boots and chest waders and hang them to dry, get dinner crackling in the skillet, and sit down with a nip of Glenlivet and a book.

Later, belly full and skillet soaking, I slip into my sleeping bag on a lower bunk, and read by lantern light. Tao rests his head on the bunk's edge until I say, "Okay." Then he leaps up, circles twice, and curls up at my feet with a moan.

The next morning I hear the steady drumming of rain on the tin roof and look outside to see the wind blowing sheets of water horizontally. If I were a duck, I'd be hunkered down, so I do the same in my sleeping bag. An hour later, I ask Tao if he's in a hurry to go hunting in the rain. His head pops up at his name. At the end of my question he merely looks straight ahead for a considered moment, then tucks back into his curl and sighs. I consider his response well thought out and we spend a delicious, unhurried morning over coffee, pancakes (with a splash of beer in the batter to fluff them up), extra-crispy bacon, and a good book.

By noon, the wind has let up so that the rain falls vertically. If we didn't play in the rain in Alaska, we'd miss a lot of play, so Tao and I suit up. I decide to head south—across the tidal flats toward the tide line. It's where I'll have the best chance at geese. And, I hope to stir up some ducks on either the way out or back, or get some flying along the tidal sloughs or tide line. It's too damn wet and cold to sit still on decoys. I need the hard hiking through water and marsh mud to stay warm.

Hunting Alaska's tidal flats brings its own spice. As I step across my first tidal slough, Tao leaping easily ahead of me, I remember the first season I hunted here with Karl. The first slough we were to cross looked unremarkable, a bit more than a yard wide. Not waiting for Karl, I stepped across. The mud on the other side was as slick as potter's slip. I slid down the bank, my hip boots topped instantly, and my feet churned in the watery abyss. I clawed at the mud, sinking fast, until Karl's broad, strong hand clamped onto my shoulder, pulled me from the water with a sucking swoosh, and dropped me on the grass. Once he determined I was okay, except for the shock of the cold, Karl sternly admonished me to take sloughs seriously.

I didn't think of complaining that Karl could've warned me: Alaska's wilderness demands personal accountability. The deeper that was drummed into me the safer I'd be—with or without Karl. My only thoughts were how lucky I'd been that Karl had been there, and that I'd better quit being a silly fool and start paying attention. From that moment, I recognized tidal sloughs for what they are—dark, bottomless, frigid, current-ridden death traps.

Alaska's tides are another pinch of spice to hunting the tidal flats. The tide out here can go from a minus four feet to a plus thirty-four feet in six hours. That can change the narrow slough you easily stepped across earlier to canal size by the time you're heading back. And it can change a boot stuck in the mud from an irritating inconvenience to an immutable death sentence.

As I walk through the tall grass toward the open flats, I replay the news account of a young couple, married a month, who set off on an ATV with a trailer across the mud flats outside of Anchorage. When the trailer got stuck, she stepped off to free it, but the mud sucked her legs in and set up hard. For two hours, her new husband tried to free her. Fire department rescuers and troopers arrived and worked ever more frantically as the tide flowed in. I imagine them all—the wife, the husband, the rescue workers—as the frigid, murky water rose to the young woman's waist, then her shoulders, until the rescue attempt had to be abandoned, and there was nothing to do except watch the young woman drown.

In the Duck Shack, under the Coleman lantern's glow, Karl and I have "what-iffed" one of us getting stuck in the mud. With a shot of Glenlivet warmth we asserted that we'd cut the other's legs off if we had to. Sipping another nip of Mr. Glen, we speculated how long it would take with a Swiss Army knife, whether we could do it quicker than it would take the stuck one of us to bleed to death, whether the one getting his or her legs cut off could remain conscious, and whether it might be better if she or he didn't. Then we quieted and changed the subject to what we'd need to spend the winter at the Duck Shack, and started making our list of supplies out loud.

These grim scenes vanish instantly as wings explode in the tall grass just ahead, and a mallard hen breaks into view. I shoot best when I haven't time to think. The bird drops straight and heavy, and Tao is out of his racing blocks. He trots back, head held high, mouth full of reflexively flapping wings. I wring the duck's neck, close its eyes with my thumb and index finger, give silent thanks, and place the bird in the billowed pocket of my coat, where I warm my hand against it as I continue to walk. And, I confess, I grin for more than a few steps.

The rain never stops. Tao and I sneak up to sloughs hoping to jump some teal and creep near ponds in search of mallards or pintails or wigeons. Hours pass, and I'm now as cold as the mallard I shot. I start seeing some birds near the tide line and walk in that direction. Where the tall grass peters out into short tufts of green moss and purple kelp clinging to the mud, I find an uprooted tree stump for Tao and me to hide on and hope for birds.

Just as I'm about to give up and head back, a distant flock grows larger heading in a straight line for me. Tao stands excitedly when he hears me take the safety off. "Sit!" I growl, willing the geese not to have seen him move. They continue toward me as if on a zip line. I wait for the geese to come into range, pick one, and begin moving my gun, leading the bird by more than a foot. I squeeze the trigger. My bird stops in mid air, wings flapping. I fire the second shot and hear the pellets hit. The goose glides jerkily to the ground, about fifty yards away in the direction of the tide line, and lands hard in the mud.

Tao is off, and I'm running after him as soon as I load two new shells. If the bird is only wounded and makes it to the tide line, we may lose it. Tao closes in and pounces as I stop. He isn't tall enough to lift all the goose off the ground, and the bird's body is too big for his mouth. He tries for a proper hold more than once, settles on the neck just above the wings, and drags his load to me. It's an effective retrieve, if not stylish. I kneel, flushed and trying to catch my breath from running across half-set Jell-O. I straighten the goose's broken wing, wipe the blood from its breast with my hand, and then wipe my hand on muddy moss. I look up at the sky.

Contentment is the weight of the goose and the mallard hanging on my shoulder as Tao and I walk toward the Duck Shack—contentment, respect, gratitude, and sweet sadness. I carry the contradictions along with the birds and feel intimate with both.

I have one more day alone at the Duck Shack. One more day of hunting. Of being outdoors. Of walking long, muddy miles on the flats with the dog. Of sitting and letting stillness find me. Of going to wild places—outside and inside. And then I get to face a bit of fear, embrace resistance, and fly again—home.

About the Contributors

ANN BAKER is a psychotherapist and organizational consultant who lives in Truro, Massachusettes.

LUCY JANE BLEDSOE is the author of two novels, *This Wild Silence* and *Working Parts*, and of *Sweat: Stories and a Novella*. She's recently traveled to Antarctica, visiting all three U.S. stations and many field camps, as a two-time recipient of the National Science Foundation's Antarctic Artists and Writers Fellowship. Her forthcoming book, *The Breath of Seals: Adventures in Fear and Grace*, features writing about those Antarctic journeys.

SHERYL CLOUGH is a graduate of the MFA program at the University of Alaska–Fairbanks, and is a poet and nonfiction writer whose favorite vehicle is a sea kayak. She currently supports her travels and writing through part-time work as a paralegal specializing in medical research. Recent publications include poetry in the Washington Water Trails Association's *Easy Current News*. Sheryl has recently completed a manuscript of essays, titled *Glaciers, Starfish, and Madwomen*, based on more than ten years of sea kayak travel on the Pacific Rim.

Former magazine editor MONIQUE COLE lives in Hawaii with her photographer husband, Phil Mislinski, and two daughters. She has traded in her snow tires for a surfboard, sailboat, and sea kayak. Occasionally, she recounts her exploits on the Iditarod trail to incredulous friends on the North Shore of Oʻahu who think that a seventy-degree evening is chilly. Although she started a second career in real estate two years ago, she still finds time to write magazine articles, and is working on a novel based loosely on her stranger-than-life experiences in property management.

CANDACE DEMPSEY is an adventure travel writer who enjoys kayaking, backcountry skiing, and mountain climbing. Her stories appear in *Gifts of the Wild, Travelers' Tales: Women in the Wild, Travelers' Tales: Turkey*, and other anthologies. She lives in Seattle with her husband, Mark, and son, Jacob.

BARBARA J. EUSER grew up sailing on reservoirs in Colorado. When she joined the U.S. Department of State Foreign Service, she moved with her husband and two daughters to Washington, D.C. They bought *Islander*, a thirty-four-foot sloop, and sailed in Chesapeake Bay. When Euser was posted to the U.S. Embassy in Paris, she and a crew sailed *Islander* across the Atlantic. After her tour ended, she sailed *Islander* back home. Barbara is the director of the International Community Development Foundation and the author of *Children of Dolpo, Somaliland*, and *Take 'Em Along: Sharing the Wilderness with Your Children*, co-author of *A Climber's Climber: On the Trail with Carl Blaurock*, and editor of *Bay Area Gardening*.

ALICE EVANS works as a magazine editor in Eugene, Oregon. She takes two daily walks in the woods with her husband and their two dogs—a Welsh corgi and a yellow lab. Their daughter, a college junior, joins them now and then. Alice's essays, poems, and stories can be found in various magazines and anthologies, including the following Seal Press collections: *The Unsavvy Traveler; Drive: Women's True Stories of the Open Road; Gifts of the Wild;* and *Another Wilderness.*

SUSAN EWING is the author of three books of nonfiction, including *The Great Rocky Mountain Nature Factbook* and *The Great Alaska Nature Factbook*, and two children's books, *Lucky Hares and Itchy Bears* and *Ten Rowdy Ravens*. Her articles, essays, and short stories have appeared in *Gray's*

Sporting Journal, Big Sky Journal, Acorn, Sports Afield, Bugle, and other publications, as well as a number of anthologies, including *Heart Shots: Women Write About Hunting, American Nature Writing*, and *Living in the Runaway West*.

KATHLEEN GASPERINI was the senior editor of *Powder* and *Snowboarder* magazines, and the editor of *Women's Sports & Fitness*. She was the technical writer for the IMAX movie *Extreme*, and is the cofounder of the nonprofit foundation Boarding for Breast Cancer, for which she received a Humanitarian Award from Snow Sports Industries of America. Kathleen was the publisher of the original action sports lifestyle magazine, *W.i.g. Magazine—for Women in General*, and has completed a book with Tina Basich for HarperCollins, *Pretty Good for a Girl: The Autobiography of a Snowboarding Pioneer*. In 2000, Kathleen cofounded Label Networks, a youth culture marketing intelligence company.

GENEEN MARIE HAUGEN's work appears in numerous anthologies and journals, among them *American Nature Writing 2000; Another Wilderness: Notes From the New Outdoorswoman; High Country News; Ring of Fire: Writers of the Yellowstone Region; Alaska Passages: 20 Voices from Above the 54th Parallel; Alligator Juniper; Heart Shots: Women Write About Hunting*. She's a contributor to the syndicated column, "Writers on the Range," and has recently completed a young adult novel. A two-time recipient of the Wyoming Arts Council literary award for "writing inspired by nature," she has also received writers' residencies from Ucross Foundation, Hedgebrook, and Soapstone. A long-time backcountry skier, backpacker, off-trail hiker, and river runner, she lives in Kelly, Wyoming.

LORI HOBKIRK is the author of two children's textbooks about Madam C. J. Walker and President Jimmy Carter. She manages an editorial services company called The Book Factory, and is currently a graduate student in the Teaching of Writing at the University of Colorado–Denver. She lives in Boulder, Colorado.

MARYBETH HOLLEMAN is author of *The Heart of the Sound: An Alaskan Paradise Found and Nearly Lost*, *The State of the Sound 2003*, and *Alaska's Prince William Sound*. Her essays, poetry, and articles have appeared in *North American Review*, *Orion*, *The Christian Science Monitor*, *Ice-Floe*, *Sierra*, *National Wildlife*, *American Nature Writing*, *Under Northern Lights*, and *The Seacoast Reader*. She also teaches creative writing and women's studies at the University of Alaska. Raised in the Appalachian mountains of North Carolina, she transplanted to Alaska nearly twenty years ago, where she lives in the foothills of the Chugach Mountains with her husband and son.

SHARYN LAYFIELD is an artist living in Vermont. She teaches at St. Michael's College and Vermont College of Union Institute and University. Her work has been published in *Ploughshares*, *Sudden Fiction*, and the *Norton Anthology of Short Fiction*.

Originally from the Pacific Northwest, SUSAN MARSH lives in Jackson Hole, Wyoming, where she leads the recreation and wilderness programs for the Bridger-Teton National Forest. She has degrees in geology and landscape architecture. Her writing has appeared in *Orion*, *North American Review*, and numerous other journals, and has been anthologized in *Ring of Fire*, *The Leap Years*, *Women Runners*, and *Going Alone*. She received the 2003 Neltje Blanchan Memorial Award, awarded by the Wyoming Arts Council for literature inspired by the natural world.

E. A. MILLER lives outside of Boston with her daughter and teaches writing at various colleges in the area. She is currently working on a first novel, a chapter of which appeared in *The Flying Dutchman*, and is contemplating purchasing a kayak. She has been an associate faculty member with the Institute for Writing and Thinking for fifteen years and has just become a lay minister at a Unitarian Universalist parish.

VERA LÚCIA MORITZ was born on an island in southern Brazil. She holds a master's degree in civil engineering and now works as an engineer in Colorado. Her latest adventure is living in and fixing up an old cabin in the Colorado mountains.

TRICIA PEARSALL quit her more-than-full-time job as Director of Minimester and Coordinator of Community Outreach for St. Catherine's School in Richmond, Virginia, to pursue her passion: traveling by foot to remote regions of the world. Writer, photographer, and now part-time St. Catherine's teacher, she has traveled extensively along the high-mountain chains of Nepal, Pakistan, China, India, and Kyrgyzstan, and is committed more than ever to the heightened consciousness and insight of the solo experience.

BRIDGET QUINN is a writer and Waldorf teacher who lives in San Francisco with her husband and two young children. "The Cliffhanger" is one of a series of essay she's working on that revolve around sports. One was included in *Two in the Wild* and one has appeared in the journal *Literal Latte*. In addition to essays, her fiction has appeared in the anthology *Brain, Child: greatest hits*, and in a variety of literary magazines.

ANN STALEY's early solo adventures included wandering the corn rows at Madar's Farm, canoeing the Susquehanna River, and a ten-thousand mile cross-country trip in a 1961 VW bug. She taught high school literature and writing in Oregon, edited the poetry journal *Fireweed*, and has spent the last fifteen years teaching with the Northwest Writing Institute at Lewis & Clark College. She is, at last, old enough to write personal essays and to understand Basho's opening lines from *Narrow Road to a Far Province*: "The passing days and months are eternal travelers in time. The years that come and go are travelers too."

VALERIE VAN BROCKLIN is a national public speaker, trainer, and consultant for law enforcement, and a freelance writer. Her past careers include working as a special education teacher and a state and federal prosecutor. She's been published in *Alaska* and *Police Chief* magazines, and has written, produced, and narrated radio essays for *Alaska Public Radio*. She's working on a book about flying, fishing, and hunting in Alaska's wilderness. She lives with her husband, Karl Johnstone, and their retriever, Tao.

KAREN WARREN is an instructor for the Outdoors Program and Recreational Athletics at Hampshire College in Amherst, Massachusetts. She teaches courses in outdoor leadership, experiential education, wilderness studies, and social justice issues in the outdoors. She is co-editor of *The Theory of Experiential Education* and editor of *Women's Voices in Experiential Education*. She lives with her partner and two daughters in the hills of Western Massachusetts and still enjoys an annual solo trip in November.

LAURA WATERMAN is a writer and climber who lives in Vermont. She co-authored with her late husband, Guy Waterman, *Backwoods Ethics: A Guide to Low-Impact Hiking and Camping*, which won a national Outdoor Book Award in 2002. Their other books include *Wilderness Ethics: Preserving the Spirit of Wildness*, *Forest and Crag*, and *Yankee Rock & Ice*, as well as a collection, *A Fine Kind of Madness*, that explores through essays and fiction the enduring mystery of why we climb and its meaning to our lives. Her memoir, *Losing the Garden: The Story of a Marriage*, is about the homesteading and climbing life she shared with Guy, and her efforts to come to terms with his suicide.

ALISON WATT came to live in the States twelve years ago, leaving behind a career in academia. She taught the sociology of health and illness, specializing in women's health and community health action, and has published extensively. She also left behind the English weather. Since working for Colorado Outward Bound, she has trained in craniosacral therapy and now has an active practice in Boulder, Colorado. She also offers group/organization development and training under the title of Interactive Dynamics. She continues to seek wilderness adventure and solace.

CHRISTINE WEEBER grew up in Grand Rapids, Michigan, and now lives near Nederland, Colorado. Her writing has appeared in *Voices*, *Dialogue*, and the *Oregon Extension Journal*. She recently completed a master's degree in Cultural Anthropology and a graduate certificate in Women's Studies from Colorado State University.

About the Editor

SUSAN FOX ROGERS is the editor of ten book anthologies, including *Another Wilderness: Notes from the New Outdoorswoman*, *Two in the Wild: Tales of Adventure from Friends, Mothers, and Daughters*, and *Going Alone: Women's Adventures in the Wild*. Her essays have appeared in several anthologies, including most recently "Searching for Cèpes" in *France, A Love Story: Women Write about the French Experience*. She teaches writing at Bard College in the Hudson Valley, and in the 2004–2005 austral summer, traveled to Antarctica as a participant in the National Science Foundation's Antarctic Artists and Writers Program.

SELECTED TITLES FROM SEAL PRESS

For more than twenty-five years, Seal Press has published groundbreaking books. By women. For women. Visit our website at www.sealpress.com.

Going Alone: Women's Adventures in the Wild edited by Susan Fox Rogers. $15.95, 1-58005-106-5. This anthology explores the many ways women find fulfillment, solace, and joy when they head out alone into the great outdoors.

Italy, A Love Story: Women Write about the Italian Experience edited by Camille Cusumano. $15.95, 1-58005-143-X. Twenty-eight women describe the country they love and why they fell under its spell.

The Risks of Sunbathing Topless: And Other Funny Stories from the Road edited by Kate Chynoweth. $15.95, 1-58005-141-3. These wry, amusing, and insightful stories capture the comical essence of bad travel, and the uniquely female experience on the road.

No Touch Monkey! And Other Travel Lessons Learned Too Late by Ayun Halliday. $14.95, 1-58005-097-2. A self-admittedly bumbling vacationer, Halliday shares—with razor-sharp wit and to hilarious effect—the travel stories most are too self-conscious to tell.

Making Connections: Mother-Daughter Travel Adventures edited by Wendy Knight. $16.95, 1-58005-087-5. What happens when mother and daughter step out of the complacent familiarity of routine into uncharted territory? This collection offers ample inspiration and insight into how travel affects this most complex and intimate of relationships.

The Pirate Queen: In Search of Grace O'Malley and Other Legendary Women of the Sea by Barbara Sjoholm. $15.95, 1-58005-109-X. A fascinating account of an intriguing Irish clan chieftan is joined by tales of cross-dressing sailors, medieval explorers, storm witches, and sea goddesses.